Gilbert

THE MAN WHO WAS
G.K. CHESTERTON

"Group Portrait," circa 1913. Photo by Alvin Langdon Coburn. From the
collection of International Museum of Photography of
George Eastman House.

Gilbert

THE MAN WHO WAS
G.K. CHESTERTON

Michael Coren

PARAGON HOUSE   NEW YORK

First U.S. edition, 1990

Published in the United States by

Paragon House Publishers
90 Fifth Avenue
New York, NY 10011

Published in a slightly different version
by Jonathan Cape, Ltd., United Kingdom, 1989

Library of Congress Cataloging-in-Publication Data
Coren, Michael.
Gilbert, the man who was G.K. Chesterton / Michael Coren. — 1st
U.S. ed.
p.   cm.
"Published in a slightly different version by Jonathan Cape, Ltd.,
United Kingdom, 1989"—T.p. verso.
Bibliography: p.
Includes index.
ISBN 1-55778-256-3
1. Chesterton, G. K. (Gilbert Keith), 1874–1936—Biography.
2. Authors, English—20th century—Biography.   I. Title.
PR4453.C4Z5876   1990
828'.91209—dc20
[B]   89-16202
                                 CIP

The paper used in this publication meets the minimum requirements of
American National Standard for Information Sciences—Permanence of
Paper for Printed Library Materials, ANSI Z39.48-1984.

Manufactured in the United States of America

To my father, Philip Coren, still my best of men.

Contents

Preface

I first became interested in and intrigued by G. K. Chesterton when I was a schoolboy and read the Father Brown stories. They were bright, bold and brilliant. Later, after having read *The Everlasting Man* and *The Man Who Was Thursday,* I searched for a study of Chesterton's life and discovered that few existed and those that did labeled him an anti-Semite and worse. I could not reconcile such sensitive prose with such barbaric views. My studies of Gilbert then began.

Years later, in the summer of 1986, on a quintessentially English afternoon, I walked across an East Anglian field with a dear old friend. As we often did on our walks, we discussed Chesterton, literature, my career, still in its inchoate stages, the state of the world. I had just finished writing my second book and my friend asked what I would write next. I answered that I did not know; that Chesterton was a love of mine, but I felt a bit too young to consider such a project. He looked down an aquiline nose at me, registered a hybrid of disgust and disappointment and told me to begin at once. I did.

The absence of notes in the book is a deliberate policy. In my jejune way I have attempted to follow in the tradition of my subject, and paint a picture as well as tell a story of a great life. For Chesterton the use of copious notes in a biography detracted from the central theme and purpose. On this project, though not for biographies in general, I concur with him. Hence sources are either quoted in the main body of the text, or referred to in the bibliography.

The American edition of *Gilbert* differs from the British edition in several ways. The publisher requested that I include another chapter dealing with the relationship between Gilbert and Bernard Shaw. I have also extended the final chapter, concentrating on Gilbert's time in the United States, and dwelling on the final months in his life. There were also, inevitably, some blemishes in the British edition which have been erased for the more discerning American reader.

I would like to express my appreciation and thanks to the following people: Aidan Mackey, Chestertonian of Chestertonians, who provided time, sources, beer and advice; I shall forever be in his debt. I should like to record my appreciation of the trust the late Miss Dorothy Collins showed me in giving me access to photographs and papers. The following people have also played a vital role in bringing this book to be: I give thanks to Dr. Tessa Beeching, Colin Welland, Monsignor F. Miles, Rev. Henry Reed, Rt. Hon. Kenneth Baker, George Smith, The Weiner Library, Col. John Hayes, Gregory Mac-Donald, Paul Goodman, Paul Pinto, Professor David Regan, Sir Stephen Hayhurst, George Marlin, Father Bocard Sewell, Capt. Moshe Ben-Avi, Iain Benson, Susan Walker, Judith Lee, J.B. Priestley, my editor at Paragon House, Donald Fehr, my parents Philip and Shiela Coren, my wife Bernadette and son Daniel Avi Gilbert.

Michael Coren
Toronto, Canada
August 1989

Gilbert

THE MAN WHO WAS
G.K. CHESTERTON

I

The God with the Golden Key

When the inevitable came, it came with a bitter sudden-
ness. Gilbert had completed his *Autobiography* early
in 1936, and his health was even then under severe strain.
Friends were relieved that the book of memoirs was finally at
an end; they did not expect the man to see out much more
than another year. Dorothy Collins, ever aware of the problems which Gilbert was facing, took him and Frances to
France, to visit the shrines of Lourdes and Lisieux. It was not
a simple sight-seeing exercise. From Lisieux he wrote a letter,
his handwriting by this time almost impossible to read, and
said he was presently "under the shadow of the shrine". He
sang a good deal on the trip, his repertoire including selec-
tions from Gilbert and Sullivan and lines of lyrical poetry.
The two ladies listened sympathetically. Lourdes appealed to
his Catholicism and his love of continental Europe. He did
not find it too commercial and relished its comfort and curious ordinariness.

On returning home Gilbert found that his study was ready
and he and Dorothy Collins moved in. By this time however
Gilbert's ill health was too serious to ignore; his pain and
suffering was for the first time controlling his actions and
dictating his way of life. On March 18th he delivered his final
radio talk, entitled "We Will End With A Bang". In a parody
of T.S. Eliot's "The Hollow Men" he stated, "And they may
end with a whimper/But we will end with a bang". But work
was becoming virtually impossible. He would walk to his
desk, sit down, and after increasingly shorter periods of time
would fall asleep. The doctors knew of Gilbert's bronchitis
and fever attacks; they also knew that the fundamental prob-

lem was the great man's heart. Heart trouble had been diag-
nosed years ago, and now with age and weight and excess
compounding the difficulties there was little that could be
done. Frances wrote to Father O'Connor

12th June, 1936

My Dear Padre,
    In case you hear the news from elsewhere I write
myself to tell you that G. is very seriously ill. The main
trouble is heart and kidney and an amount of fluid in the
body that sets up a dropsical condition. I have had a
specialist to see him, who says that though he is desper-
ately ill there is a fighting chance. I think possibly he is a
little better today. He has had Extreme Unction this
morning and received Holy Communion.
    Will you, as I know you will, pray for him and get
others to do so and say some Masses for him.

Frances was adamant that the press should not know of or
exploit Gilbert's illness. She personally asked editors not to
publicise the fact, anxious that her husband should have
peace and quiet, also quite terrified that the probability of
death should become even more real and immediate through
its publicity. She was a brave, terrified and loving woman. He
did fight back to something like full consciousness at one
point, proclaiming in his storm before the lull that, "The issue
is now quite clear. It is between light and darkness and every
one must choose his side." Frances had experienced the 1916
recovery, thought of it as a miracle and "did not dare" to
hope this would be yet another. She kept vigil by his bed, and
prayed.
    On June 12th Monsignor Smith, the parish priest, arrived
at Top Meadow to anoint Gilbert with chrism and to give
communion. Gilbert was partly conscious for the rite, as he
had been for brief periods over the previous two days. Father
Vincent McNabb followed soon afterwards. He sang the
Salve Regina over Gilbert, the hymn which is sung over dying
Dominican priests; how appropriate for the biographer of St
Thomas Aquinas, the jewel of the Dominican order. He saw

4

Gilbert's pen lying by the side of the bed, blessed and kissed it and then returned to London.

On the night of 13th June he seemed a little better, almost calm and clear as he struggled to cope with his breathing. In one of these fleeting moments of alertness he managed to see Frances, and said simply "Hello, my darling." Turning to Dorothy Collins, who was also in the room, he said "Hello, my dear." He was to speak no more, and slipped under a blanket of painful and unnatural sleep. His condition grew worse through the night, and around 10.15 on the morning of 14th June 1936, Gilbert's soul passed gently from this earth.

Because of Frances's efforts to keep the newspapers at a safe distance the news was all the more shocking. She wrote to Father O'Connor: "Our beloved Gilbert passed away this morning at 10.15. He was unconscious for some time before but had received the Last Sacraments and Extreme Unction whilst he was still in possession of his understanding ..." Tributes were not long in coming. E.C. Bentley spoke of the genius of his friend on the radio, Cardinal Pacelli (later to become Pope Pius XII) cabled "Holy Father deeply grieved death Mr. Gilbert Keith Chesterton devoted son Holy Church gifted Defender of the Catholic Faith. His Holiness offers paternal sympathy people of England assures prayers dear departed, bestows Apostolic Benediction." George Bernard Shaw wrote to Frances immediately on hearing the news, asking if she was financially secure and lamenting that he, eighteen years the senior of Gilbert, should out-live his friend and foe. Maurice Baring, scribbling painfully in pencil, worked through his shaking palsy to write: "Too paralysed with neuritis and 'agitance' to hold pen or pencil. Saw incredible news in Times. Then your letter came. All my prayers and thought are with you. I'm not allowed to travel except once a week to see doctor, but I'll have a mass said here." Written messages of respect and sorrow came from J.M. Barrie, Ronald Knox, Eric Gill and a host of admirers both known and unknown to Gilbert. Writing to a companion, Hugh Kingsmill stated: "My friend Hesketh Pearson was staying with me when I read of Chesterton's death. I told him of it through the bathroom door, and he sent up a hollow groan

which must have echoed that morning all over England."
Gilbert had stridden both literary and social worlds, and both
registered their shock and regret. To some the loss was agonising and confusing; a friend and ally in the most important
of all conflicts. To others a gracious opponent and witty
antagonist had left them, leaving a vacuum impossible to fill.
To many the response on hearing of his death was to say
"What will we ever do without him?"

The sun greeted those attending Gilbert's funeral. It was
very hot, and the town of Beaconsfield bathed in the glow of
fine weather. Such conditions had not always suited Gilbert's
huge frame when he was alive; and the sheer size and weight
of his coffin caused logistical problems for the undertakers.
Baring, Gilbert's closest friend during the last decade, could
not attend. "I wish I could come down tomorrow," he wrote,
"but I cannot go even to mass here on Sundays because
directly I get into a church where there are people I have a sort
of attack of palpitations and have to come out at once. . . ."
But the small church of St Teresa's near the railway was more
than full. Hilaire Belloc had left his Sussex home at dawn to
be in time. He was found after the funeral at a nearby hotel,
crying tears of isolation.

Such was Gilbert's popularity that the procession took a
prolonged route, passing through the town so that last respects could be paid. William Titterton, friend and biographer, noted

> Now I am at his peaceful funeral at Beaconsfield in the
> great company of his friends. (I have gone down by train
> with some of them, arguing furiously and joyously all the
> way about his views on machinery.) I see the coffin that
> holds all that is mortal of my captain. I pass with it along
> the little town's winding ways. It is a roundabout way we
> go. For the police of the place will have it that Gilbert
> Chesterton shall make his last earthly journey past the
> homes of the people who knew him and loved him best.
> And there they were, crowding the pavements, and all,
> like us, bereaved. Yet it was almost a gala day. There was
> no moping, no gush of tears. Nay, there was laughter as

one of us recalled him and his heroic jollity to another's ready remembrance. A policeman at the gate of the cemetery said to Edward Macdonald, "Most of the lads are on duty, else they would all have been here." As Edward Macdonald says, "He was the Lord of the Manor. And he never knew it." So we left him.

There were some tears though. Young Harold Soref, later to become a Conservative Member of Parliament, had helped to bring back the *Debater* magazine at St Paul's School, inspired by the heady days of Gilbert's time at the institution. He attended the funeral, and was seen to weep. An elderly man approached the teenager and told him that he shouldn't be embarrassed by his tears. Soref replied that he wasn't, mainly because they were due to his chronic hay-fever, accentuated by the hot weather. It was the sort of humour that Gilbert would have appreciated.

On 27th June at Westminster Cathedral a Solemn Requiem was held. The mass was sung by Father O'Connor, aided by Father McNabb, and Ronald Knox gave an eloquent and fitting eulogy. Through all of this Frances Chesterton was resolute, acting in the faith that she would have only to live out a few more years before she joined her husband. She wrote a moving, touchingly sincere note to Father O'Connor: "I find it increasingly difficult to keep going. The feeling that he needs me no longer is almost unbearable. How do lovers love without each other? We were always lovers ..." She seemed to miss the children she could never have more and more, surrounding herself with other people's offspring and spending large amounts of time with them. She was not a woman to take herself out of the living world and wait ascetically for death. She had never been an intellectual in the Chestertonian manner, nor had she been a socialiser in the Chestertonian manner. For the woman behind the man, and that is most certainly what she was, life would now be a struggle. She was present when Eric Gill designed a crucifixion headstone for Gilbert's grave, and for the publication of Gilbert's *Autobiography* in November 1936.

In his will he left £2,000 to Dorothy Collins, £500 to the

local Catholic church and priest, and the rest to his wife. She also took over Top Meadow, their beloved home, which was eventually to transfer to the Converts' Aid Society, an organisation to take care of Anglican priests who convert to Roman Catholicism. It is also a shrine for readers of Gilbert Chesterton, and serves both purposes rather well. Gilbert's books and papers were left to his wife and to Dorothy Collins.

Frances died in 1938, two years after her husband. George Bernard Shaw wondered if the cause of death had been "widowhood," and he may have been correct. The doctors said it was cancer. She suffered, like her husband, with tolerance and complete confidence in her future life. Friend and biographer Maisie Ward was told by one who saw Frances in hospital shortly before her death that "Her arms were spread out and there was a lovely expression of happiness on her face. I felt that Gilbert had come to tell her everything was all right and to welcome her."

II

The Napoleon of Campden Hill

Bowing down in blind credulity, as is my custom, before mere authority and the tradition of the elders, superstitiously swallowing a story I could not test at the time by experiment of private judgement, I am firmly of opinion that I was born on the 29th of May, 1874, on Campden Hill, Kensington; and baptised according to the formalities of the Church of England in the little church of St George opposite the large Waterworks Tower that dominates the ridge. I do not allege any significance in the relation of the two buildings; and I indignantly deny that the church was chosen because it needed the whole water-power of West London to turn me into a Christian.

Thus begins Gilbert's *Autobiography*. The specific place of the birth was 32 Sheffield Terrace, a hauntingly quiet and attractive little road between Holland Park and Kensington Palace Gardens. It was in this geographical setting that Father Brown would face many dangers and the fictional hero of one of Gilbert's finest works would come to life.

The Chestertons sometimes claimed to have originated in the quaint Cambridgeshire village of the same name, nowadays clearly signposted to those entering the university city by road. Gilbert was always sceptical about the claim, aware that several other small towns and villages existed under the name Chesterton and that the family clan tradition was founded on little other than imaginative reasoning and uninformed guesswork. Writing an introduction to a volume on Old Cambridge he stated: "I have never been to Cambridge

9

except as an admiring visitor; I have never been to Chesterton at all, either from a sense of unworthiness or from a faint superstitious feeling that I might be fulfilling a prophecy in the countryside. Anyone with a sense of the savour of the old English country rhymes and tales will share my vague alarm that the steeple might crack or the market cross fall down, for a smaller thing than the coincidence of a man named Chesterton going to Chesterton."

Another romantic notion which clung to the Chesterton family mentality until the early years of this century was that an ancestor was a close friend, supporter and drinking companion of the Prince Regent. The story had it that the Chesterton in question squandered his time and fortune away in the profligate company of the "fat friend" who was soon to be King of England. That a Chesterton of the period did fall foul of the debtors' laws of the period and go to prison is in some doubt; the letters he wrote from his cell certainly existed and were read to the family well into the nineteenth century, but scholars of the Regency period have yet to discover any princely companion by the name of Chesterton. Gilbert rarely spoke about the issue with a serious demeanour.

Captain George Laval Chesterton did exist. What we know of his life makes for fascinating reading. He served in the Peninsular War, where Wellington established his fame, and then joined the British army and its loyalist and Indian allies in the war of 1812 against the Americans. The Captain observed the intricate details of military life during the age of Waterloo, recalling hardened soldiers being "made ill by the sight of a private receiving five hundred strokes of the lash." A professional fighting man, he was apparently unhappy with his treatment at the hands of the British authorities, offered his services as a mercenary in the South American rebellion which took place soon after and finally settled for being made governor of Cold Bath Fields Prison. It was here that he became friendly with the prison reformer Elizabeth Fry and her fellow social critic Charles Dickens. Maisie Ward recorded that a relative of the family remembered the line "I cried, Dickens cried, we all cried" from a letter from Captain Chesterton; alas, the complete document no longer exists.

Two books were left for posterity: an autobiography, and *Revelations of Prison Life*. Both are incisive views into the man and his time, neither rival or predict the literary genius of the Chesterton to come.

The bulk of the Chesterton family archives survived, in what would seem to be good order and repair. When Gilbert's mother died, however, he mysteriously threw out almost all of the papers and documents in his late father's study, leaving a hiatus in Chestertonian genealogy. The modern period presents no such difficulties. Gilbert's paternal grandfather was Arthur, who had sailed for Jamaica in 1829 on the *Lune*, and was to take over and run the firm of estate agents which had been started by his father, Charles, a former poulterer who had a small shop in Kensington High Street. Gilbert remembered his grandfather well

> My grandfather, my father's father, was a fine-looking old man with white hair and beard and manners that had something of that rounded solemnity that went with the old-fashioned customs of proposing toasts and sentiments. He kept up the ancient Christian custom of singing at the dinner-table, and it did not seem incongruous when he sang "The Fine Old English Gentleman" as well as more pompous songs of the period of Waterloo and Trafalgar. [And speaking of his grandfather's class status] For the particular sort of British bourgeoisie of which I am speaking has been so much altered or diminished, that it cannot exactly be said to exist today. Nothing quite like it at least can be found in England; nothing in the least like it, I fancy, was ever found in America. One peculiarity of this middle-class was that it really was a class and it really was in the middle. Both for good and evil, and certainly often to excess, it was separated both from the class above it and the class below. It knew far too little of the working-classes, to the grave peril of a later generation.

Gilbert's mother, Marie Louise Grosjean, poses more of a problem. Whereas the difficulty with Gilbert's memories of his family is usually the staggering amount of anecdote and incident, when it comes to his mother there is scarcely any reference at all. There is no physical description of her in the *Autobiography,* only three petty references which depict her in relation to her husband, Gilbert's beloved father. Gilbert noted a family legend when talking of his mother's people "they were descended from a French private soldier of the Revolutionary Wars, who had been a prisoner in England and remained there; as some certainly did." It would seem in fact that the family had come to Britain from the French-speaking region of Switzerland two generations earlier and were of a wealthy background. Ironically, Marie Louise's father had been a Temperance Movement pioneer, a Wesleyan lay preacher and a man who was readily dominated by his wife. Little was inherited from this strand of the family. Her mother passed on more to Gilbert, principally a Celtic passion and flamboyance. She was of the Keith family from Aberdeen – hence Gilbert's second name – and provided her grandson with "a certain vividness in any infusion of Scots blood or patriotism . . . a sort of Scottish romance in my childhood."

Marie Louise herself came from a very large family and inherited her mother's tendency to dominate and organise. She was not a particularly attractive woman, often indifferent to how she appeared in dress and the least conscientious of housewives, but she was an intellectually gifted woman, erudite and powerful in conversation. Cecil Chesterton, not always a reliable witness, thought of his mother as the cleverest woman in London. Her mental strength was all the greater because of her physical weakness. She suffered from an unusual brittleness in her bones, often having to endure painful breaks which did not heal easily. She suffered, like her son, with patience and good nature. Her massive energy, penchant for serving and eating vast meals and bodily fragility were inherited by both Gilbert and Cecil Chesterton.

Why then only the fleeting acknowledgment of his mother in Gilbert's writings? It would be facile to read too much into this. In his book on George Bernard Shaw he wrote "A man should always be tied to his mother's apron strings; he should always have a hold on his childhood; and be ready at intervals to start anew from a childish standpoint." The simple fact is that in spite of what Gilbert may have said or wished he was and always would be influenced by men rather than women. His relationship with his mother would have bearing on his marriage with a woman he loved very much, but also sometimes neglected. He did not understand women particularly well, had little experience of their sexuality and motivations and treated them according to his own perceptions rather than their own sense of identity. He was a man of his age. And better his noble if archaic concepts of chivalry and childishness than the fear or downright misogyny exhibited by so many other writers of the period.

The father of the family was Edward, one of six sons. He was put in charge of the estate agent business with his brother Sydney but was never happy as surveyor or seller. "My father might have reminded people of Mr Pickwick, except that he was always bearded and never bald; he wore spectacles and had all the Pickwickian evenness of temper and pleasure in the humours of travel," wrote Gilbert. "I remember, to give one example of a hundred such inventions, how he gravely instructed some grave ladies in the names of flowers; dwelling especially on the rustic names given in certain localities. 'The country people call them Sailors' Pen-Knives,' he would say in an off-hand manner, after affecting to provide them with the full scientific name, or, 'They call them Bakers' Bootlaces down in Lincolnshire, I believe;' and it is a fine example of human simplicity to note how far he found he could safely go in such instructive discourse."

It was not only this evident delight in teasing which Gilbert was to rival. Edward Chesterton was a man who cared less than nought for fashion and tidiness, seemingly apathetic as to how others viewed him. He wore a pince-nez and a short, evenly cut beard. His clothes were well-worn and consistently creased, with a strong emphasis on comfort. Although he was a competent businessman, knowing when to leave matters to his brother Sydney, he was never settled or enthusiastic about the family property firm, and when ill health forced him to retire he accepted his fate with a robust resignation. Heart palpitations had bothered, pained and frightened him for some years, and he was easily susceptible to those who suggested that his heart was dangerously weak and serious work should be put aside. Early retirement left room for Edward Chesterton's real pleasures. He would now devote time and energy to photography, model making, painting and conversation. In an early letter to E.C. Bentley, Gilbert spoke of another of his father's great hobbies: "I went to a party at my uncle's where my father, known in those regions as 'Uncle Ned,' showed a magic lantern display, most of the slides I had seen before with the exception of one beautiful series, copied and coloured by my cousin, illustrating the tragical story of Hookybeak the Raven."

A sense of the spiritual was not passed on, at least not directly. Gilbert would always proclaim that his life was a living example of how a nominally non-Christian family could produce Christian children. Edward was a product of that late Victorian progressive humanism which Gilbert eventually set his sword so strongly against. He was a radical, a loving man who saw a future for mankind but only a present and a past for God. It worried Gilbert greatly. Writing to Ronald Knox shortly before his father died Gilbert explained: "My father is the very best man I ever knew of that generation that never understood the new need of a spiritual authority; and lives almost perfectly by the sort of religion men had when rationalism was rational. I think he was always subconsciously prepared for the next generation having less theology than he has; and is rather puzzled at its having more." The two men were close, friends as well as father and son. The father was an avid reader, an authority on English literature and of a gentle, open nature. He was supremely that most English of types, the amateur. Gilbert was pleased that his father had declined becoming a professional painter or craftsman. "It might," he thought, "have spoilt his career, his private career. He could never have made a vulgar success of all the thousand things he did so successfully."

The delicate, sanguine, at times child-like world of Edward Chesterton received a shattering blow when his first child, a daughter named Beatrice, died at the age of eight. The family lived at Sheffield Terrace at the time, and when the poor child died her brother Gilbert was aged only three, barely communicating in broken sentences. He did not remember her death but did recall her "falling off a rocking horse. I know from experience of bereavements only a little later, that children feel with exactitude, without a word of explanation, the emotional tone or tint of a house in mourning. But in this case, the greater catastrophe must somehow have become confused and identified with a smaller one. I always felt it as a tragic memory, as if she had been thrown by a real horse and killed." It is a moving explanation. His father reacted in a different manner. Birdie, as the girl was known to all friends and family, was to no longer exist in memory or conversation. Death, in mid- and late-Victorian families, was so much a part of everyday life in a world where most families lost children and loved ones at an early age that its morbidity and fear, so terrifying today, was usually discussed and accepted. Not so with the Chesterton family. Edward Chesterton was transformed by the loss. The girl would not be spoken of, cried over or lamented. Her portrait was turned to the wall so it could not be seen; her name was not to be heard or spoken. The motives of the distraught father were two-fold: he loved his first child with a passion, she sharing aspects of his character and he enjoying the childish qualities which had filled the house. Her death seemed to be beyond his understanding. His heart was broken, and instead of gradually coming to terms with the pain as a natural balance and counter to the joy in his life, he let himself be drowned by his terror and sorrow. He could not cope. The second motive was not as understandable, not as noble. Edward Chesterton was a man petrified by ill health and death. The passing of his daughter was a reminder of his own mortality and a shock too great to be tolerated. The answer was to pretend it had not happened. From now on if a funeral procession passed by the house the children, sometimes the entire family, were to rush into the back room so as not to witness the dark tones of death and end. On no account would anyone actually attend a funeral. Some of this phobia was passed on to Gilbert, who was subsequently disturbed by illness and death for most of his life. His character was greater and stronger than that of his father however; he tried to overcome his weakness, and by

15

the time of his own death he had almost done so. What a contrast there was between Gilbert's running from the dinner-table when his brother Cecil would cough on a piece of food or choke on a morsel, and his quiet peaceful decline and death when he was accepting and in control. Gilbert inherited both faults and virtues from his parents, but his adult humanity, intellect and genius were products of his own development and will. If any person made Gilbert Keith Chesterton it was Gilbert Keith Chesterton.

The family moved to 11 Warwick Gardens soon after the bereavement. It was here that Cecil Chesterton was born on 12th November 1879. Gilbert was five years old when his brother came into the world, and he welcomed him with "Now I shall always have an audience." The environment into which both boys were born was stable, secure and endlessly fecund. E.C. Bentley, companion and school-mate of Gilbert's, was to write in his memoirs "Nothing could harm us – nothing! This was the solid, well-founded conviction at the back of the British national mind in the days of my boyhood. As far as security from attack was concerned, no people had ever been in such a position . . . . We were by far the richest people in the world. We manufactured goods for all the world . . . . Over a quarter of the world was included in the British Empire." Bentley was representing the attitudes of the British people of the late nineteenth and early twentieth century. He spoke for most of the country, he certainly spoke for Gilbert.

If Britain and the British middle-class psyche was granite-like in its sense of stability, the Chesterton household was equally assured and reliable. The house in Warwick Gardens, nestling in a sheltered corner of Kensington, was the habitat for a consummate childhood, universally acknowledged as one of the happiest in English literature. Cecil Chesterton's wife, Ada, sometimes hostile to Gilbert and his wife because of the attention they received in relation to Cecil and herself, wrote of the family home long after Gilbert's childhood

> It stood out from its neighbours . . . . [with] flowers in dark green window boxes and the sheen of paint the

colour of West Country bricks, that seemed to hold the sunshine. The setting of the house never altered. The walls of the dining-room renewed their original shade of bronze-green year after year. The mantel-piece was perennially wine colour, and the tiles of the hearth [were] Edward Chesterton's own design .... Books lined as much of the wall space as was feasible and the shelves reached from floor to ceiling .... The furniture was graceful .... [but] there were deep chairs .... On party nights wide folding doors stood open and through the vista of a warm yet delicate rose-coloured drawing-room, you saw a long and lovely garden [with] walls and tall trees .... where on special occasions Edward Chesterton .... would hang up fairy lamps among the flowers and trees.

In his *Autobiography* Gilbert dwelt on his childhood, with love and lamentation. "What was wonderful about childhood is that anything in it was a wonder. It was not merely a world full of miracles; it was a miraculous world. What gives me this shock is almost anything. I really recall; not the things I should think most worth recalling. This is where it differs from the great thrill of the past, all that is connected with first love and the romantic passion; for that, though equally poignant, comes always to a point; and is narrow like a rapier piercing the heart, whereas the other was more like a hundred windows opened on all sides of the head." He was conscious of what the critics, the analysts would say if they had the chance in years to come. "If some laborious reader of little books on child psychology cries out to me in glee and cunning: 'You only like romantic things because your father showed you a toy theatre in your childhood,' I shall reply with gentle and Christian patience: 'Yes, fool, yes. Undoubtedly your explanation is, in that sense, the true one. But what you are saying, in your witty way, is simply that I associate these things with happiness because I was so happy.' "

The toy theatre was a constant friend and source of amusement and delight for Gilbert. His brother, Cecil, believed in adult years that this childish fascination led Gilbert away from the hardened, political reality of journalistic life and drew him towards the ethereal. To Cecil, who always perceived the political and the treasonable even when his imagination was the only evidence, Gilbert had over-balanced in favour of the dream. Cecil, of course, never attained the literary heights which his brother so often scaled; gifted writer and thinker though he was, he lacked that generosity of mind and width of wondering which Gilbert may well have learnt first in the front stalls of his father's miniature dramas. Gilbert remembered his first sensation of happiness when he saw a young man on a bridge

> He had a curly moustache and an attitude of confidence verging on swagger. He carried in his hand . . . . a large key of a shining yellow metal and wore a large golden crown. The bridge he was crossing sprang on the one side from the edge of a highly perilous mountain chasm . . . . and at the other it joined the upper part of the tower . . . . of a castle. In the castle tower there was one window, out of which a young lady was looking.

Castle, young man and fair lady were only a few inches tall, and made of painted board.

At Warwick Gardens Cecil had a small den, a tiny home from home where the untidy, sometimes dirty, child kept cockroaches as pets and fed them on scraps of food, watching as the ugly creatures nibbled at bits of bread and butter. He also looked after a tom-cat which responded to the name of Faustine. Gilbert did not particularly share his brother's partiality for animals and insects. The kitchen and servants' lodgings were in the basement of the house and at the top were the sleeping quarters for the family. The upper floor also contained a nursery and Gilbert's den. His room was always littered with books, which would fill up a wall of the room and then collect in piles on the floor. Gilbert took the habit of reading as he walked, or dined, into his adult life, and endearing as this was it inevitably led to the loss of books and papers. As a child he would read in the garden, underneath a tree, run in when it rained and later find all that remained of a prized volume was a soggy mess. His books would be found

18

in every room in the house. Paints, lumps of clay, drawings and poetic attempts would mingle delightfully with learned books and the remains of midnight feasts or hurried break-fasts in the rooms of the Chesterton brothers. Gilbert was an eclectic child, discovering jewels on his boyish travels as he adventured in the garden jungle or the basement dungeons, and taking them home to his personal castle at the top of his world.

Gilbert was not a lonely child. He welcomed the birth of his brother with the gusto of one who wished to share, but that is nothing unusual in an only child. In fact there is a certain irony in Gilbert's expectations that Cecil would provide him with an infant audience. It was Cecil who would become the stronger of the pair, always more determined to triumph in discussion. Cecil had strong opinions. He would become opinionated at a young age and his spirit of compromise was seldom as developed or as sensitive as that of Gilbert. They rarely argued, but they constantly debated. It was Gilbert who did most of the listening and the observing, lovingly looking on as his precocious younger brother held court. Early friends included cousins and local children, and the daughters of his mother's close friends, Lizzie and Annie Firmin. Gilbert's mother never hid the fact that she would have liked her elder son to marry Annie Firmin. "One of my first memories is playing in the garden under the care of a girl with ropes of golden hair," he was to say, and "The two Firmin girls had more to do with enlivening my earlier years than most." The band of young cowboys and Indians would fight it out to the gory end or run to a pirate king for an alliance.

There is throughout the anecdotes of Gilbert's childhood, both from himself and others, an overwhelming flavour of comfort and warmth; of fire-side relief after a busy day of playing and running, always rejoicing in the knowledge that all would be well. Annie Firmin, Mrs Kidd as she would become, remembered that the authority in the Chesterton home would always come from Mrs Chesterton, or Aunt Marie as she called her. She would call the children in from the garden, or admonish a stray arrow or cracked window.

Her stern character was felt by others as well. "Aunt Marie was a bit of a tyrant in her own family! I have been many times at dinner, when there might be a joint, say, and a chicken – and she would say positively to Mr Ed, 'Which will you have Edward?' Edward: 'I think I'd like a bit of chicken!' Aunt M, fiercely: 'No, you won't, you'll have mutton!' That happened so often . . ."

Marie Chesterton was not a mother who avoided favouritism. Her choice was clearly Cecil, who reciprocated the special treatment by his adoration. Gilbert was his father's child, which is reflected in the book which so transformed his early days, a gift from his father entitled *The Princess and the Goblin*. It is a timeless volume by George MacDonald, a sadly neglected author today. MacDonald was a major influence on C.S. Lewis, who also included Gilbert Chesterton amongst his philosophical and theological mentors, and the three writers are spoken of as having striking similarities. The book made "a difference to my whole existence, which helped me to see things in a certain way from the start." It is a tale of goblins in the hidden corners and rooms of a house, fairy allies in others. Writing an introduction to Greville MacDonald's biography entitled "George MacDonald and His Wife," Gilbert wrote: ". . . a house that is our home, that is rightly loved as our home, but of which we hardly know the best or the worst, and must always wait for the one and watch against the other . . . . Since I first read that story some five alternative philosophies of the universe have come to our colleges out of Germany, blowing through the world like the east wind. But for me that castle is still standing in the mountains, its light is not put out."

For all Edward Chesterton's modernity in matters spiritual he took his children to church, albeit an institution which Gilbert would vehemently attack in the years to come. They attended Bedford Chapel, where a Unitarian minister named Stopford Brooke preached. He was an Irishman of some charisma and wit who had at one time been a royal chaplain in the Church of England. He left the Anglican church because of, amongst other obstacles, his lack of belief in miracles. In 1880 he declared his commitment to Unitarianism and socialism, and began to put forward his own brand of New

Theology, something Cecil described as "The Fatherhood of God, the Brotherhood of Man, the non-eternity of evil, the final salvation of souls." Gilbert was to dedicate one of his first clerihews to the bewildering theologian who pointed the young man in all the correct directions; that is, diametrically away from what the minister was preaching

> The Rev. Stopford Brooke
> The Church forsook.
> He preached about an apple
> In Bedford Chapel.

One cannot escape the comparison between the man Brooke and another Anglican clergyman, the Bishop of Durham, who one century later would cause outrage and uproar as he lectured about his own apples in his own Bedford Chapel.

Religion did, however, break through the cloud of unknowing apathy. Gilbert's parents read him the story of St Francis, a journey of magic and child-like love with universal appeal. His own biography of St Francis was published shortly after he was received into the Roman Catholic Church, with heavy doses of gratitude for the example and strength which *Le Jongleur de Dieu* had set. Did the Franciscan road begin as early as those fire-side stories told by parents who discerned little more than a humble man of spirit who cared for the weak? Gilbert always put an emphasis on the indirect conversion of his sceptical family. A certain reason for his joining the Church was that only that body could have produced a St Francis

> ... we find [the counsels of perfection] produced by the same religious system which claims continuity and authority from the scenes in which they first appeared. Any number of philosophies will repeat the platitudes of Christianity. But it is the ancient Church that can again startle the world with the paradoxes of Christianity.

While Gilbert drank in the goodness of Francis he swallowed hardily at the symbolism and mystery of Christmas.

His early Christmas experiences were Dickensian in the richest sense, with that strange and inexplicable mixture of atheistic [the doing of good once a year for the sake of goodness and human goodwill] and religious [good for the sake of a higher order and command] which has perplexed the most hardened of cynics. The magic of the time was obvious; for Gilbert the magic had a more noble origin, he "believed in the spirit of Christmas before I believed in Christ . . . and from my earliest years I had an affection for the Blessed Virgin and the Holy Family [for] Bethlehem and the story of Nazareth." The spirit of the Christmas season was to stay with Gilbert until the last. The Reverend Stopford Brooke's views on miracles were no match for the miraculous.

Gilbert's childhood was touched with the institutional for the first time when he was prepared for senior school by his parents. They decided to send their son to St Paul's, as was the case with several Chesterton cousins and nephews, and chose as a prep school Colet House. Gilbert says nothing about the establishment in any of his writings, and the precise date of his first term is unknown. The school opened its doors in 1881, which could have been when Gilbert arrived; but we also know that he did not begin to read with any understanding until two years later. Colet House was a direct prep school for St Paul's – today it is known as Colet Court and is the junior department of the well-known public school – and was headed and inspired by Samuel Bewsher. It was situated in Edith Road, West Kensington, until enrollment figures necessitated an expansion. The new development was built adjacent to St Paul's, and was staffed with a set of teachers who were mostly Oxford and Cambridge scholars with what seems to have been a distinct flair for their vocation. Stafford Aston remembered Gilbert at the time

When I was about seven years old, I went to St Paul's Preparatory School (Head Master, Mr S. Bewsher), and at this school I met G.K.C. who, no doubt, would be about seven years old too. His home was in Warwick Gardens, mine in Pembroke Gardens, and we used to walk to school along the Hammersmith Road together.

The master of our class (I think a Mr Alexander) once said to G.K.C., "You know, Chesterton, if we could open up your head, we should not find any brain, but only a lump of white fat!"

On our way to and from school, we passed a very entrancing toy shop in the Hammersmith Road, but I had very little money. Chesterton once said to me, "I have ten shillings at home, I will give it to you – I do not want it." Of course, my people would never have let me take it.

When I was at University College, G.K.C. once came up to me and asked me if my name was Aston. I told him "Yes," and he said that he thought he recognised "the twilight of past years" – we were both about eighteen-years-old then, I should think.

One cannot help recalling the passage from *As You Like It,* which Gilbert was always so fond of quoting in his adult years: "And then the whining schoolboy, with his satchel,/ And shining morning face, creeping like snail/Unwillingly to school." At "Bewsher's" there may have been some reason for a lackadaisical journey to school, for though the education was in most respects first class the discipline was harsh and the amount of corporal punishment would be unacceptable today to even the sternest of teachers. E.C. Bentley noted that a fondness for the cane "still lingered in the mind of Samuel Bewsher . . . . I used to see him going the round of the classes with a cane, picking out a boy here and there for questions about the work in hand, and dealing him a few hearty whacks if the replies were unsatisfactory." Such a method would never have achieved any lasting results in Gilbert.

It is now quite clear that a lot of the suffering which Gilbert experienced as a young schoolboy was due to his short-sightedness. Gilbert was not perceived as being myopic and hence was beaten or scolded for his educational failures when a simple pair of glasses would have raised his marks immediately. There are no photographs of, or references to, Gilbert actually wearing spectacles until he was into his teens. He did not read until he was nine, but he was drawing well-crafted and considered illustrations over anything and everything he could get his hands on from a much earlier age. The drawings show understanding and intelligence, and a keen sense of wit; so why the apparent dullness at school and such concern on the part of teachers and parents alike?

Gilbert's eye-sight problems were a major cause; he frequently wore a "brooding expression" as a child and it was only when a relative or friend came within recognition distance that his face transformed itself into a glow of affection. The poor child was not brooding, he could not see and was squinting. It was at this stage that his mother took him to a doctor, worried that his apparent lust for learning at home became an inept failure at school. The boy had an unusually large brain she was told, and would either be an idiot or a genius. Nor was he a physically indifferent child, he enjoyed long, sometimes lonely, walks where he would take in miles of London streets, thinking to himself and relishing hours of contemplation. Yet at Colet House he frequently came last or at the bottom of the list in any organised game or sport. The contrast between home and school was a painful one for Gilbert. He was not a conscious rebel, and respected the teachers and masters, but he was a misfit. The tone of authority which he would seek throughout his life was not to be found at Colet House, at least not in the form for which Gilbert was searching. His docility at the school is at times so humble and accepting as to be quite moving. He was not bullied, but he was teased and laughed at. When it snowed, it would certainly be Gilbert who was pelted with snowballs and have snow put into his pockets. At gym class the rest of the boys would break from their frenzied activities to watch Gilbert fail to jump over the exercise horse, or make no headway on the climbing frame. In his *Autobiography* he was to write

> The change from childhood to boyhood, and the mysterious transformation that produces that monster the schoolboy, might be very well summed-up in one small fact. To me the ancient capital letters of the Greek alphabet, the great Theta, a sphere barred across the midst like

24

Saturn, or the great Upsilon, standing up like a tall curved chalice, have still a quite unaccountable charm and mystery, as if they were the characters traced in wide welcome over Eden of the dawn. The ordinary small Greek letters, though I am now much more familiar with them, seem to me quite nasty little things like a swarm of gnats .... I say this merely to show that I was a much wiser and wider-minded person at the age of six than at the age of sixteen.

Many of the problems which he encountered at Colet House were to follow him to St Paul's, to which he moved in January 1887, aged a vulnerable and not altogether happy twelve. St Paul's was a school with a noble past and an honourable future. It was founded in the early part of the reign of Henry VIII. It was wealthy and prestigious, noted for its scholarship as well as standing in the class-obsessed world of late-Victorian England. The Reverend A.M. Mead, present Chaplain and Librarian at the school, describes St Paul's at the time of Gilbert's entry as "still a Christian and a classical school, not necessarily in that order. There was no chapel and the chaplain's designation had been secularised into 'Third Master,' though he, like many of the other masters, was in holy orders. However, the whole school still attended Latin prayers, some of which had been composed by Colet and his circle. Most of the boys were members of the Church of England, although Jewish boys were not uncommon. The High Master, F.W. Walker, a layman who was himself an Old Pauline, was probably, if a believer at all, a very free-thinking one. There were compulsory divinity lessons, which included reading the Greek Testament. Though it was no longer true that 'at St Paul's we teach only Latin and Greek,' the emphasis on the classics was still very strong and to specialise in them was considered the normal path of the abler Pauline . . ."

Gilbert's first year at St Paul's was not a happy one. Apart from the problem of his sight he was also at a disadvantage in terms of size. Obesity was not yet a problem, but he was an extremely tall boy for his age, with none of the strength or athleticism which so often accompany height. He was quite

25

simply growing too quickly. And his voice, always to be rather high for a man of his imposing stature, was high pitched and at times out of control in its tones and sounds. He was first-class schoolboy tease material. His clothes were often untidy and dusty; if there was any possibility of leaning against a chalk-covered wall or a dirty table Gilbert would certainly exploit the opportunity. He was also a dreamer, which at such an age gave the appearance of absent-mindedness. He was seen as being vacant, a boy who was to be spoken about rather than spoken with. Matters were not helped by the fact that Gilbert had not been able to maintain the pace of his contemporaries; most of his companions were two or even three years younger than himself: the humiliation was apparent and obvious to all. Edward Fordham, a friend and school-mate, remembered that "He sat at the back of the room and never distinguished himself. We thought him the most curious thing that ever was. I can see him now very tall and lanky, striding untidily along Kensington High Street, smiling and sometimes scowling as he talked to himself, apparently oblivious of everything he passed; but in reality a far closer observer than most, and one who had not only observed but remembered what he had seen." Lucian Oldershaw, later to become Gilbert's brother-in-law, looked on one day when Gilbert's pockets, not for the first or last time, were filled with snow. When the class left the playground the heat melted the content of Gilbert's pockets and his jacket began to soak through. "Please, Sir," shouted a horribly observant boy from the side of the room, "I think the laboratory sink must be leaking again. The water is coming through and falling all over Chesterton." The teacher believed the story and sent Gilbert outside to inform the powers that be that the sink was broken. It is sad that the master was so deceived; it is pathetic that Gilbert was throughout the escapade totally believing and never aware that most of the class were laughing at his trusting misfortune.

He became something of a school mascot, accepted as the archetypal eccentric and tolerated as such. If his homework was not given in on time, or not at all, the most absurd of explanations would be given and taken; "It's only Chesterton." On one occasion he was seen by boys and masters wandering aimlessly around the school playground when he should have been attending classes. He justified the action by explaining that he was under the misapprehension that it was a Saturday. No punishment was given, it just might have been true.

Gilbert's 1887 form master had an affectionate but critical opinion of the young dreamer: "Too much for me: means well by me, I believe, but has an inconceivable knack of forgetting at the shortest notice, is consequently always in trouble, though some of his work is well done, when he does remember to do it. He ought to be in a studio not at school. Never troublesome, but for his lack of memory and absence of mind." It is difficult not to judge this period with the iniquitous benefit of hindsight and to pour scorn on the teachers and other boys who failed to perceive Gilbert's budding genius. Only those closest to him, and not always they, were aware that his exercise books and volumes of fiction and non-fiction were covered with scribbled passages revealing insight and intellect, and delicate illustrations of all things from Christ on the Cross to railway engines. Here was a mind bursting to learn and comment. He was now reading with a burning passion. He drove himself through the great classical works of English literature in a remarkably short space of time, and devoured them with such an interest that he could recite by heart long passages of Dickens and Shakespeare. When a nineteenth-century novel was not at hand he would turn to the *Chambers Encyclopaedia* or at one juncture *A History of English Trade* which was in the house. Sir Walter Scott was another particular favourite, and Gilbert revealed in his *Autobiography* an early tendency which was to shape his future writing. "I was one day wandering about the streets in that part of North Kensington, telling myself stories of feudal sallies and sieges, in the manner of Walter Scott, and vaguely trying to apply them to the wilderness of bricks and mortar around me." Not lazy wanderings and vacuous dreams. His grasp of the main Latin works increased with a weekly intake of volumes with which most boys of his age had no intention of coming to grips. Still the master discerned no

27

spark. In July 1888 his report claimed that he was "Wildly inaccurate about everything; never thinks for two consecutive moments to judge by his work: plenty of ability, perhaps in other directions than classics."

By the December of the following year progress was described as "Fair. Improving in neatness. Has a very fair stock of general knowledge." More praise but harsher criticism in July 1889 with "A great blunderer with much intelligence." Blunderer he may have been, but his memory was sufficiently acute for him to remember and appreciate the Book of Job, *Lays of Ancient Rome* and several of the more esoteric of Shakespeare's plays and poems. This was a period of non-recognition for Gilbert, an immensely frustrating time of upset and barely any encouragement. Here was a young, developing man with an intellectual tendency superior to that of anybody in the school; yet he was considered a poor scholar, something of a buffoon. For any budding novelist, of course, the enforced loneliness and sense of failure was an inimitable learning process. Gilbert's grasp of isolation was to serve him well when he built layer on layer over his fictional characters, creating haunting degrees of individualism. For a schoolboy, however, being alone simply meant being alone. The result was a great amount of pain.

Salvation appeared in the form of a school playground fight, lasting some forty-five minutes, but with an affectionate conclusion. Gilbert was probably fifteen, possibly sixteen, at the time; Edmund Clerihew Bentley was two years younger. "The supreme importance to me of my schooldays lies in the fact that they were the time when I saw most of Gilbert Keith Chesterton," wrote Bentley in his memoirs. "If this were an autobiography, I should have more to say upon that subject than upon almost any other; and as it is, such account as I can give of G.K.C. must include a reference to his extraordinary power – of which he was and always remained quite unconscious – of inspiring affection and trust in all who had anything to do with him. It is as much a part of his story as of mine that we could form a friendship that was to last quite unchanged through life, even through years when we did not often meet and hardly ever wrote to each other: that was to become, speaking for myself, a part of the permanent background of existence, so that whatever happened to me, there was always somewhere in my mind the thought of the impression that it would make upon him . . ."

It was to become one of the greatest of literary friendships. Gilbert had not noticed the younger boy during his time at St Paul's and Bentley seems to have been unaware of the existence of Gilbert. The conflict which brought them together could never be recalled by Bentley, and Gilbert, always heavily influenced by his readings and imagination, was not beyond elaborating romantically on a quite uneventful meeting. However, his account tells of an energetic struggle, followed the next day by an even more tiring combat. The fisticuffs stopped when one of them quoted a line from Macaulay, the other was familiar with it and continued the quotation; the battle over, they set about becoming allies. Gilbert's home became a form of retreat for them both, a refreshment point where nourishment of an intellectual as well as a calorific kind could be obtained. Bentley was one of those prodigies which appear every generation or so to enliven schoolboy mythology. While dreaming the day away during the extremely dull chemistry lesson at St Paul's the vibrant young man began to doodle on the blotting paper in front of him. What he wrote was to edge its way into literary history and begin an entirely new poetic style.

> Sir Humphrey Davy
> Abominated gravy,
> He lived in the odium
> Of having discovered sodium.

As Bentley's middle name was Clerihew this distinctive title – which he scrupulously kept to himself all through his schooldays, knowing that years of teasing would follow such a revelation – was awarded to the verses which he was to write. Light-hearted and even absurd at times they may have been, but clerihews have retained their appeal throughout the years, still provoking a wry smile from readers.

The finest of the breed were to be published in *Biography*

for Beginners, with illustrations from Gilbert Chesterton, and
the first thing which was to be learned from the book was that
Biography differs from Geography because the latter is about
maps, the former about chaps. And did the Spanish people
believe Cervantes equal to half-a-dozen Dantes? It was very
much the humour of Gilbert and Bentley, ridiculous but
heavily tinged with learning and thought. The intimacy of the
friendship is indicated by the dedication in Bentley's most
famous work, the immortal detective story *Trent's Last Case.*
"Dear Gilbert," he wrote, ". . . I have been thinking again
today of those astonishing times when neither of us ever
looked at a newspaper; when we were purely happy in the
boundless consumption of paper, pencils, tea, and our elders'
patience; when we embraced the most severe literature and
ourselves produced such light reading as was necessary. . . in
short, when we were extremely young." The friendship was
the most influential happening of Bentley's life, with an importance which surpasses most schoolboy affections. Their
bond was deeply emotional, known to the rest of the school
and respected as something special rather than sinister. If
there was any homosexual aspect to the relationship, as some
have alleged, it was of the most innocent kind which is not
uncommon amongst adolescent boys; the physical was never
hinted at or suggested, they were simply two people involved
in healthy, noble love. Platonic partnerships between men
during the 1890s were frequent, usually encouraged. Attitudes of the times discerned a masculine quality in the close
companionship of males, without any of the homosexual
connotations which hold sway today. Until the 1950s, for
example, television could present two male friends in the
same bed without the physical being considered. External
attitudes have altered modern interpretations, and it would
be a dangerous anachronism to apply this to Gilbert and
Bentley. Gilbert was aware of possible accusations however,
and vehemently denied and condemned "the sin of Oscar
Wilde."

In an article in the *Spectator* shortly after Gilbert's death
Bentley would write, "This friend of all men and respecter of
every honest opinion had among his foremost qualities an

enormous intellectual pugnacity; for the love of his kind involved, for him, the intolerance of wrong, of error, of the abuse of power or influence." He continued, "Anyone who shares my memory of 11 Warwick Gardens in his boyhood will agree that vigorous and long-sustained arguments with anyone who would take up the cudgels were the most keenly felt pleasures of G.K.C. – sweeter even than the joy in books, or that collaboration in the producing of oceans of nonsense with pencil and paper which was the favourite amusement in that schoolboy circle." And concluded with, "The parents made their home a place of happiness for their two boys' many friends, a place that none of them can ever have forgotten." Home was still Gilbert's favourite place, not the school or the library. If a friend became special, if a book became precious, he would endeavour to involve person or object in his family base.

The next individual to be invited to the endearingly chaotic Chesterton household was to be the missing link in the "three" ("Three is certainly the symbolic number for friendship," Gilbert stated.) He was Lucian Oldershaw. Oldershaw differed from the other two-thirds of this sparkling triumvirate in many ways; he was from a totally different background, was of a distinct character. The son of an actor, he had travelled widely and lived in various towns and houses. This enforced change in location had meant a wide experience of schools, and when the dark, thin youth with a mature face and tested social manners joined Gilbert and Bentley he stood out as the publicist of the three, the boy who would get things done and also talk about his achievements. Gilbert believed that Oldershaw "brought into our secrets the breath of ambition and the air of a great world," and with his talent for magic tricks and conjuring he impressed his class-mates with a reputation for being unpredictable, out of the ordinary in an impressive heroic way.

For all Gilbert's support of the trio in youthful friendships the maxim of "two's company, three's a crowd" did have its sting. Oldershaw wanted Gilbert as his best friend, his personal companion in the new school. He tried hard, but never succeeded. The subsequent tension which this introduced would have strained the pull of friendship in a young man less affectionate and forgiving than Gilbert. Oldershaw's greatest contribution – apart from later becoming Gilbert's brother-in-law – was to provide the impetus behind the formation of the Junior Debating Club. Literary, semi-political and debating organisations were being formed all over England at this time, and the venture which the three embarked upon was by no means unique; it was, however, probably the most mature and successful project of its kind anywhere in the country. The St Paul's School Union Society already existed, but was looked on with some scorn, seen as a means of collaborating with masters and enhancing the prestige of the already bloated senior boys. Nor was the school magazine to be contributed to, regarded in Gilbert's eyes as beneath the efforts of any serious writer. The boys already met together on an informal basis, and Oldershaw proposed that a regular venue and time be arranged. The first meeting would be held at Oldershaw's house, in Talgarth Road, and the date would be 1st July 1890. The minutes of that first meeting were taken by Oldershaw, and are quite clear on points of purpose and nature.

> The object of the above Club is to get a few friends together to amuse one another with a literary or something approaching a literary subject. It was thought best to have someone to manage it, so a Chairman and Secretary have been elected, and the rules given below have been framed. It was thought at first to confine it only to Shakespeare, but it was decided to let it be any literary subject.

The elected Chairman was to be Gilbert, Oldershaw was made Secretary. The members represented something of an outcast, non-conformist group within St Paul's, and were to produce some startlingly polished writings and talks.

Twelve boys made up the original group, all of them agreeing with the Debating Club's motto of "Hence loathed Melancholy" and accepting the rule that any member failing to read a literary paper to the assembled members when re-

32

quired to do so would be fined sixpence; the same fine was levied on any boy absent from meetings twice in succession without a valid and convincing excuse. Meetings would take place in the members' houses, after school and sometimes on Saturdays. The founding sons of the Junior Debating Club were an intriguing group. First came Gilbert, Bentley and Oldershaw. Then there was Robert Vernède, a promising and skilled poet of French ancestry who sadly was killed in the First World War. The Solomon brothers, Lawrence and Maurice, were Jewish boys, once described by Gilbert in front of them as "the children of Israel"; Lawrence died in 1940, he was a Senior Tutor at University College, London. His brother, Maurice, became a leading director of the General Electric Company. Lawrence Solomon, a respected Latin don, became a close friend of Gilbert's, a companion who was to maintain Gilbert's sense of moderation and tolerance on the issue of anti-Semitism when many around him were indulging in crass Jew-baiting. Edward Fordham was a writer of satiric poetry, and used his caustic wit as a successful barrister. A second pair of brothers, Digby and Waldo d'Avigdor, two young men named Salter (later a Principal in the Treasury and Gilbert's solicitor) and Bertram (Director of Civil Aviation in the then Air Ministry) and B.N. Langdon-Davies completed the set.

The club took itself seriously, having photographs taken and feeling itself to be a somewhat exclusive body. In the group photograph of the J.D.C. reproduced here a pyramid has been formed with the aid of a step-ladder. Bentley is on top, an ambiguous expression on his face, possibly due to his having to perch in a precarious position. Gilbert is a few feet down, hands in pockets, bored by the whole thing. The rest of the group pose with arms folded or in positions of affected informality. At the bottom of the picture, almost hidden away is the small Cecil Chesterton, who ran along in the slipstream of the J.D.C., at first in short trousers. Bentley did not like Cecil and was prepared to show it; Cecil was never one to take a hint.

The good-fellowship and hours of laughter and discussion which centred on these young scholars and the other St Paul's pupils who would come along was not sufficient for all of the members, particularly Lucian Oldershaw. Always bursting with the urge to create and organise, Oldershaw perceived the need for a magazine in which the members could write and publish their views. Bentley was later to write that Oldershaw was not content with the simple founding of a well-organised and productive school society, "he founded, edited, published and actually sold within the school a J.D.C. magazine, the *Debater,* which contained, in addition to reports of the club's proceedings, literary contributions by most of its members. These included the first of Chesterton's poems to appear in print; poems which, as he declared many years afterwards, he never so much as glanced at again after leaving St Paul's."

Eighteen issues of the *Debater* were to see the light of day written in studious and laborious longhand by the leading members of the J.D.C. and then transported, sometimes by ludicrous means, to the typewriting studio of Miss Davidson at 13 Charleville Road in West Kensington. The circulation of the magazine was between sixty and one hundred copies, sold at sixpence each. Pale fawn covers held the journal together, and by the end of the first day of circulation the initial issue of the *Debater* had been completely sold out. "It is patent to an awe-struck universe," the first issue reported in a delightfully self-mocking manner, "that this paper is the offspring of that illustrious Society, the Junior Debating Club, whose fame has reached so many remote out-posts of the Empire, and whose ranks contain so many of the most able and distinguished men of the day." The issue contained an article by Gilbert entitled "Dragons," in which he demonstrated the style and grasp of argument and imagination which was to serve him so well

> The dragon is certainly the most cosmopolitan of impossibilities. His eccentric figure has walked through the romances of all ages and of all nations ... this scaly intruder has appeared from the earliest times, and appeared apparently with the sole object of being killed, whether by the lance of St George, the club of Herakles, the sword of Siegfried, or the arrows of Hiawatha. We

have even seen a dragon, together with some dubious-looking quadrupeds, in the arabesques of Moham-medans...

The first line of the piece was used by other members of the J.D.C. as a password, an alternative motto. The first edition also contained contributions by Oldershaw on Chaucer and "Misinterpretation of Design" by Bentley. Gilbert himself recalled many years later that to have his thoughts and words recorded in print was "blood-curdling.... I contributed to it turgid poems, in which bad imitations of Swinburne were so exactly balanced with worse imitations of the Lays of Ancient Rome, that many of my simpler friends fell under the illusion that I had a style of my own .... But I must admit that, for whatever reason, they attracted a certain amount of attention; and our experiment began to float to the surface of the school life and come within the range of official attention, which was the last thing I had ever desired."

He is referring to the notice given to the *Debater* by Frederick Walker, the High Master of St Paul's. Walker was an imposing man, respected by the boys but also capable of instilling fear and some dislike. He had arrived from Manchester Grammar School in 1876 after taking a first from Corpus Christi College, Oxford. His memory and ability to organise were gigantic, his sense of authority over the boys, and their subsequent acceptance of his standing, quite remarkable. His bellowing voice was notorious, his brusque manners ranging between the eccentrically amusing and the downright rude. Gilbert, and others, remembered the occasion when a protective and concerned mother wrote to Walker, anxious about the social standing of the boys at the school. "Madam," he replied, "so long as your son behaves himself and the fees are paid, no question will be asked about his social standing."

It was this daunting figure who came across a copy of the *Debater* on his table; it had been nervously placed there by one of the boys. He announced in a voice which, according to Gilbert "began like an organ and ended like a penny whistle," that the magazine "showed some glimmerings of talent"; he also announced on Speech Day that if he had been consulted about the magazine before its launch he may not have been willing to give it his blessing. This was one of the prime reasons why he was not involved in the early stages. The writings of Bentley and Gilbert had particularly impressed him, especially since Gilbert had little intellectual reputation amongst the masters at the school up until then. Walker showed his appreciation one day in Kensington High Street when Gilbert was innocently walking along, his mind centuries and countries away. The High Master positively shouted at the startled and severely embarrassed young man that he had some literary merit and capability, as long as he could "solidify" his potential.

In May 1891 Gilbert reached the age of seventeen. The J.D.C. noted the event with its usual thoroughness. "The Secretary then rose and in a speech in which he extolled the merits of the Chairman as a chairman, and mentioned the benefits which the Junior Debating Club received on the day of which this was the anniversary, viz., the natal day of Mr Chesterton, proposed that a vote wishing him many happy returns of the day and a long continuance in the Chair of the Club should be passed. This was carried with acclamations. The Chairman replied after restoring order." Gilbert's life had improved; he was recognised by his friends as a wit and a good companion, someone to be seen with, to learn from. Wider acknowledgment was still a problem, and the school was only to discern his true worth later. The pupils at St Paul's knew that Gilbert was an extraordinary peer, but some of the masters still found it difficult to recognise a promising author and poet in the slow, awkward youth who was frequently so difficult to teach, so reluctant to shine in their classes.

With each article he wrote Gilbert was developing, maturing. The month of his seventeenth birthday he wrote of Milton

His earliest recollections were of Greene and Marlowe, Fletcher and Shakespeare, and all the crowd of reckless, impoverished, dissolute geniuses who wrote in garrets and taverns the works which are the glory of the Elizabethan age. Their classical learning and their daring imagination he imbibed and carried with him into the narrower and sterner sphere of Puritan piety, and forms, as it were, a link between the two Englands differing in everything but their glory, the England of Elizabeth and the England of Cromwell.

One year later he took on the character of Shelley

He was not a bad man; he was not a good man; he was not an ordinary man; he was a sincere philanthropist and Republican; yet he was often as lonely and ill-tempered as a misanthrope; he had far purer feelings towards women than either Burns or Byron, yet he was a far worse husband than they: he was one of those men whose faults and failures seem due, not to the presence of tempting passions or threatening disasters, so much as to a mysterious inner weakness, a certain helplessness in the hands of circumstances.

At eighteen the completely inexperienced Gilbert was delving deeply into the minds and matters of profoundly complex individuals.

There was also a political demeanour emerging. Examples of anger against injustice are scattered throughout these early writings, particularly in the context of the Jewish people and their suffering. Four members of the J.D.C. were Jewish and although Gilbert was to sometimes make fun of them in his letters to Bentley his genuine sympathies were undoubtedly with the Jews – "No Jews; that is, if I except the elder tribe coming over on Sunday to take me to see Oldershaw . . . . I tried an experiment with Lawrence on Friday night, to see if he would accept on its real ground of friendliness our Semitic jocularity; so I took the bull by the horns and said that 'I would walk with him to the gates of the Ghetto'. . . . I don't think we need fear the misunderstanding which, I must say, would be imminent in the case of less sensible and well-feeling pagans."

He showed this clearly enough when composing his youthful outline of religious freedom. He quoted from Macaulay's monumental speech in favour of admitting Jews into Parliament. "The points on which Jews and Christians differ have a great deal to do with a man's fitness to be a bishop or a rabbi, but they have no more to do with his fitness to be a member of parliament than with his fitness to be a cobbler." He reacted with emotion and bewilderment to the news of the pogroms, those hellish massacres and violent attacks which the Ukrainian, Russian and Polish Jews had to suffer at the hands of the mob and the government-backed Black Hundreds, morbid bands of manic anti-Semites; one report forced him to write: "Made me feel strongly inclined to knock somebody down, but refrained." This predicament in Eastern Europe, which was provoking hundreds of thousands of Jews to emigrate from their adopted homes to the United States, Britain and any nation with doors open, remained on Gilbert's mind. He penned a poem called "Before a Statue of Cromwell, At the Time of the Persecution of the Jews in Russia;" in which he recalled how Oliver Cromwell had enabled the Jews to settle in England in the 1650s and contrasted this with the murderings in Russia, "While a brave and tortured people cry the shame of men to God!" There are indications here of an early leaning towards the paradox as a literary style, a fascination with the medieval world and a faith in the "ordinary" people of England who have not yet spoken.

As the *Debater* increased its importance and its circulation it was decided to improve the quality of its appearance. A professional printer, J.W. Wakeham of Bedford Terrace, Kensington, was awarded the task. Gilbert's writings had so impressed his contemporaries that he was persuaded to send one of his poems to the *Speaker,* a radical magazine then circulating. It was published.

God has struck all into chaos, princes and priests down-
   hurled,
But he leaves the place of the toiler, the old estate of the
   world.
When the old Priest fades to a phantom, when the old
   King nods on his throne,

The old, old hand of labour is mighty and holdeth
its own.

Gilbert's view on labour and socialism were undergoing a
period of acute ambivalence. He wrote to Lawrence Solomon: "With what you say about Socialism I most cordially
assent. It is utterly impracticable as things stand: that is why I
am so fond of it. It is almost as impracticable as Christianity."
The members of the club were not political on a party basis
and seldom held constant beliefs. Gilbert was enamoured
with some of the trappings of the theory, never seriously with
the realities of it. It was the camaraderie of the group which
for Gilbert had a socialistic appeal; whereas in reality the
J.D.C. was exclusive, élite and individualistic. The singing of
songs, which was to be so important in the Distributist days
of the future, transported Gilbert into an egalitarian life of
healthy peasants and earthy honesty. That the entire enterprise took place in one of the most conservative and class-
ridden establishments in the country made little impression.
The boys sang, and sang with conviction

I'm a Member, I'm a Member, Member of the J.D.C.
    I'll belong to it for ever,
Don't you wish that you were me?

The drinking of tea was compulsory and almost oriental in its
significance. So important was the ceremony of liquid refreshment that the boys put it to music and lyric. The last verse
went as follows

Then pass the cup, debaters all
    And fill the tea-pot high,
And o'er the joy of wild debate
    May hours like moments fly.
As critics quiet and composed,
    As brothers kind and free,
Join hand in hand the tea-pot round.
    Joy to the J.D.C.

39

The ranks of the Junior Debating Club rose as one man in 1892 to share in Gilbert's glory when he was awarded the Milton Prize for English verse at St Paul's School. Issue no. 15 of the *Debater* announced that "as we go to press we hear the pleasant news that our Chairman, Mr Chesterton, has gained the Milton Prize . . . the subject for treatment being St Francis Xavier, the apostle of the Indies . . ." The giving of the prize to Gilbert came as a shock, even a minor scandal, to the school as the Milton Prize had in the past been jealously in the preserve of the Eighth form. There was a deal of snobbery about it, and the bad feeling which was shown towards Gilbert by the boys who were also in the running left an unsavoury taste in the mouths of those who knew that his writing and imaginative skills were far in excess of anything any rival could offer. He had exhibited a depth of understanding of Xavier which was extraordinary for a teenager, even though it may have been overly romantic and lacked the realism which he was to demonstrate later when writing of St Francis and St Thomas Aquinas. Bentley remembered Gilbert "wiping the sweat from his brow as he stood, tall, gawky and untidy, reading the poem to a great audience of parents as well as boys at the end of the school year." The original copies have been lost, the only remaining version being that recorded by Maisie Ward, which had the warning "This is not exactly the same as given in the prize poem" written over it. He began the piece with

> He left his dust, by all the myriad tread
> Of yon dense millions trampled to the strand,
> Or 'neath some cross forgotten lays his head
> Where dark seas whiten on a lonely land:
> He left his work, what all his life had planned,
> A wanting flame to flicker and to fall,
> Mid the huge myths his toil could scarce withstand,
> And the light died in temple and in hall,
> And the old twilight sank and settled over all.

And concluded the fifty-four line poem with

This then we say: let all things further rest
And this brave life, with many thousands more,
Be gathered up in the eternal's breast
In that dim past his love is bending o'er:
Healing all shattered hopes and failure sore:
Since he had bravely looked on death and pain
For what he chose to worship and adore,
Cast boldly down his life for loss or gain
In the eternal lottery: not to be in vain.

   High Master Walker took good notice of the achievement, and posted on the school bulletin board that "G.K. Chesterton to rank with the Eighth." Gilbert never did reach that academic position, remaining in form 6B, some two years behind most boys of his own age, but now enjoying the privileges which the members of "the Eighth" coveted so dearly. It was a confused, confusing period for Gilbert; judged a boy genius by some, a slow learner well below the average by others. At least Frederick Walker began to back this St Paul's enigma, and when Gilbert's mother met him in 1894 to discuss her son's future life and education he was to reply, "Six foot of genius. Cherish him, Mrs Chesterton, cherish him."

III

Learning and Lunacy

Gilbert was never fully aware of the importance and prestige attached to literary prizes, and certainly failed to appreciate just how influential the Milton Award was in shaping other people's opinions of him as a poet and a character. It is to his credit that modesty, and a degree of *naïveté*, dominated the youthful personality who was generally regarded as a promising writer and thinker. Edward Chesterton recognised the talent, but preferred to pay more attention to his son's skills with the brush and pencil. Gilbert's short-term future would be decided for him. But first came a holiday, and a gift. For winning the Milton and for graduating – he would not be returning to St Paul's the next term – Gilbert was taken to France, his first journey out of the country. Father and son took the train to Rouen, visited some picturesque towns in the Normandy countryside and then travelled to Paris. France and the French had long been a subject of deep interest for Gilbert, and a fascination with the French Revolution was never to leave him. He liked the people of France, found them to be attractive and amusing, but detected a habit of talking too much. At Notre Dame Cathedral he was entertained by a kindly tour guide, and was touched by his willingness to compromise with the English language. He recorded his impressions in letter form, to E.C. Bentley.

A foreign town is a very funny sight with solemn old abbés in their broad brims and black robes and sashes and fiery bronzed little French soldiers staring right and left under their red caps, dotted everywhere among the blue blouses of the labourers and the white caps of the women. [And after encountering a pair of young French boys] My pater having discovered that the book they had with them was a prize at a Paris school, some slight conversation arose. Not thinking my French altogether equal to a prolonged interview, I took out a scrap of paper and began, with a fine carelessness, to draw a picture of Napoleon . . .

On arriving back in England Gilbert was faced with the most difficult period of his early years. It was a time of change, and here was a young man who was always more comfortable with evolution rather than revolution, no matter how much he waxed lyrical about great movements forward or backward. The first few months in London are vaguely recorded, with little more known than what was noted at the meetings of the Junior Debating Club. On 16th December 1892 a meeting argued over the very existence of itself: "A constitutional discussion was held regarding the future of the Club. This was opened by the Secretary, who remarked on the necessity for holding such a discussion, as members were already beginning to leave St Paul's School, and in a year or so more would be scattered over different parts of the world." The *Debater* closed its pages. The final issue appeared in the February of 1893, and announced that "With this number the *Debater* ceases to exist. Regretful though we may be at losing our Magazine, we may still claim that enthusiasm which prompted us to start it, and a belief that the idea which it was intended to embody, has been helped rather than hindered by its championship." It was a depressing day for Gilbert.

His sense of isolation began to grow again, a feeling which had entirely left him since the beginning of his friendship with Bentley and the others in the J.D.C. Unsure as to where his real talents lay, he knew he had a contribution to make to the world but had no idea where, or why. All he could realistically see about him was a break-up of contentment and joy. He hadn't questioned the life-style of debate, walks with good friends, comfortable argument and the warm safety of home and companions. He was confused, facing a painful experience without any weapons to fight back. He turned to his notebooks, treasure chests of revelation and explanation. His drawings in these are expertly crafted, sensitive and sanguine at times, horribly grotesque and dark at others. At all times they are clever and worked with an easy expertise. He was to turn to them more and more in the coming, unhappy months.

In his *Autobiography* he would write: "I deal here with the darkest and most difficult part of my task; the period of youth which is full of doubts and morbidities and temptations; and which, though in my case mainly subjective, has left in my mind for ever a certitude upon the objective solidity of Sin . . ." The notebooks reveal this. Devils and goblins rival each other in degrees of terror, angels join combat with soldiers and quite lovely depictions of the Virgin Mary. And there are shapeless creatures as well, undefined in form or gender, looking out of the pages in wonderment and fear. He was writing in the books too. Often only half sentences or a few words would be recorded, sometimes the beginnings of novels, poems and diatribes on any matter which sparked off an interest or a thought. There are no dates on the exercise books, and the only reliable, or almost reliable, method of placing them in any chronological order is to judge by the handwriting of the author. Gilbert's St Paul's writing was always accomplished in a large, untidy, scribbled type of scrawl, readily announcing his outward style. He later wrote in a form of italic, neat but sometimes difficult to read. The notebooks written up until the age of around seventeen, are full of flying dreams and typical teenage attitudes. He did write "Half-hours in Hades, an Elementary Handbook of Demonology," but it has no real bearing on his inner pain and suffering which was to ensue. There were verses as well, some clumsy and sloppy, others not so.

> O strange old shadow among us, O sweet-
> voiced mystery,
> Now in the hour of question I lift my voice
> unto thee.
> Stricken, unstable the creeds and old things
> fall and are not.

The temples shake and groan and whisper we
    know not what.
The shapes and the forms of worship wherein
    the divine was seen
Are scattered and cast away on the fields of
    the things that have been . . .

In the notebooks which cover the following year and a half certain themes appear again and again. People with hands bound behind them, awaiting punishment, or pleasure. Knights in armour gallop across the page, ladies in distress cry out for help and revenge. Naked figures are tormented and whipped, murdered and chastised. The sexual motive is obvious, though to dwell too much on this obscures the reality. If Gilbert were not undergoing that intricate transformation of sexuality at this stage in his life there would be a problem; the fact that he was experiencing conflicting emotions and desires is healthy and understandable. That a young man thinks of sadistic, or masochistic, images during his private times has little influence on his sexual maturity, any more than a schoolboy who sniggers at a softly pornographic magazine in the playground will be obsessed with hard pornography as an adult. What was far more damaging was the loneliness which he was to face as a result of his educational future.

In the 1890s a young man fresh out of public school who desired a career requiring an education, or a wealthy teenager who simply looked for three or four years of learning in beautiful and comfortable surroundings, would opt for a place at Oxford or Cambridge. This was what the majority of Gilbert's close friends did, along with thousands of others. For a boy with a middle- or upper-class background and a good brain it was natural, expected. Not so Gilbert. He was to attend art school, and learn the trade to which his father was so devoted. Edward Chesterton had influenced his son. It was a close, loving relationship and Gilbert's arm was not twisted, no bumptious pressure was brought to bear. If there is criticism of Edward Chesterton it must be in the realm of the child living out the parent's hopes. Edward was dedicated

45

to his art, and would have much preferred to have studied and become a professional than waste early years in a business and then indulge himself as a gifted amateur. Gilbert may have been fired with the control of words, but he could also control the pencil. It was not an evil decision, but it was a short-sighted one.

He first studied at a small art college in St John's Wood which boasted a fine reputation and called itself "Calderon's," after its leading light and teacher. Less an art college, more a band of artists with like-minded tastes and aspirations, it was known locally and amongst the artistic community as the "St John's Wood Clique," and its reputation did not outlive its existence. A number of practical jokes took place, and from the cartoons in Gilbert's notebooks no alteration in style as an artist is apparent; work was seldom allowed to interfere with play. In the middle of 1893 the Chestertons took a holiday in the lowlands of Scotland. Gilbert attempted the game of golf, and was confirmed in his view that sport was not his particular vocation. He wrote to Bentley, as always. "I am enjoying myself very much down here, though our time is drawing to a close. One of the nicest things about it is the way you mix with strangers and the absence of the cursed class feeling which makes me feel as if we were all humbugs. Whenever I feel tired of writing the novel [he had been working on this project for some time] I sally out in the evenings and play with children on the sands: coastguards' and visitors' children alike, except that the coastguards' are rather the more refined. Our Christian names are known all over the sands, and we behave generally like the inhabitants of one sandy nursery." It is a description of "merrily doing nothing." For Gilbert was drifting without purpose, and purpose was just what his contemporaries had in abundance.

Friends wrote to him from Oxford University, enthusiastic and fully in love with their colleges and studies. Agonising to Gilbert was the information that "a younger brother" of the J.D.C. had been formed at Oxford, obviously without Gilbert. Had then he been necessary in the debating club at St Paul's? He was evidently not necessary now. The world was continuing without him, the life which he had enjoyed so much still moved along, but without Gilbert. The emptiness which this made him feel was not unlike that felt by a lover after a broken romance, the belief that for the other person everything continued with the same gusto and warmth, whereas for the lover all was broken and destroyed. He had built a pyramid of values, with the J.D.C. and his friends, particularly Bentley, placed at the very top. When they suddenly disappeared the rest became meaningless, without merit or reason. He had no faith at the time, no spiritual lifeline, and no telescope of ambition to maintain his mental health. There was too little to share, too few to share with. Bentley wrote from Merton

> You will be charmed to hear that the Human Club exists .... It was decided that it would be well to discuss things, and read papers, until it got homogeneous enough to come together for the fun of the thing alone, like the J.D.C. – one of the surest indicia of the remarkable effect of that club on its members, don't you think? We are asking people to join whom we like, no intellectual standard, I needn't say. We come to bring not the etc., but and so forth. The title exercised us much. Vernède suggested the Whitmen; ruled out as being of an exclusive sound. Oldershaw wanted the S.U. (Some of Us) or the Hugger Mugger Club ... very Eighteenth-Century. I suggested the Tinkling Symbols. Vernède said the Cosmic Club was rather good. I had a long series of names, among them the Christ and Culture, the Anti-Philistines, and finally, by a sudden flash of memory, the Human Club. ... By the way, will you write to Vernède and tell him there is a God? He's getting frightfully dogmatic in his Agnosticism and wants somebody to unreason with him on the point.

The cutting stabs of loneliness continued, always with the friends at Oxford believing they were doing the best thing by keeping Gilbert informed, not leaving him out even though he was not present. Salter wrote that "There was a meeting of the Human one night last week at Oldershaw's, but nobody

read a paper" and "I went to breakfast with Bentley yesterday. You ought to come up, if only to see his new rooms. He
had just had them packed full overnight with some twenty-
two men come to hear a paper of his on Chaucer." His closest
friend, the romantic notion of the academic breakfast, his
adored Chaucer being debated. Not only Bentley, but Salter,
Oldershaw and Vernède at Oxford and together. The strain
was monumental.

Gilbert's response was full of pathos. When he received
letters telling of love lost and found, of pretty young things
and sporting heroics, he could only reply with suburban gossip and family news. When he told of the progress of locals
who were known by the group the information seemed sterile,
the tellings of a time and place far away, of children and
playing. He became overly concerned with his friends, who
were themselves undergoing the often difficult process of
becoming students, with all of the consequent assumptions
and poses; as well as the realisation that large intellectual
reputations in small schools do not dictate large intellectual
reputations in large universities. He wrote a poem about
them, hopeful but ultimately maudlin. It was titled "An Idyll"

> Tea is made; the red fogs shut round the house
>   but the gas burns.
> I wish I had at this moment round the table
> A company of fine people.
> Two of them are at Oxford and one in Scotland
>   and two at other places.
> But I wish they would all walk in now, for the
>   tea is made.

Bentley professed his love for Nina Vivian, one of a family
who lived near to Gilbert in Warwick Gardens. Gilbert knew
of this, and in a notebook poem he dwelt on her characteristics, as well as those of her sister Ida. "What are little girls
made of? .... Nina is made of water-colours, three lilies and
an apron; Ida of three good novels and a paper cracker . . ."
He also recorded in his notebook the composition of Bentley:
"hard wood with a knot in it, a complete set of Browning and

a strong spring." Of Oldershaw he perceived Lucifer matches and a pen, Lawrence Solomon was a barrister's wig, salt and copies of *Punch,* and his brother Maurice a clean collar and watch-wheels. Knowing of Bentley's interest in the Vivian family he wrote to him of them. "Today is Sunday, and Ida's birthday. Thus it commemorates two things, the creation of Ida and the creation of the world. And the Lord looked and beheld they were good. Really it is most interesting to think that nineteen years ago the Cosmic Factory was at work; the vast wheel of stars revolved, the archangels had a conference and the result was another person . . . . I should imagine that sun, wind, colours, chopsticks, circulating library books, ribbons, caricatures and the grace of God were used." Gilbert's frustration is beyond question, but the notebooks which have been relied upon to give shape and form to those unhappy years of his life are mostly what they appear to be: notebooks. They are not profound sexual admissions or nightmares of the real Gilbert. And Gilbert probably worried about his "lunatic" years more than was strictly necessary. He had nobody of his own age and experience to confess to or be guided by. It was too much for a boy alone. In his *Autobiography* he dwelt on the period, and was harsh with himself

. . . . I am not proud of believing in the Devil. To put it more correctly, I am not proud of knowing the Devil. I made his acquaintance by my own fault; and followed it up along lines which, had they been followed further, might have led me to devil-worship or the devil knows what . . . . What I may call my period of madness coincided with a period of drifting and doing nothing; in which I could not settle down to any regular work. I dabbled in a number of things; and some of them may have had something to do with the psychology of the affair. I would not for a moment suggest it as a cause, far less as an excuse, but it is a contributory fact that among these dabblings in this dubious time, I dabbled in Spiritualism without having even the decision to be a Spiritualist. Indeed I was, in a rather unusual manner, not only detached but indifferent. My brother and I used to play with planchette, or what the Americans call the ouija board; but we were among the few, I imagine, who played in a mere spirit of play . . . . I saw quite enough of the thing to be able to testify, with complete certainty, that something happens which is not in the ordinary sense natural, or produced by the normal and conscious human will. Whether it is produced by some sub-conscious but still human force, or by some powers, good, bad or indifferent, which are external to humanity, I would not myself attempt to decide. The only thing I will say with complete confidence, about that mystic and invisible power, is that it tells lies. The lies may be larks or they may be lures to the imperilled soul or they may be a thousand other things; but whatever they are, they are not truths about the other world; or for that matter about this world.

Spiritualism, and those pseudo-sciences on the fringes of the occult, are often the preserve of the vulnerable and the lonely. For men and women who find no contentment with the established order of events and lack an appropriate number of stable relationships a contact with powers beyond the day-to-day is highly valuable. It is in essence an escape, and Gilbert knew what he wanted to escape from, and to an extent where he wanted to escape to. Many have looked into the world of the psychic; indeed Sir Arthur Conan Doyle, that sanest of Englishmen, was obsessed with spiritualism and at times appallingly gullible. A need, rather than an inclination, to search for meaning and understanding in what may loosely be termed black magic is not particularly sinister. And if, as Gilbert later believed, there was only one true path and only that path could provide complete satisfaction it was only natural for a young man then without that truth to look elsewhere.

If there was a deeper mental anxiety plaguing Gilbert at the time it was almost certainly his struggle with a late blooming of sexual awareness. He only began noticing women after he left St Paul's and consequently had no one with whom to share his observations. Such a feeling as "I am the only person undergoing this, the only man wanting to masturbate and to be physically intimate with women" is entirely typical in lonely boys at the time of puberty. It is usually those coming from a close circle of brothers and friends who manage to discover that their emotions and desires are neither unique, nor evil and wrong. Gilbert's only close male companion was his brother Cecil, still too young to hear such stuff.

So he continued to explore the world which he so hated and feared. Its very darkness attracted him, for Gilbert was always an adventurer searching without success for an adventure. He gave examples of his undertakings with candour

> We asked planchette, in our usual random fashion, what advice it would give to an acquaintance of ours, a solid and rather dull Member of Parliament who had the misfortune to be an authority on education. Planchette wrote down with brazen promptitude (in these later times it was always very prompt, though not always very clear) the simple words, "Get a divorce." The wife of the politician was so respectable, and I will add so hideous, that the materials of a scandalous romance seemed to be lacking. So we sternly enquired of our familiar spirit what the devil he meant; possibly an appropriate invocation. The result was rather curious. It wrote down very rapidly an immensely and indeed incredibly long word, which was at first quite illegible. It wrote again; it wrote it four or five times; it was always quite obviously the same word; and towards the end it was apparent that it began with the three letters Orr .... I said, "This is all nonsense; there is no word in the English language beginning Orr, let alone a word as long as that." Finally it tried again and wrote the word out quite clearly; and it ran: Orriblerevelationsinighlife.

Gilbert's rationality broke through the artificial tension. He recalled how he felt after the experience, which runs the border between chilling horror and ludicrous hoax

> If it was our subconsciousness, our subconsciousness at least had a simple sense of humour. But that it was our subconsciousness rather than our consciousness (if it was not something outside both) is proved by the practical

fact that we did go on puzzling over the written word, when it was again and again rewritten, and really never had a notion of what it was, until it burst upon us at last. Nobody who knew us, I think, would suppose us capable of playing a long and solemn and silly deception on each other.

He concluded his anecdote with a warning

But cases of this kind fill me with wonder and a faint alarm, when I consider the number of people who seem to be taking spirit communications seriously, and founding religions and moral philosophies upon them. There would indeed have been some Orrible Revelations in Igh Life, and some Orrible Revelations about our own mental state and moral behaviour, if we had trotted off to the M.P. with our little message from the higher sphere.

Some purpose was injected into Gilbert's life when he began to study at University College, London. His course was Fine Art and included English, French and Latin. He had the monumental opportunity of studying Latin under Alfred Edward Housman. Housman had had an undistinguished career at Oxford, only managing a pass degree, and was forced into employment as a civil servant in London for the first ten working years of his life. It was only later that he began to shine as a scholar, building a reputation in the academic journals of the time. From 1892 until 1911 he was Professor of Latin at University College, during which time he wrote the profound and picquant *A Shropshire Lad*. In 1911 he was appointed to the chair of Latin at Cambridge, and continued to write until the mid 1930s. He died in 1936, the same year as Gilbert. It was rare for Gilbert to miss the flavour of genius in those with whom he made contact, but he did so with his Latin teacher at University College. After one year of the course he was asked, and agreed, to give up the subject. Yet Latin had been, and was to be, always a particular joy for Gilbert. It was not the theme of the lectures which disappointed him but the lectures on the theme. His studies were anarchic, as was his personality. He loved to learn at his own pace – which was frequently faster than that of his contemporaries – and along his own criteria and values. Rigid structures of education could not hold him, and neither could controlled intellectual curiosity. Gilbert's journey was one of startled, larger-than-life discovery, learning for learning's sake and not for somebody else's narrow concept of education.

Gilbert's butterfly mind – he would settle on one subject for a time, absorb all the beauty and wisdom he could from it and then move to another issue, often completely neglecting the initial area for years – found difficulty in coping with the other academic disciplines at the College as well. He studied English for two years, and achieved indifferent results. But his professor, W.P. Ker, was a popular teacher and recognised Gilbert's promise. Gilbert wrote

.... I am able to boast myself among the many pupils who are grateful to the extraordinarily lively and stimulating learning of Professor W.P. Ker. Most of the other students were studying for examinations; but I had not even that object in this objectless period of my life. The result was that I gained an entirely undeserved reputation for disinterested devotion to culture for its own sake; and I once had the honour of constituting the whole of Professor Ker's audience. But he gave as thorough and thoughtful a lecture as I have ever heard given, in a slightly more colloquial style; asked me some questions about my reading; and, on my mentioning something from the poetry of Pope, said with great satisfaction: "Ah, I see you have been well brought up." Pope had much less than justice from that generation of the admirers of Shelley and Swinburne.

The only close friend he made during his time at University College was Ernest Hodder Williams, a member of the publishing family Hodder and Stoughton. Hodder Williams was to help Gilbert begin his literary career, and Gilbert was to acknowledge that "in the case of my association with Hodder Williams, it was against all reason that so unbusinesslike a person should have so businesslike a friend." The friendship pleased Gilbert, but was never as intense as the relationship which existed between himself and Bentley or the others in the J.D.C; in fairness, it was not supposed to have been. The loneliness was still there, still digging away at the foundations of his sanity and composure. He later wrote a description of a companion of these heavy days for the *Daily News*. There are overwhelmingly autobiographical currents in the piece. He called it "The Diabolist."

... It was strange, perhaps, that I liked his dirty, drunken society; it was stranger still, perhaps, that he liked my society. For hours of the day he would talk with me about Milton or Gothic architecture; for hours of the night he would go where I have no wish to follow him, even in speculation. He was a man with a long, ironical face, and red hair; he was by class a gentleman, and could walk like one, but preferred, for some reason, to walk like a groom carrying two pails. He looked like a sort of super-jockey; as if some archangel had gone on the Turf. And I shall never forget the half-hour in which he and I argued about real things for the first and last time.... He had a horrible fairness of the intellect that made me despair of his soul. A common, harmless atheist would have denied that religion produced humility or humility a simple joy; but he admitted both. He only said, "But shall I not find in evil a life of its own? Granted that for every woman I ruin one of those red sparks will go out; will not the expanding pleasure of ruin ..."

"Do you see that fire?" I asked. "If we had a real fighting democracy, some one would burn you in it; like the devil-worshipper that you are."

"Perhaps," he said, in his tired, fair way. "Only what you call evil I call good."

He went down the great steps alone, and I felt as if I wanted the steps swept and cleaned. I followed later, and as I went to find my hat in the low, dark passage where it hung, I suddenly heard his voice again, but the words were inaudible. I stopped, startled; but then I heard the voice of one of the vilest of his associates saying, "Nobody can possibly know." And then I heard those two or three words which I remember in every syllable and cannot forget. I heard the Diabolist say, "I tell you I have done everything else. If I do that I shan't know the difference between right and wrong." I rushed out without daring to pause; and, as I passed the fire I did not know whether it was hell or the furious love of God.

I have since heard that he died; it may be said, I think, that he committed suicide; though he did it with tools of pleasure, not with tools of pain. God help him, I know the road he went; but I have never known or even dared to think what was that place at which he stopped and refrained.

The pattern of self-analysis is clear, as is a form of cathartic imagining. How much is a real encounter, how much an artificial construction and how much a revelation of Gilbert's own feelings and actions, both real and mental, is not known. There are undeniable traits displayed which clear some of the mud from his own predicament at the time. There is no record, either from himself or from any friend or relative or enemy, of his having committed any hideous sins, or any minor ones outside of the usual transgressions. Fear would not have held him back – cowardice was not one of Gilbert's shortcomings – and the London of the 1890s presented opportunities for the hopeful sinner. An innate sense of morality and ethics held him in place, securely within the realm of conscience. His black crimes would have to be lived out vicariously, through the pen and the fictional actions of others.

The Fine Art part of his course took place at the Slade School, a department of University College, which was then beginning to build a reputation which would become international. It had opened its doors in 1871, part of the new thrust in learning which was enabling the middle classes, as opposed to upper and upper-middle, to take advantage of higher education. Felix Slade, a Victorian benefactor and art collector, had founded the institution, leaving enough money for art professorships to be maintained and a college to be entirely devoted to an English school of painting. Women were admitted, and it was also the fashion to let the students draw and paint from live models as well as mannequins and plaster figures. Both aspects of the Slade were considered radical, going beyond the bounds of modern education. The tone of the whole college was modernity, whether it needed it or not; change and progress come what may. Such a quality never appealed to Gilbert. He was not at home there, and nobody attempted to alter the fact. His understanding of art and the artistic differed fundamentally from the dominant notions of the teachers and the students. He was different from the majority; worse, he was seen as being behind the times.

"Art may be long, but schools of art are short and very fleeting; and there have been five or six since I attended an art school!" he wrote. "Mine was the time of Impressionism; and nobody dared to dream there could be such a thing as Post-Impressionism or Post-Post-Impressionism. The very latest thing was to keep abreast of Whistler, and take him by the white forelock, as if he were Time himself. Since then that conspicuous white forelock has rather faded into a harmony of white and grey, and what was once so young has in its turn grown hoary . . ." Nor was he content to leave it there. He suffered, both in hurt pride and humiliating criticisms, and he would reply. "An art school is a place where about three people work with feverish energy and everybody else idles to a degree that I should have conceived unattainable by human nature. Moreover, those who work are, I will not say the least intelligent, but, by the very nature of the case, for the moment the most narrow; those whose keen intelligence is for the time narrowed to a strictly technical problem."

His Fine Art professor, Frederick Brown, had joined the Slade in 1892 and had much of the authority of Gilbert's High Master at St Paul's, with far less of his attraction. After one year of study Gilbert was asked to leave. The teachers claimed that they could teach him nothing. His notebook art at this period was quite exceptional, full of delicate illustrations and products of a fertile artistic mind. Nothing, however, is as vulnerable as a fashion; and those teachers were at the sharp end of the new artistic trends. Gilbert could always, would always, be a threat to those who regarded themselves as comfortably entrenched in either old philosophies or new ideas. He challenged. What could be more annoying than a student arguing with the intense wit and understanding of a genius against concepts which one knew to be correct, knew were going to transform the artistic environment? There was no room for this youth with a high-pitched voice and a ridiculous laugh, who could be moved to breathlessness by objects of natural beauty.

Shortly after Gilbert's time at the Slade students were definitely painting from female models who were seated naked in front of them. It seems likely that Gilbert also would have been painting nudes. If so, it would have been his first vision of adult nudity in women, and to his wandering mind the shock must have been great. He was interested in girls, and showed a healthy envy of his friends who had begun even the most innocuous relationships with young ladies from Oxford and London. He wrote to Lawrence Solomon after hearing that his St Paul's friend was seeing a young lady, "It is with deep pain that I hear of your 'carryings on.' You too, my poor friend, are being driven on the rock of the sirens (I allude to the fascinating Miss. . . .)" Bentley was proving himself a success with the female population of Oxford, and Gilbert looked upon all this as a heroic battle, with his friend the knight rescuing distressed damsels, and, a little less child-like and romantic, giving Gilbert the passed on pleasure of female companionship. Because, although he was not to be particularly slow in asking girls out or approaching women, at this stage in his life there was no woman, and he regretted it bitterly. News of his close friend's conquests – often only to the extent of winning a kiss or a hand held – would give him pleasure and a sense of satisfaction. He may not have been the handsome youth in demand at every society party in the university town of Oxford and the fine districts of London, but his friend was. Touches of pathos, hints of innocent longing.

In the summer of 1894 Gilbert travelled more widely. Scotland was visited again; more important, he saw Italy. He wrote to Bentley often, informing him of the delights of the country. From Florence, in the Hotel New York he sent his second letter, telling of a chance encounter with an elderly American colonel. The two tourists compared notes on Botticelli, Ruskin, Carlyle and Emerson, discussed their respective homelands and debated world issues. The American was a well informed and experienced traveller. Gilbert enjoyed and exploited the conversation

> .... I asked him what he thought of Whitman. He answered frankly that in America they were "hardly up to him." "We have one town, Boston," he said precisely, "that has got up to Browning." He then added that there was one thing everyone in America remembered: Whitman himself. The old gentleman quite kindled on this topic. "Whitman was a real Man. A man who was so pure and strong that we could not imagine him doing an unmanly thing anywhere." It was odd words to hear at a table d'hôte, from your next door neighbour: it made me quite excited over my salad. You see that this humanitarianism in which we are entangled asserts itself where, by all guidebook laws, it should not. When I take up my pen to write to you, I am thinking more of a white-moustached old Yankee at an hotel than about the things I have seen within the same 24 hours: the frescoes of Santa Croce, the illuminations of St Marco; the white marbles of the tower of Giotto; the very Madonnas of Raphael, the very David of Michelangelo. Throughout this tour, in pursuance of our theory of travelling, we have avoided the guide: he is the death-knell of individual liberty. Once only we broke through our rule and that was in favour of an extremely intelligent, nay impulsive young Italian in Santa Maria Novella, a church where we saw some of the most interesting pieces of mediaeval paintings I have ever seen, interesting not so much from an artistic as from a moral and historical point of view. Particularly noticeable was the great fresco expressive of the grandest mediaeval conception of the Communion of Saints, a figure of Christ surmounting a crowd of all ages and stations, among whom were not only Dante, Petrarca, Giotto, etc., etc., but Plato, Cicero, and best of all, Arius. I said to the guide, in a tone of expostulation, "Heretico!" (a word of impromptu manufacture). Whereupon he nodded, smiled

and was positively radiant with the latitudinarianism of the old Italian painter. It was interesting for it was fresh proof that even the early Church had a period of thought and tolerance before the dark ages closed around it. There is one thing that I must tell you more of when we meet, the tower of Giotto. It was built in a square of Florence, near the Cathedral, by a self-made young painter and architect who had kept sheep as a boy on the Tuscan hills. It is still called "The Shepherd's Tower."

What I want to tell you about is a series of bas-reliefs, which Giotto traced on it, representing the creation and progress of man, his discovery of navigation, astronomy, law, music and so on. It is religious in the grandest sense, but there is not a shred of doctrine (even the Fall is omitted) about this history in stone. If Walt Whitman had been an architect, he would have built such a tower, with such a story on it. As I want to go out and have a good look at it before we start for Venice tomorrow, I must cut this short. I hope you are enjoying yourself as much as I am, and thinking about me half as much as I am about you.

The affection for Bentley and subsequent missing of him is evident. The affection for Walt Whitman stemmed from an introduction to the author by Lucian Oldershaw; they had read *Leaves of Grass* to each other in Oldershaw's bedroom for over three hours during their last year at St Paul's, breaking only for drinks at Oldershaw's Talgarth Road house in Kensington. Whitman had gone a long way towards saving Gilbert in the earlier days of his depression, instilling in him a new lust for life and an instinct for survival.

Whitman is usually remembered by his portrait in the first edition of *Leaves of Grass* in 1855. In it the bearded poet wears an open shirt and slouch hat, with his head cocked to one side, full of that zestful enthusiasm and vibrance which Gilbert found so attractive and reassuring. He had been born in 1819 in Long Island, one of a family of ten children. He was raised on the literature of the Bible, Homer, Shakespeare and Scott – the similarities with Gilbert are striking here – and became a teacher and printer. After a period as a journalist and editor Whitman travelled with his brothers to the south, and for the next few years shared his life between the urban growth of nineteenth-century New York and the expanse of the American south-east and mid-west. He began to see man as a part of nature, with love being at the root of humanity. He read the German school of thought which was so pessimistic about the future of humanity, and dismissed it.

In 1855 came *Leaves of Grass,* a series of thirteen poems which earned him as much dislike as praise. It was in England that his reputation grew most, not in his native United States. As the poet of democracy, who was to suffer during the Civil War and become an ill man in middle age, recognition was not forthcoming. His poetry is full of warmth and a sense of the transcendental qualities which mattered much to Gilbert. In his book *The Thing: Why I Am A Catholic,* published in 1930, Gilbert would write of Whitman that "he seemed to me something like a crowd turned to a giant, or like Adam, the first man . . . . I did not care about whether his unmetrical poetry were a wise form or no, any more than whether the true Gospel of Jesus was scrawled on parchment or stone . . . . What I saluted was a new equality, which was not a dull levelling, but an enthusiastic lifting . . . . Real men were greater than unreal gods; and each remained as mystic and majestic as a god, while he became as frank and comforting as a comrade . . . . A glory was to cling about men . . . . the least and lowest of men . . . . A hump-backed negro half-wit, with one eye and homicidal mania, must not be painted without his numbus of gold-coloured light."

Whitman's influence on Gilbert both at this time and later was vast. As a poet he helped to shape Gilbert's writings, as a thinker he helped to shape Gilbert's life. If it were not for literature the young man, alone and aware of it, may have found his life too shallow to continue. His 1894 notebook contains a number of ideas and verses clearly based upon Whitman themes, and throughout his Italian holiday, in Verona and Venice and Milan, he read and thought of his new literary mentor. He was to need the Whitmanesque attitude towards optimism when he returned from Italy, for October 1894 was the month he dropped Latin from his studies at

60

University College and instead attempted to come to terms with the college classes in History and Political Economy. He wrote and remembered little of this term of study, unhappy with content and methods. For him it was "failure."

Any suicidal impulses which may have entered Gilbert's mind were not recorded outside the most cryptic of drawings, far too disguised for any serious study. Suicide, or attempts at it, by people in his situation are not uncommon: isolation, friends from the earliest days discovering new lives and doing well, a belief that one is failing in so many things, no partner or even best friend. University students between the ages of eighteen and twenty are particularly prone to severe depression and suicidal thoughts when their familiar supports and props simply drop away. Gilbert did indulge in "mad" thoughts, but gives no literal reference to the "madness" of suicide. "There is something truly menacing in the thought of how quickly I could imagine the maddest, when I had never committed the mildest crime. Something may have been due to the atmosphere of the Decadents [he saw them as in direct conflict with Whitman] and their perpetual hints of the luxurious horrors of paganism; but I am not disposed to dwell much on that defence, I suspect I manufactured most of my morbidities for myself. But anyhow, it is true that there was a time when I had reached that condition of moral anarchy within, in which a man says, in the words of Wilde, that 'Atys with the blood-stained knife were better than the thing I am.' I have never felt the faintest temptation to the particular madness of Wilde; but I could at this time imagine the worst and the wildest disproportions of more normal passion; the point is that the whole mood was overpowered and oppressed with a sort of congestion of imagination. As Bunyan, in his morbid period, described himself as prompted to utter blasphemies, I had an overpowering impulse to record or draw horrible ideas and images; plunging deeper and deeper as in a blind spiritual suicide." Suicide of the spirit was Gilbert's particular ailment, and he was only to fully recover from the near fatality when he threw off those childish things which tied him firmly to unhappiness; the comfortable late-Victorian family and the comfortable late-Victorian suburb would not follow him into adult life. When he came to terms with this, painful though it was, he was virtually cured.

Writing and writings eased the path. Of the latter it was of course Whitman who did most of the good work. Oscar Wilde also contributed. As a great man to argue against with friends and oppose as a point of principle Mr Wilde had no rivals. His fame and infamy during the 1890s made him an easy hero and even easier target. Gilbert knew that he was against what Wilde stood for, but was conscious that what Wilde actually wrote was great literature. He emulated Wilde's "The Fisherman and His Soul" in one of his notebooks, and frequently referred to him in the course of debate and conversation.

Of Robert Louis Stevenson's writings Gilbert admired the notion of the lone hero battling against forces greater and more sinister than himself. He showed when he wrote his biography of Stevenson in 1926 and 1927 that he felt a parallel between that author's boyhood and his own. His admiration for Stevenson clearly extended beyond mere love of his writings, he experienced a sense of identification. In a cleansing style he would write in the biography: "What was the matter with Stevenson, I fancy . . . was that there was too sharp a contrast between the shelter and delicate fancies of his childhood and the sort of world which met him like a wind on the front doorstep. The ideal development of a man's destiny is . . . from the child's garden of verses to the man's garden of vows. I do not think that time of transition went right with Stevenson; I think that something thwarted or misled him . . . . I think that in his childhood he had the worst luck in the world; and that this explains most of his story."

No leaps of imagination are required; Gilbert's own story is strikingly similar. He gained a solid platform of comfort from the lives of authors and poets of the past; an experience shared was an experience partially understood and, with the greatest of efforts, almost accepted. He was searching out paths back to calmness and sanity, and discovering them in the lives of great men. It was as though the supreme authors of ages past were holding out a hand of salvation.

Stevenson's outstretched arm was always the strongest.

"He stood up suddenly amid all these things and shook himself with a sort of impatient sanity; a shrug of scepticism about scepticism," Gilbert wrote about the man who provided such help. "His real distinction is that he had the sense to see that there is nothing to be done with Nothing. He saw that in that staggering universe it was absolutely necessary to stand somehow on something . . . he did seek for a ledge on which he could really stand. He did definitely and even dramatically refuse to go mad; or, what is very much worse, to remain futile." He continued the theme in *The Poet and the Lunatics,* published in July 1929. In the chapter entitled "The Crime of Gabriel Gale" Gilbert discussed madness, a subject which would appear time and again in his books. He clearly had a fascination both for the liberation as well as the agony of insanity by the time he came out of his black period; it was the interest of one who had seen the door, knocked hard, but recoiled when the first lock was opened.

A very large number of young men nearly go mad. But nearly all of them only nearly do it; and normally they recover the normal. You might almost say it's normal to have an abnormal period. It comes when there's a lack of adjustment in the scale of things outside and within. Lots of those boys, those big healthy schoolboys you hear about, who care for nothing but cricket or the tuckshop, are busting with a secret and swelling morbidity. [He then went on to describe an individual case] . . . . in this young man it was rather symbolically expressed even in the look of him. It was like his growing out of his clothes, or being too big for his boots. The inside gets too big for the outside. He doesn't know how to relate to two things; and generally he doesn't relate them at all. In one way his own mind and self seem to be colossal and cosmic and everything outside them small or distant. In another way the world is much too big for him; and his thoughts are fragile things to be hidden away. There are any number of cases of that disproportionate secretiveness.

The tunnel had seemed interminable, ever dark. There was now some light at the end, some ripples of hope. Gilbert's descent into instability was akin to a man slipping down a muddy hill, no matter how far he dug his fingers into the dirt his slide continued, and when he rested his hands for a moment the drop resumed with even greater velocity. It was a nightmare image. As he neared his twenty-first birthday the conclusion suddenly appeared to be reachable. Peace and calm had in fact been growing steadily more accessible for eighteen months, but by its very nature such a mental quandary does not allow the sufferer to perceive any ray of hope until the end is upon him. He began to grapple with perspective, and the concept of existence. If only he would relax, he told himself, and accept the joy of the present, the problems of the future would no longer be problems. He was finding meaning. In a notebook of the time he wrote

> If I set the sun beside the moon,
> And if I set the land behind the sea,
> And if I set the tower beside the country,
> And if I set the man beside the woman,
> I suppose some fool would talk about one
> being better.

And in another, which he called "The Daisy," he penned

> Colossal leagues of powers
> Went to make one daisy.
> And colossal choirs of angels
> Could not give thanks for it.

Gilbert's life was beginning to be filled with a vague image of god; God would come later. He was grateful for life, grateful for what he now saw to be wonderful gifts and opportunities. Gratitude was something to be considered and relished, and he made notes on the subject

> You say grace before meals.
> All right.
> But I say grace before the play and the opera,
> And grace before the concert and pantomime,

64

And grace before I open a book,
And grace before sketching, painting,
Swimming, fencing, boxing, walking, playing,
    dancing;
And grace before I dip the pen in the ink.

He was excited about his partial recovery, and felt well enough to inform Bentley of the news. Writing to other people on the history of his suffering was a major breakthrough. Bentley was no longer a loved friend to be envied and mourned for while he was away at Oxford, but someone who could be trusted completely with a profound example of openness. "Inwardly speaking I have had a funny time. A meaningless fit of depression, taking the form of certain absurd psychological worries, came upon me, and instead of dismissing it and talking to people, I had it out and went very far into the abysses, indeed. The result was that I found that things, when examined, necessarily spelt such a mystically satisfactory state of things, that without getting back to earth, I saw lots that made me certain it is all right. The vision is fading into common day now, and I am glad. It is embarrassing, talking with God face to face, as a man speaketh to a friend."

Of a higher being, a force behind creation, he now spoke often. He was reading the Bible, especially the Old Testament, with his usual passion for words. His notebooks contain fewer drawings and illustrations, more passages from proposed novels and short poems. He became convinced that his future – he now had a future he believed – lay in the world of literature and not in the realm of fine art. The paradox makes an early appearance: "The stone that gathers most moss is the gravestone," and one which was to occur much later in his life under a different heading: "About what else than serious subjects can one possibly make jokes?" Most important of all in the notebooks was a statement hidden between idle jottings and careless aphorisms. "The right way is the Christian way, to believe there is a positive evil somewhere and fight it." Out of an experience of hell, a taste of evil, came a dim vision of heaven. He proceeded to write more poetry on his new, evolving philosophy

The axe falls on the wood in thuds, "God, God."
The cry of the rook, "God," answers it,
The crack of the fire on the hearth, the voice
of the brook, says the same name;
All things, dog, cat, fiddle, baby,
Wind, breaker, sea, thunderclap
Repeat in a thousand languages –
"God."

He was beginning to embrace the outer boundaries of orthodox Christianity, not because of a cold decision when all around was contentment and satisfaction, but because he was floating in an ocean of uncertainty. Literature, writers, old friends and the control of inner feelings could only place a hold on depression; a greater bond was needed if the tranquillity was going to continue. There were no striking appearances or resounding orders – his full conversion was to come later – but there was a constant ringing in his ears.

Whether Gilbert approached God as an end, as the goal of mankind, the inevitable conclusion to any search for trust; or as a means, a route to happiness, is impossible to judge from his actions and writings at this stage in his life. Orthodox theology would reject the latter approach as selfish; one should ask and pray to God for what one can do for Him, not what He can do for you. God is not a path to fulfilment, He is fulfilment. C.S. Lewis, a devotee of Gilbert's, was to say that if God was seen as a road, he was not seen at all. Gilbert saw God, but he saw through the twisted vision of pain. Only when he regained his sense of equilibrium was he to explore his Christianity from a different standpoint, and embrace it wholeheartedly. Until then he would constantly philosophise

Man is a spark flying upwards. God is everlasting.
Who are we, to whom this cup of human life has
    been given, to ask for more?
Let us love mercy and walk humbly.
What is man, that thou regardest him?
Man is a star unquenchable. God is in him incarnate.
His life is planned upon a scale colossal,
    of which he sees glimpses.

The man who was Gilbert.

Gilbert's mother aged twenty-one, with Aunt Marie Chesterton.

The young misfit, finding comfort in his books.

At St. Paul's, aged fifteen. The headmaster, returning him to his mother, directed her to 'Cherish him.'

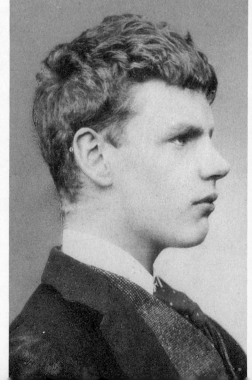

The last photograph taken during his 'happy' days at St. Paul's, before the group of friends went off to separate universities. Gilbert is the center man in the left side of the pyramid.

The Junior Debating Club at St. Paul's. G.K. is in the center of the bottom row.

The young journalist in his twenties. His later obesity is
beginning to develop.

Let him dare all things, claim all things:
He is the son of Man, who shall come in clouds of glory.
I saw these two strands mingling to make the religion
  of man.

In May 1895 Gilbert reached the age of twenty-one, full of the inquiring intensity so common in intellectually minded men and women of that age. He stood a little over six feet two inches, and was still a slim man with a tendency to stand with his hands in his pockets and his stomach pushed a little forward, his head slightly back from the rest of his body. With a crumpled waistcoat, badly knotted bow-tie and hair hastily combed he resembled a youthful professor of the absent-minded variety. He smiled often, but when he adopted a serious face it seemed as if all of the cares in the world rested on those young, slender shoulders.

His mother wrote to him on his birthday, enclosing some money for expenses and any books he may wish to buy (he was staying in Oxford). "My heart is full of thanks to God for the day you were born and for the day on which you attain your manhood. Words will not express my pride and joy in your boyhood which has been without stain and a source of pleasure and good to so many – I wish you a long happy and useful life. May God grant it. Nothing I can say or give would express my love and pleasure in having such a son . . ." Gilbert himself was delighted at his coming of age. He wrote to Bentley, describing the event as "really rather good fun." He continued

It is one of those occasions when you remember the existence of all sorts of miscellaneous people. A cousin of mine, Alice Chesterton, daughter of my uncle Arthur, writes me a delightfully cordial letter from Berlin, where she is a governess; and better still, my mother has received a most amusing letter from an old nurse of mine, an exceptionally nice and intelligent nurse, who writes on hearing that it is my twenty-first birthday . . . . Yes, it is not bad being twenty-one, in a world so full of kind people.

Gilbert's becoming of age also marked the final stages of his years of "lunacy." He ended his autobiographical chapter on the period with the comment, ". . . it flatters me to think that, in this my period of lunacy, I may have been a little useful to other lunatics." It had been an excruciating lesson.

IV

In Work and In Love

Gilbert was to leave University College at the end of the summer of 1895, without a degree, and without any serious respect for the English system of further education as he had experienced it. He had arrived at the far end of his tunnel of darkness, but still had no firm idea of where his future lay, or to what his career in life would lead. He knew that words rather than pictures were his foremost attraction; but more than an inclination towards the literary was required. Gilbert had no formula for beginning a journalistic life. As was so often the way in his story events came to him, and gave him no option but to follow. Such fortune occurred just as he was about to leave the Slade, in extreme need of a sign of encouragement. Bentley remembered that Gilbert's "phase of emptiness" was short-lived, and that in that summer of leaving his studies he was asked to review a book for the *Academy;* the editor enthused over the article, "told me to make it longer, and published it," Gilbert wrote to his friend, exuberant at having seen the first indications of his vocation appear in full focus

> Mr. Cotton is a little bristly, bohemian man, as fidgety as a kitten, who runs round the table while he talks to you. When he agrees with you he shuts his eyes tight and shakes his head. When he means anything rather seriously he ends up with a loud nervous laugh. He talks incessantly and is mad on the history of Oxford. I sent him my review of Ruskin and he read it before me (Note. Hell) and delivered himself with astonishing rapidity to the following effect: This is very good: you've got some-

69

thing to say: Oh, yes: this is worth saying: I agree with you about Ruskin and about the Century: this is good: you've no idea: if you saw some stuff: some reviews I get: the fellows are practised but of all the damned fools: you've no idea: they know the trade in a way: but such infernal asses . . .

The excited editor gave Gilbert the book, *A Ruskin Reader,* and then offered a second volume for review. "Here I got a word in: one of protest and thanks. But Mr Cotton insisted on my accepting the Ruskin . . . . At one point he said, literally dancing with glee: 'Oh, the other day I stuck some pins into Andrew Lang.' I said, 'Dear me, that must be a very good game.' It was something about an edition of Scott, but I was told that Andrew took the painful operation 'very well.' We sat up horribly late together talking about Browning, Afghans, Notes, the Yellow Book, the French Revolution, William Morris, Norsemen and Mr Richard le Gallienne. 'I don't despair for anyone,' he said suddenly. 'Hang it all, that's what you mean by humanity.' This appears to be a rather good editor of the Academy. And my joy in having begun my life is very great. 'I am tired,' I said to Mr Brodribb (Cotton), 'of writing only what I like.' 'Oh, well,' he said heartily, 'you'll have no reason to make that complaint in journalism.' "

Cotton did not remain for very long in the editor's chair, soon being appointed to a position in India. It was not of any great importance, because first impressions of Gilbert usually opened all doors for him; he was a much-liked young man. More disappointing was that he was given no by-line in the magazine, and his review appeared anonymously. In the editions for the years 1895 and 1896 most reviews are signed or initialled, but there is no indication of authorship from Gilbert. It was rather a false start, and he would not exploit his early success as a reviewer for four years. Instead he found employment in a publishing house, working for the firm of Redway. It was a small outfit, and when he began there in September 1895 they were concentrating on books on the occult; Gilbert had all of the correct qualifications, and all of the wrong ones. He enjoyed the work, but didn't find it fulfilling. He still wrote in the evenings, and in the odd moments which were left free for him in the working day. The disciplined structure of daily responsibility made depression – or what was remaining of it – a luxury which simply could not be afforded; he was too busy.

He wrote to Bentley one late night, telling of his experiences. He had been working on "a recast of that 'Picture of Tuesday' " for a Slade magazine.

. . . Like you, I am beastly busy, but there is something exciting about it. If I must be busy (as I certainly must, being an approximately honest man) I had much rather be busy in a varied, mixed up way, with half a hundred things to attend to, than with one blank day of monotonous "study" before me. To give you some idea of what I mean. I have been engaged in 3 different tiring occupations and enjoyed them all. (1) Redway says, "We've got too many MSS.; read through them, will you, and send back those that are too bad at once." I go slap through a room full of MSS., criticising deuced conscientiously, with the result that I post back some years of MSS. to addresses, which I should imagine, must be private asylums. But one feels worried, somehow. (2) Redway says, "I'm going to give you entire charge of the press department, sending copies to Reviews etc." Consequence is, one has to keep an elaborate book and make it tally with other elaborate books, and one has to remember all the magazines that exist and what sort of books they'd crack up. I used to think I hated responsibility: I am positively getting to enjoy it. (3) There is that confounded "Picture of Tuesday" which I have been scribbling at the whole evening, and have at last got it presentable. This sounds like mere amusement, but, now that I have tried other kinds of hurry and bustle, I solemnly pledge myself to the opinion that there is no work so tiring as writing, that is, not for fun, but for publication. Other work has a repetition, a machinery, a reflex action about it somewhere, but to be on the stretch inventing things, making them out of nothing, making them as good as you can for a matter of four hours leaves me more inclined to lie down

71

and read Dickens than I ever feel after nine hours' ramp at Redway's. The worst of it is that you always think the thing so bad, too, when you're in that state.

I can't imagine anything more idiotic than what I've just finished. Well, enough of work and all its works. By all means come on Monday evening, but don't be frightened if by any chance I'm not in till about 6.30, as Monday is a busy day . . .

Publishing may have held a certain appeal, but the house of Redway lost its attraction before very long. After only a few months he moved on, to the larger and far more prestigious organisation of T. Fisher Unwin, with offices at 11 Paternoster Buildings. He was to spend the next six years of his life working here, building his reputation within the publishing house, and outside in the larger world as a promising journalist and author. He claimed in later years to have read some ten thousand novels during his time at Fisher Unwin, and invited anyone to challenge his memory of the plots and characters of each book. When tested, and few had the courage to do so, he was invariably proved to be accurate. The variety of volumes which were given to him over the years was astounding, for there was at the time no strait-jacket of specialisation; a literary mind signified a literary ability no matter what the theme or author. The subsidised education which Gilbert received was unparalleled. He recorded his impressions of the day-to-day activities at his work-place in letters. He was evidently happy, if sometimes pushed to his extreme limit.

. . . The book I have to deal with for Unwin is an exhaustive and I am told interesting work on "Rome and the Empire" a kind of realistic, modern account of the life of the ancient world. I have got to fix it up, choose illustrations, introductions, notes, etc., and all because I am the only person who knows a little Latin and precious little Roman history and no more archaeology than a blind cat. It is entertaining, and just like our firm's casual way. The work ought to be done by an authority on Roman antiquities. If I hadn't been there they would have given it to the office boy.

However, I shall get through it all right: the more I see of the publishing world, the more I come to the conclusion that I know next to nothing, but that the vast mass of literary people know less. This is something called having "a public-school education."

The letter is an exaggeration and a revealing example of Gilbert's modesty. There were others present who could have done the work; he was considered to be the most able.

He thrived on the amount of work, as well as the content. The copious number of pages he would turn out over the next forty years had its foundation at this time. He was forced to learn self-discipline, he was usually left entirely to himself to get the work done at Fisher Unwin, and the difficult skill of pace and control; he would extend his hours of work without a break by the day, until he could write and read for up to six hours without a single interlude. Knowing his previous reluctance to indulge in work of any ordered kind, friends and relatives sometimes doubted his endeavours. He was at pains to prove them wrong. ". . . For fear that you should really suppose that my observations about being busy are the subterfuges of a habitual liar, I may give you briefly some idea of the irons at present in the fire. As far as I can make out there are at least seven things that I have undertaken to do and every one of them I ought to do before any of the others." He proceeded to list them. First came the book on Ancient Rome, second was Captain Webster

Who is Captain Webster? I will tell you. Captain Webster is a small man with a carefully waxed moustache and a very Bond Street get-up, living at the Grosvenor Hotel. Talking to him you would say: he is an ass, but an agreeable ass, a humble, transparent honourable ass. He is an innocent and idiotic butterfly. The interesting finishing touch is that he has been to New Guinea for four years or so, and had some of the most hideous and extravagant adventures that could befall a modern man. His yacht was surrounded by shoals of canoes full of myriads of cannibals of a race who file their teeth to look like the teeth of dogs, and hang weights in their ears till the ears hang like dogs' ears, on the shoulder. He held his yacht at the point of the revolver and got away, leaving some of his men dead on the shore. All night long he heard the horrible noise of the banqueting songs and saw the huge fires that told him his friends were being eaten. Now he lives in the Grosvenor Hotel. Captain Webster finds the pen, not only mightier than the sword, but also much more difficult.

Gilbert's task was to improve the grammar and style of the Captain's English, and although this proved to be at times an impossible undertaking the two men built up a respect for each other, both being without pretence of what they were not. The heroics of an English eccentric were more to Gilbert's liking than a history of China, the third point in his list of burdens. He claimed to know no more of China than the man in the moon. ". . . I shall make the most of what I do know" he wrote, "and airily talk of La-o-tsee and Wu-sank-Wei, criticise Chung-tang and Fu-Tche, compare Tchieu Lung with his great successor, whose name I have forgotten, and the Napoleonic vigour of Li with the weak opportunism of Woo. Before I have done I hope people will be looking behind for my pig-tail. The name I shall adopt will be Tches-Ter-Ton."

Next came a manuscript to read which had been translated from Norwegian. It was a History of the Kiss, and made Gilbert extremely angry with its author; he doubted that he would even send up a report on it. His own project, his first book of poetry, occupied much of his time, as did his ideas for a novel. He ended his letter with ". . . and all these things, with the exception of the last one, are supposed to be really urgent, and to be done immediately . . . . Now I hope I have sickened you forever of wanting to know the details of my dull affairs. But I hope it may give you some notion of how hard it really is to get time for writing just now. For you see they are none of them even mechanical things: they all require some thinking about. I am afraid . . . that if you really want to know what I do, you must forgive me for seeming egoistic. That is the tragedy of the literary person: his very existence is an assertion of his own mental vanity: he must pretend to be conceited even if he isn't . . ."

It was at Fisher Unwin that the legend of Gilbert Chesterton the character began to take root. His peculiarities at St Paul's had been seen as amusing, sometimes a little ridiculous. At university he was beyond the bounds of eccentricity, mainly because he was not in the slightest sense fashionable. When he carried his eccentric behaviour into the world of publishing with its cultivated ways and niceties, his oddities became a mark of distinction, particular blemishes on an outstanding young man. His untidiness, which was always a characteristic was seen in its full absurdity by those who worked at the publisher's and in nearby offices, who would observe this increasingly obese and idiosyncratic figure going out for lunch or leaving for home. He seemed to possess an uncanny gift of covering himself with ink. It would begin on his hands, travel upwards to his cuff and sleeve, and then be transferred by means of a careless wipe to the face, hair and neck. After a busy day at the press, where the cyclostyle skin which held the text was placed in a duplicating machine, he would be covered in thick, black ink. He was dressed, as was required for the office and demanded by the era, in a black frock-coat and matching top hat on these working days and this rendered a battle with the ink pot completely absurd. He resembled a huge schoolboy, somehow apishly copying his father. Gilbert was well aware of how he appeared to the others at the office, indulging their well-meant but too frequent jokes and parodies.

When his costume escaped the perils of ink it was battered by Gilbert's lack of respect for anything which was placed on his back. It looked as if he had slept in his day clothes, and periodically that was the case. Collars rarely fitted and seldom remained in place, shirt fronts transformed themselves into menus, advertising what he had eaten for a long, heavily lubricated lunch. His drinking habits were now being talked about in the office; but he always had a reputation for being a drinker, never a drunk. The difference is subtle, and vital. Considering the volume of alcohol consumed by him at this time it is staggering that he was hardly ever seen out of control, or truly inebriated.

An essential part of Gilbert's dress was the ubiquitous sword-stick. The sword, the walking stick and the cane were to arise time and again in his writing, a symbol of romantic chivalry and pure indications of noble gestures. In an essay entitled "The Universal Stick" he would write "The stick is meant partly to hold a man up, partly to knock a man down; partly to point with like a finger-post, partly to balance with like a balancing pole, partly to trifle with like a cigarette, partly to kill with like a club of a giant; it is a crutch and a cudgel; an elongated finger and an extra leg." He always wished to fight with his weapon, and was prepared to kill; that, of course, never happened. He would have to be content with archaic notions as he marched or waddled down the streets of west and central London, settling for the finger or the leg rather than the cudgel. The stick which he carried in his early twenties was a rapier inside an elegant and sturdy outer cane. One disadvantage such an object did have was essential to its design; so as to be available for a rapid and surprising defence, it was possible to draw the sword from the stick by simply twisting the handle and pulling. Hence it was similarly easy to fidget with the device, and watch helplessly as the cane rolled on to the ground, leaving the owner grasping a naked blade, much to the shock and embarrassment of all present. There were few of his friends who had not at least one memory of Gilbert standing with a child-like smile as some eager young helper rushed to retrieve half a sword-stick. As the entrance to Fisher Unwin was at the top of a set of stone steps the noise of a falling cane would be apparent to all in the vicinity. So common did the accident become that when the rattle of an object bouncing from step to step was heard through a closed door only a round of smiles would follow, from his fellow workers at the publishing house, everybody knowing that it was only Chesterton being Chesterton. He was already a man apart, liked by everyone but understood by not a soul. If Gilbert was content and optimistic, he was still lonely.

He was still in regular communication with Bentley and Oldershaw at Oxford, both cutting their own figures at the University. They were first-class debaters, becoming presidents of the Oxford Union, and had developed oratorical skills which the young members of the J.D.C. would have looked upon with awe and admiration. Bentley had always been Gilbert's most important influence – he was to remain a constant and consistent friend – but it was Lucian Oldershaw who now turned Gilbert's life towards other directions. Oldershaw was one of nature's young romantics, falling in love without undue difficulty, and relishing the challenge of courtship. His heart was broken by one girl in an area of London called Bedford Park; through her he came into contact with other families in the suburb, and other attractive young women.

Bedford Park in the late-nineteenth century was typical of one of the outbursts of the Victorian obsession to improve, progress, perfect. It had not evolved, as most London suburbs had done, but was constructed to an idea, an ideal. It was the first garden suburb in the world. Based upon a dream and plan by Jonathan Comyns Carr, who was financially ruined by the project, the architect was Norman Shaw. It was near Chiswick, not too far from Gilbert's home, and had a reputation in London for being an artistic colony, or at least a colony of people who would like to be thought of as artistic. Rows of red-brick buildings stood in good order around one another, having as their centre a village green, although this was certainly no village. There was a note of the ludicrous about the whole thing. To live there carried an impression; Bedford Park was said to be bohemian, full of doctors and lawyers and writers, with middle-class thinkers announcing their thoughts to their friends in the pub and in the frequent parties and dances which were arranged. It also contained some of the cheapest middle-class housing in London, less idealistic than the villas of Bedford Park, but rather more practical.

Economy had been the motivation behind the Blogg family

moving to No 6 Bath Road, Bedford Park, and the Blogg family had been the motivation for Mr Oldershaw coming to Bedford Park. He had fallen for the daughter, Ethel, and was eventually to marry her. Her family was respected in the district for its hard work and intellectualism. Their name, provoking a grin in those hearing it for the first time, was considered to lack the gentility of the expected residents of Bedford Park. In fact it was the anglicised version of de Blogue, the title of a family from France which had moved to England many years ago. Blanche Blogg, the mother of the family, had lost her diamond merchant husband and was a deeply unhappy woman; all three of her daughters had to go out to work to support the family in its fairly meagre circumstances. The brother of the three, Knollys, was a difficult man; self-obsessed, perhaps neurotic and undoubtedly spoilt by his mother. Ethel, Oldershaw's love, was secretary to a panel of doctors, Gertrude worked for a period as secretary to Rudyard Kipling, and Frances Blogg, the eldest of the girls, was a secretary at the Westminster office of the Parents' National Educational Union, whose aim it was to single out the high-flying children in Britain's schools and ensure that the best young minds were taught by the best older minds. Gilbert went to the Blogg household to attend a debate with Oldershaw and was introduced to some of the family, but Frances was not present

The secretary of this debating-club always proved her efficiency by entirely refusing to debate. She was one of a family of sisters, with one brother, whom I had grown to know through the offices of Oldershaw; and they had a cousin on the premises, who was engaged to a German professor and permanently fascinated by the subject of German fairy-tales. She was naturally attracted also to the Celtic fairy-tales that were loose in the neighbourhood; and one day she came back glowing with the news that Willie Yeats had cast her horoscope, or performed some such occult rite, and told her that she was especially under the influence of the moon . . .

He mentioned this dialogue to Frances, who announced that she herself hated the moon

She really had an obstinate objection to all those natural forces that seemed to be sterile or aimless; she disliked loud winds that seemed to be going nowhere; she did not care much for the sea, a spectacle of which I was very fond; and by the same instinct she was up against the moon, which she said looked like an imbecile. On the other hand, she had a sort of hungry appetite for all the fruitful things like fields and gardens and anything connected with production; about which she was quite practical. She practised gardening; in that curious Cockney culture she would have been quite ready to practise farming; and on the same perverse principle, she actually practised a religion. This was something utterly unaccountable both to me and to the whole fussy culture in which she lived. Any number of people proclaimed religions, chiefly oriental religions, analysed or argued about them; but that anybody could regard religion as a practical thing like gardening was something quite new to me and, to her neighbours, new and incomprehensible. She had been, by an accident, brought up in the school of an Anglo-Catholic convent; and, to all that agnostic or mystic world, practising a religion was much more puzzling than professing it. She was a queer card. She wore a green velvet dress barred with grey fur, which I should have called artistic, but that she hated all the talk about art; and she had an attractive face, which I should have called elvish, but that she hated all the talk about elves. But what was arresting and almost blood-curdling about her, in that social atmosphere, was not so much that she hated it, as that she was entirely unaffected by it. She never knew what was meant by being "under the influence" of Yeats or Shaw or Tolstoy or anybody else. She was intelligent, with a great love of literature, and especially of Stevenson. But if Stevenson had walked into the room and explained his personal doubts about personal immortality, she would have regretted that he

79

should be wrong upon the point; but would otherwise have been utterly unaffected . . .

Frances was twenty-seven when she met Gilbert. She was small and prone to ill health. As Gilbert was already becoming fleshy and plump, her tiny frame and height of just over five feet two inches appeared toy-like in comparison. Later, Ada Chesterton, Cecil's wife, was frequently to be unfair to her sister-in-law, and described her first meeting with Frances in darkened tones. "She had a queer elusive attraction in those days, with her pale face, quite devoid of powder or the least tinge of make-up, and curiously vague eyes. She looked charming in blue or green, but she rarely wore those shades, and usually affected dim browns or greys. We did not find much mutual ground of understanding . . ." There is without a doubt a mystique about the young Frances Blogg, and in the photographs of her of the period her eyes seem to be constantly focused on a thought, a subject, far beyond the camera and the photographer; it was as though she were looking deeply into the future, searching for a safe place to look. Her hair is more often than not tangled, blown in directions it does not appear to be comfortable with. It is a happy face though, probing but contented. Foremost, it is a face of understanding, of depth. Gilbert fell in love with her at first sight, even though months of diffident anguish would ensue before either of them could or would announce their feelings. They flirted harmlessly, exchanging smiles and giggles; at social gatherings they would wander around, waiting for the chance to begin conversation with each other, disguising these meetings under the cloak of chance.

Gilbert's notebooks began to be dominated by this all-embracing theme: love, love of a woman, his love of a woman, his love for Frances Blogg. The entire process seemed quite natural to him, with no particular surprises or shocks. He suffered all of the expected pains of young and first love, but nothing to cause particular alarm. Because although the two people were shy to the point of pretended non-recognition at times, both knew that their respective emotions were reciprocated. Gilbert wrote in his notebook of the Blogg household

In Work and In Love
An Afternoon Call

Three sisters, and there has been a quarrel.
The eldest is dignified and very uncomfortable.
She talks with an exaggerated friendliness
    and triviality,
Dealing bravely with the social embarrassment.
Another seems moody and fretful,
But shakes it off bit by bit
And comes to her sister's help,
Smiling against her will.
The third sits and reads Tennyson
As one reads Tennyson when one is very angry,
With no work except when questioned.
Probably they were all wrong in the quarrel.
(In all family quarrels and most other ones
    everyone is wrong.)
But would anyone decide for me
Which I felt most for
And should most have liked to assist?

He did not need any help in deciding. He wrote of Frances just
a little while after the lines of the sisterly argument

A harmony in green and brown. There is some gold
somewhere in it, but cannot be located on examination.
Probably the golden crown. Harp not yet arrived. Physically there is not quite enough of her to carry all that
temperament; she looks slight, fiery and wasted, with a
face which could be a Burne Jones if it were not brave: it
has the asceticism of cheerfulness, not the easier asceticism of melancholy. Devouring appetite for sensations;
very fond of the Bible; very fond of dancing. When she is
enjoying herself thoroughly, one has the sense that it
would be well for her to go to sleep for a hundred years.
It would be jolly fine for some prince too. One of the few
girls . . . who have souls . . .

The world of Bedford Park, epitomised by the versatile Blogg
sisters was a fitting home for Gilbert. He was surprised to
discover that while he and Bentley and Oldershaw and their

friends had been organising a life of tea and debating around St Paul's, other fraternal units of young people had been doing the same, with their own particular leanings and penchant. The Blogg family had been at the centre of a debating circle known as the I.D.K. When curious friends and acquaintances enquired for what the initials stood, as they always were supposed to do, they were told quite firmly "I don't know." The confusion which followed ("What do you mean, you don't know, you're a member aren't you?" "Yes, that is why I tell you 'I don't know.' " And so on) caused uproar and hilarity amongst the informed members; it was only the most subtle and aware of minds which instantly realised that I.D.K. stood for exactly that: "I Don't Know." It was a delightful piece of light-heartedness, and appealed directly to Gilbert's sense of the absurd.

Bentley and Oldershaw had been resident speakers at the I.D.K. for some time, and Cecil Chesterton was to join their ranks. Gilbert adored the atmosphere immediately. Ethel Blogg was the secretary, Knollys Blogg the treasurer and Frances one of the founding members. Their debates were of a very high quality, given impetus by the new styles brought down from Oxford by Bentley and Oldershaw, the enthusiasm of the Bloggs and the growing brilliance of Gilbert, ever anxious to impress his new found love. In his *Autobiography* he described the Bedford Park set as "frightful fun," an inviting scene where he felt at home, a place of belonging found once again. "It was called the 'I.D.K.,' and an awful seal of secrecy was supposed to attach to the true meaning of the initials. Perhaps the Theosophists did really believe that it meant India's Divine Karma. Possibly the Socialists did interpret it as Individualists Deserve Kicking. But it was a strict rule of the club that its members should profess ignorance of the meaning of its name . . ." The sparkling conversation, the robust singing, the steaming tea, all contributed to Gilbert's feelings of love. His emotions were deeper than mere feelings of satisfaction however; he missed Frances all the time they were apart. She travelled to work in Westminster each day by means of the new underground system, something to which Gilbert never managed to adapt himself. On his way to and from his publishing office he would stop by at Frances's place of work and leave a letter or a few lines of poetry for her to read. If he managed to arrive at Westminster before she started work he would write a note of affection or a witty observation on her blotting pad. He had professed his love, she had returned hers. Doubt would not enter their relationship. She too was a poet, and acknowledged Gilbert's ability; affirmation was precisely what he needed at this time. She was suitably impressed by his being published, and would not enjoy the I.D.K. debates until Gilbert would stand up and deliver his speech; his memory and organised mind fascinated her, his disorganised body charmed her.

They began to write to each other on a daily basis, with the communication to lovers being the central theme and purpose of the day's activities; all revolved around their relationship. Gilbert experienced the pains of love more strongly than Frances; he did not love her more than she loved him – nor would there ever be a visible lack of balance in their feelings for one another – but he was vulnerable to the upsets and insecurities of such deep emotions, to a greater degree than the often phlegmatic Frances. He had waited for a long time for the chasm in his life to be filled, and now that that appeared to have happened he was not going to let this sudden joy escape him. He held on hard, perhaps a little too hard, but that was understandable in a man who had been lonely for the past few years, constantly searching for a road back into his former happy state.

In one of the last formal letters of his pre-marriage courtship with Frances he created a semi-authentic honour roll of the articles and qualities which he had accumulated for the battle of Frances's hand

> . . . I am looking over the sea and endeavouring to reckon up the estate I have to offer you. As far as I can make out my equipment for starting on a journey to fairyland consists of the following items:
>
> 1st. A Straw Hat. The oldest part of this admirable relic shows traces of pure Norman work. The vandalism of

Cromwell's soldiers has left us little of the original hat-band.

2nd. A Walking Stick, very knobby and heavy: admirably fitted to break the head of any denizen of Suffolk who denies that you are the noblest of ladies, but of no other manifest use.

3rd. A copy of Walt Whitman's poems, once nearly given to Salter, but quite forgotten. It has his name in it still with an affectionate inscription from his sincere friend Gilbert Chesterton. I wonder if he will ever have it.

4th. A number of letters from a young lady, containing everything good and generous and loyal and holy and wise that isn't in Walt Whitman's poems.

5th. An unwieldy sort of a pocket knife, the blades mostly having an edge of a more varied and picturesque outline than is provided by the prosaic cutler. The chief element however is a thing "to take stones out of a horse's hoof." What a beautiful sensation of security it gives one to reflect that if one should ever have money enough to buy a horse and should happen to buy one and the horse should happen to have a stone in his hoof – that one is ready; one stands prepared, with a defiant smile!

6th. Passing from the last miracle of practical foresight, we come to a box of matches. Every now and then I strike one of these, because fire is beautiful and burns your fingers. Some people think this a waste of matches: the same people who object to the building of Cathedrals.

7th. About three pounds in gold and silver, the remains of one of Mr Unwin's bursts of affection: those explosions of spontaneous love for myself, which, such is the perfect order and harmony of his mind, occur at startlingly exact intervals of time.

8th. A book of Children's Rhymes, in manuscript, called "The Weather Book" about 3/4 finished, and destined for Mr Nutt. I have been working at it fairly steadily, which I think jolly creditable under the circumstances. One can't put anything interesting in it. They'll understand those things when they grow up.

9th. A tennis racket – nay, start not. It is a part of the new régime, and the only new and neat-looking thing in the Museum. We'll soon mellow it – like the straw hat. My brother and I are teaching each other lawn tennis.

10th. A soul, hitherto idle and omnivorous but now happy enough to be ashamed of itself.

11th. A body, equally idle and quite equally omnivorous, absorbing tea, coffee, claret, sea-water and oxygen to its own perfect satisfaction. It is happiest swimming, I think, the sea being about a convenient size.

12th. A Heart – mislaid somewhere.

And that is about all the property of which an inventory can be made at present. After all, my tastes are stoically simple. A straw hat, a stick, a box of matches and some of his own poetry. What else does man require . . . ?

It has never been fully explained why Frances destroyed so much of the poetry and the romantic notes which she received from Gilbert. Part of her reason was the grief which followed his death; but material was also lost or thrown away before Gilbert's death. The more personal revelations in the love letters were only for the eyes of Gilbert and Frances, and not for the inquisitive mentality of posterity; Frances had no intention of letting future generations dwell on her secrets and her husband's most heartfelt desires.

Nevertheless, some of the writings have survived, and illuminate with at least a ray of light the tracks of their journey together. Gilbert would often hide his true feelings behind a mask of humour, or diminish their intensity by placing them in the middle of a light-hearted verse or boyish giggle. He employed euphemism. Chivalry in the abstract was not a stranger to Gilbert, but the reality of winning another heart proved a different matter. In the early days of the courtship he built up a transparently ridiculous scenario, believing that by showing equal affection – or what he took to be equal affection – to Frances's sisters as well as to her, he would be able to advance his suit without the least hint of embarrassment.

His early poems to Frances were seldom forthright, and often coy to the point of childishness. He occasionally managed to please both himself and his love

> 'Twixt Bedford Park and Westminster
> Oft would a lady hurry,
> Inside she was divine and deep
> And outside green and furry.
> The golden armoury of God
> In truth was round her buckled.
> The son of man that is a worm
> He blew his nose and chuckled.
> For weary weeks and maddening months
> In sunny days and shady
> That amateurish Satan bored
> That green and brown young lady.
> And he would slay the cynic thought
> That whispered Ver non semper
> Viret – The spring will lose its crown
> And she will lose her temper.

In the notebook, often snatched from a cupboard the moment he returned home from visiting Frances, would be more colourful, more honest recordings of his sentiments; the poems written only for his eyes also tended to be of a higher quality, as though the thought of such an important and exclusive audience marred his verses for Frances. Two connected but distinct loves were taking place. One involved Gilbert's active pursuit of Frances and his strategy for gaining her. The other was for a woman who, though she happened to be Frances Blogg, was in reality a product of Gilbert's own imagination and desire; his dream partner would adapt to fit Miss Blogg, and vice versa. The twin romances taking place in Gilbert's mind would frequently show themselves almost simultaneously. On a Monday he would write of his ideal woman, the stuff of teenage longings and perfect balance between man and woman. On Tuesday morning he would

compose a sonnet to Frances, the flesh-and-blood reality of
his love life. He perceived no conflict, perhaps there was none.
In a notebook poem entitled "Madonna Mia" he wrote

> About Her whom I have not yet met
>   I wonder what she is doing
>   Now, at this sunset hour,
> Working perhaps, or playing, worrying or laughing,
> Is she making tea, or singing a song, or writing,
>   or praying, or reading?
> Is she thoughtful, as I am thoughtful?
>   Is she looking now out of the window
>   As I am looking out of the window?

And in "To My Lady," written a short while later

> God made you very carefully,
> He set a star apart for it,
> He stained it green and gold with fields
> And aureoled it with sunshine;
> He peopled it with kings, people, republics,
> And so made you, very carefully.
> All nature is God's book, filled with His
>   rough sketches for you.

The poetry continued apace. When Gilbert had finally
made up his mind to ask Frances for her hand in marriage he
experienced a sudden attack of anxiety. He worked through
it, as ever, by thinking and writing long and hard about his
future. Serenity returned to him, and he celebrated his decision with a much longer poem, fully prepared and constructed, taking time and wine. He called it "In The Balance"

> A poet scrawled upon a page of verse
> Wherein a priest and king battled: whose bones
> Are grown to grass for eight dead centuries
> The words that through the dark and through the day
> Rang in my ears.

87

Even as Becket, graced
By perilous pleasure of the Angevin –
Cried out "Am I the man for cross of Christ?"
In the vast fane filled with one presence dark
That spoke and shook the stars . . . "Thou art the Man."
So do I stand.

A mitre and a cross!
God's blood – ! A cross is but a pair of sticks,
A mitre is a fool's cap out of school,
Candles are fireworks – fling them in the street –
Why should he fear to fill so poor a place?
When I stand up 'neath seven staring heavens,
Naked and arrogant and insolent
And ask for the crown jewels of the Lord.

Lord I have been a Waster of the sun
A sleeper on the highways of the world
A garnerer of thistles and of weeds
A hewer of waste wood that no man buys
A lover of things violent, things perverse
Grotesque and grinning and inscrutable
A savage and a clown – and there she stands
Straight as the living lily of the Lord.
O thy world-wisdom speak – am I the man?

Lo: I am man, even the son of man
Thou knowest these things: in my blood's heritage
Is every sin that shrieked in Babylon,
All tales untold and lost that reddened Heaven
In falling fire above the monstrous domes
Of cities damned and done with . . . there she goes
White in the living sunlight on the lawn,
Alive and bearing flowers . . . My God . . . my God,
Am I the man?

Strong keeper of the world,
O King thou knowest man of woman born,
How weak as water and how strong as fire,
Judge Thou O Lord for I am sick of love,
And may not judge: . . .

Comparisons between his love for a woman and the martyr-dom of Thomas Becket may appear to be rhetorical, even presumptuous. He considered his sacrifice, his commitment, to be that of vocation. Love was not in question, but a life-long partnership with Frances was a matter of frightening proportions. The poem articulated those fears, which were overcome. Once his future was decided he felt a huge sense of release, of liberation. He could now run, tumble, into marriage.

The actual spot chosen by Gilbert to propose to Frances was, and is, one of the most beautiful and mysterious locations in all of London. In a warm summer lunch-hour in 1898 Gilbert met Frances from work, and they walked together to St James's Park. It is perhaps the finest small park in the world, with a fairy-tale-like view of Buckingham Palace at one end, the red, royal road of the Mall running alongside it, Whitehall and Horse Guard's Parade to one side, and the magnificent Admiralty Arch at the other. In the 1890s it was not uncommon to see a cabinet minister hurrying through the Park's green paths from his ministry of state towards Downing Street for a prime-ministerial consultation, or a royal escort on horseback out for an early afternoon exercise. The Park vibrated with romance; with its fountains, young couples, ripples of importance and glamour. On a small bridge near the middle of St James's it is possible to stand so as to see only the tall towers of Whitehall, the higher trees at the edge of the Park and the cascading water forced up from the lake. Here the London of times gone can be imagined, and no traffic – either motorised or horse-drawn – is visible. In this charming place Gilbert asked Frances if she would marry him. Her reply was swift, and certain. Eleven hours later on that same night the sleepless Gilbert wrote his new fiancée a letter.

You will, I am sure, forgive one so recently appointed to the post of Emperor of Creation, for having had a great deal to do tonight before he had time to do the only thing worth doing. I have just dismissed with costs a case between two planets and am still keeping a comet (accused of furious driving) in the ante-chamber.

Little as you may suppose it at the first glance, I have discovered that my existence until today has been, in truth, passed in the most intense gloom. Comparatively speaking, Pain, Hatred, Despair and Madness have been the companions of my days and nights. Nothing could woo a smile from my sombre and forbidding visage. Such (comparatively speaking) had been my previous condition. Intrinsically speaking it has been very jolly. But I never knew what being happy meant before tonight. Happiness is not at all smug: it is not peaceful or contented, as I have always been until today. Happiness brings not peace but a sword; it shakes you like rattling dice; it breaks your speech and darkens your sight. Happiness is stronger than oneself and sets its palpable foot upon one's neck.

When I was going home tonight upon an omnibus – a curious thing came upon me. In flat contradiction to my normal physical habit and for the first time since I was about seven, I felt myself in a kind of fierce proximity to tears. If you knew what a weird feeling it was to me you would have some idea of the state I am in.

Another thing I have discovered is that if there is such a thing as falling in love with anyone over again, I did it in St James's Park. (St James seems to be our patron saint somehow – Hall – Station – Park, etc.) I think it is no exaggeration to say that I never saw you in my life without thinking that I underrated you the time before. But today was something more than usual: you went up seven heavens at a run. I will tell you one thing about the male character. You can always tell the real love from the slight by the fact that the latter weakens at the moment of success; the former is quadrupled. Really and truly, dearest, I feel as if I never thought you so brave and beautiful as I do now. Before I was only groping (frantically indeed) for my own soul.

I will not say that I am unworthy of all this, for that suggests that some-one might be thought worthy of it. But this love is not bought, dear. Even mine you could not have bought with all your virtues. Somewhere in Addison's tragedy of Cato (which you read every morning in the train) that person is made to say – " 'Tis not in mortals to command success, but we'll do more, Sempronius, we'll deserve it." As an epigram it is well enough, but as a philosophy I think it most impudent, and if applied to success in things like ours, downright indecent. Allow me to express my attitude in this amendment – " 'Tis not in mortals to deserve Miss Blogg, but we'll do more, Sempronius – we'll obtain her." Which strikes me as much more humble and reverent – and also much more fun. But Cato was never in love and was an old fool – which is, in fact, the same thing.

I cannot write connectedly or explain my position now; we will have sensible conversation later. I am overwhelmed with an enormous sense of my own worthlessness – which is very nice and makes me dance and sing – neither with great technical charm. I shall of course see you tomorrow. Should you then be inclined to spurn me, pray do so. I can't think why you don't but I suppose you know your own business best.

People are shouting for me to go to bed, and they ought to be listened to. It will be their turn to listen soon. Don't worry about your Mother; as long as we keep right she is sure to be with us. God bless you, my dear girl.

Indeed it would be the turn of other people to listen soon. Because Gilbert and Frances decided to delay the announcement of their engagement for a while; and neither of their mothers had indicated any enthusiasm for the marriage in the past. It was Gilbert's responsibility to break the news, and as responsibility was never his strongest quality procrastination drew on and on. Frances was at times upset, other times angry at the hiatus between their private decision and public acknowledgment. "Please tell your mother soon," she wrote. "Tell her I am not so silly as to expect her to think me good enough, but really I will try to be."

Marie Chesterton had witnessed her first son's attitude to crushes and childish affection and infatuation in the past, and was convinced that the entire affair with Frances was based upon similar lines. She had expected a marriage between Gilbert and Annie Firmin, and was firmly in support of such a bond. She did not see a grown man when she looked at untidy, short-sighted Gilbert; only an over-grown boy, full of play and pleasantries, but not a suitable husband or father. During a family holiday at Felixstowe Gilbert took the plunge, but in his own particular style felt the water inch by inch. Instead of speaking to his mother he wrote to her, despite her being in the same seaside house where they were staying. He explained his actions in the first paragraph of the letter by saying that by discovering the news of the engagement in letter form she would have time and opportunity to dwell on the matter, before replying. He went on

I am going to tell you the whole of a situation in which I believe I have acted rightly, though I am not absolutely certain, and to ask for your advice on it. It was a somewhat complicated one, and I repeat that I do not think I could rightly have acted otherwise, but if I were the greatest fool in the three kingdoms and had made nothing but a mess of it there is one person I should always turn to and trust. Mothers know more of their son's idiocies than other people can, and this has been peculiarly true in your case. I have always rejoiced at this, and not been ashamed of it: this has always been true and always will be. These things are easier written than said, but you know it is true, don't you?

I am inexpressibly anxious that you should give me credit for having done my best, and for having constantly had in mind the way in which you would be affected by the letter I am now writing. I do hope you will be pleased. [Such preambles when writing to his mother, and often when talking to her about matters of importance where he knew she might disagree, are especially defensive to modern eyes and minds. Gilbert's relationship with his mother was particularly close, she was a woman of strength and character, and it was an age when filial loyalty and respect was expected.]

About eight years ago, you made a remark – this may

show you that if we "jeer" at your remarks, we remember them. The remark applied to the hypothetical young lady with whom I should fall in love and took the form of saying "If she is good, I shan't mind who she is." I don't know how many times I said that over to myself in the last two or three days in which I have decided on this letter.

Do not be frightened; or suppose that anything sensational or final has occurred. I am not married, my dear mother, neither am I engaged. [The fear he had for his mother is clearly on display; he was engaged, and was telling a lie, albeit a small one – a highly unusual act for Gilbert.] You are called to the council of chiefs very early in its deliberations. If you don't mind I will tell you, briefly, the whole story.

You are, I think, the shrewdest person for seeing things whom I ever knew: consequently I imagine that you do not think that I go down to Bedford Park every Sunday for the sake of the scenery. I should not wonder if you know nearly as much about the matter as I can tell in a letter. Suffice it to say, however briefly (for neither of us care much for gushing: this letter is not on Mrs Ratcliffe lines), that the first half of my time of acquaintance with the Bloggs was spent in enjoying a very intimate, but quite breezy and Platonic friendship with Frances Blogg, reading, talking and enjoying life together, having great sympathies on all subjects; and the second half in making the thrilling, but painfully responsible discovery that Platonism, on my side, had not the field by any means to itself. That is how we stand now. No one knows, except her family and yourself.

My dearest mother, I am sure you are at least not unsympathetic. Indeed we love each other more than we shall either of us ever be able to say. I have refrained from sentiment in this letter – for I don't think you like it very much. But love is a very different thing from sentiment and you will never laugh at that. I will not say that you are sure to like Frances, for all young men say that to their mothers, quite naturally, and their mothers never believe them, also, quite naturally. Besides, I am so confident, I should like you to find her out for yourself. She is, in reality, very much the sort of woman you like, what is called, I believe, "a Woman's Woman," very humorous, inconsequent and sympathetic and defiled with no offensive exuberance of good health.

He ended the letter by explaining that he had thought of little else but Frances and his mother for the past week; and then thanked her for the cup of cocoa she had just handed to him.

Gilbert had stage-managed the announcement – the hour, the means, the delivery – so as to minimise any risk of an argument. His mother's precise reaction is not known, because neither Gilbert nor Cecil recorded it. Could it be that the anger of her reply made such a recollection too painful to put down on paper? Frances was not informed of her prospective mother-in-law's response in writing, and the engagement was not seriously questioned by the Chesterton family. We can only assume that parental permission was granted. More than that, Edward Chesterton always had a special place in his affections for Frances. He detected her sense of loneliness when in the middle of the exuberant Chesterton clan and endeavoured to compensate for his wife's lack of warmth. Both Cecil Chesterton and his future wife disliked Frances, the former not understanding her at all, the latter being vindictive at times towards a gentle, loving woman. Marie Louise never grew to like or love Frances, a continuous source of pain and confusion for Gilbert.

Frances's mother was no less an obstacle. She was not particularly fond of Gilbert – he was "a self-opinionated scarecrow" – and was jealously loving towards her daughters. Gilbert did not provoke a feeling of security in other people; his dress was becoming increasingly disorganised, his mannerisms more and more ridiculous. As a publishing assistant he was not a highly paid man, earning just over one pound a week. As Frances would have to sacrifice her job, as was demanded by custom, the couple would be forced to live solely on his income; it seemed impossible. Nor were Gilbert's chances of promotion very great, he was quite content to remain in his position, and as long as he adopted that attitude his employers would be in no hurry to pay him more money or raise his position in the company. It was not an enthusiastic Mrs Blogg who heard and consented to the news of her daughter's engagement, but she was determined to make the best of it. Attempting to restore a note of balance to the evening after she had heard the startling news, Mrs Blogg looked round her drawing-room for a conversation piece to alter the subject. "How do you like my new wallpaper, Gilbert?" she asked. He bounded over to the new, expensive paper, stared at it in deep thought for a few moments, and then after searching and finding a piece of chalk in his pocket drew a portrait of Frances over the wall. We have no description of Mrs Blogg's expression after this! She did insist that the couple maintain a silence on the subject of their engagement, and inform as few people as possible for the time being.

Taciturnity was not Gilbert's forte. He ached to tell people the good news, as any recently betrothed man would. The matter took his mind from his work, kept him awake at night and even managed to distract him from his food and drink. Each day of quiet on this subject so very dear to his whole self was a day of bland indifference. The smoke-screen of silence surrounding the good news was becoming thicker; how long would it be before Frances started to doubt the existence of their engagement? Mrs Blogg was now insisting that because of financial difficulties there would be no marriage for a long time. Rumours were spreading however. Gilbert wrote to Frances, thanking her for a gift of some pressed flowers, but he could only contain himself until the second paragraph

Yourself and your Mother are the only guardians of reticence you have any need to appease or satisfy. For my part, it is no exaggeration but the simple fact if any fine morning you feel inclined to send the news on a postcard to Queen Victoria, I should merely be pleased at the incident. I want everybody to know: I want even the Siberian standing beside his dog-sledge to have something to rejoice his soul: I hunger for the congratulations of the Tasmanian black. Always tell anyone you feel inclined to and the instant you feel inclined to. For the sake of your Mother's anxieties I cheerfully put off the time when I can appear in my regalia, but it is rather rough to be timidly appealed to as if I were the mystery-mongering blackguard adventurer of the secret engagement, "despised even by the Editress of Home Chat . . ."

They were not the only engaged couple in their circle, both at work and amongst friends. As far as they knew, of course, they were the only couple who were not proclaiming their news to all around. "Why, in Heaven's name, dear love," he wrote, "do you talk as if I were endeavouring to hide you like stolen property in a cupboard?" Gradually the news began to spread. Miss Mason, a working companion of Frances's, was told the secret – she probably already had a strong idea, as she would frequently observe the letters, poetry and messages on the blotting-pad left for Frances by Gilbert most mornings. Frances's cousin, Margaret Heaton, pleased the Chesterton family and made Gilbert feel more welcomed and encouraged when she sent her congratulations to him, speaking as one of the Blogg family. "I wish you both the most perfect union and God's blessing. I have known you pretty intimately for some time now, and I have never heard you say an unkind word of anyone and have often observed how you championed the cause of the weak, this makes me feel more confident than anything of my dear cousin's happiness with you . . ." Gertrude Blogg also wrote to him: "Please don't be afraid of me any more," and "Of course you are quite unworthy of Frances but the sooner you forget it the better." The Bloggs always fascinated Gilbert, and terrified him. Gertrude's forthright ways were indicative of how strident, at times rude, the family could be. They were caring and compassionate, also mildly eccentric and deeply Victorian English. Gilbert wrote to Frances

. . . It is a mystic and refreshing thought that I shall never understand Bloggs. That is the truth of it . . . that this remarkable family atmosphere . . . this temperament with its changing moods and its everlasting will, its divine trust in one's soul and its tremulous speculations as to one's "future," its sensitiveness like a tempered sword, vibrating but never broken: its patience that can wait for Eternity and its impatience that cannot wait for tea: its power of bearing huge calamities, and its queer little moods that even those calamities can never overshadow or wipe out: its brusqueness that always pleases and its over-tactfulness that sometimes wounds: its terrific intensity of feeling, that sometimes paralyses the outsider with conversational responsibility: its untranslatable humour of courage and poverty and its unfathomed epics of past tragedy and triumph – all this glorious confusion of family traits, which, in no exaggerative sense, makes the Gentiles come to your light and the folk of the nations to the brightness of your house – is a thing so utterly outside my own temperament that I was formed by nature to admire and not understand it. God made me very simply – as He made a tree or a pig or an oyster: to perform certain functions. The best thing He gave me was a perfect and unshakable trust in those I love . . .

His undoubted love for Frances brought some irritating truths home to Gilbert. Happy though he was at his work, it would not suffice in the future. His financial demands, as his mother-in-law had pointed out, were easily met at present, but married life would alter all that. He paid no rent while living at home in Warwick Gardens, his travel expenses came to only four or five shillings a week, and it would take more than his prodigious eating and drinking habits to get through the remaining money. He was to be a rich man no longer. Work in publishing was notoriously under-paid, with nobody at Fisher Unwin earning more than a meagre salary in the closing years of the nineteenth and opening decade of the twentieth century. If he enjoyed working at the publisher's, and if circumstances demanded extra income, he would have to supplement his wages with some extra labours. As so many writers have done since, he worked at his articles during the few free moments he had at work. It was difficult and at times overwhelming but Frances and her world made it all worthwhile. The I.D.K. was still meeting, still full of verve and passions. Gilbert was never happier than at the centre of it.

He designed a menu for one of the Society's Ladies' Nights, and came to dominate the discussions with his piercing ability to be able to get straight to the heart of a problem which seemed to possess none. He also bathed in the attention of those kindly souls who were attempting to change his appearance. Frances's mother was constantly, through others and by herself, encouraging him to smarten himself up; from her point of view a wealthy and successful man necessitated a tidy man. He was teased, and sometimes cajoled. Mostly it was good-natured, and Gilbert interpreted it so – he was always the best of victims. The poking of fun was part of the camaraderie of the Bedford Park set, and its latest recruit played his full part when he wrote of his appearance in the July of 1899

... I am clean. I am wearing a frockcoat, which from a superficial survey seems to have no end of buttons. It must be admitted that I am wearing a bow-tie: but on careful research I find that these were constantly worn by Vikings. A distinct allusion to them is made in that fine fragment, the Tryggvhessa Saga, where the poet says, in the short alliterative lines of Early Norse poetry:

Frockcoat Folding then
Hakon Hardrada
Bow-tie Buckled
Waited for war

(Brit. Mus. MSS. CCCLXIX, lines 99981–99985)

I resume. My appearance, as I have suggested, is singularly exemplary. My boots are placed, after the fastidious London fashion, on the feet: the laces are done up, the watch is going, the hair is brushed, the sleeve-links are inserted, for of such is the Kingdom of Heaven. As for my straw hat, I put it on eighteen times consecutively, taking a run and a jump to each try, till at last I hit the right angle. I have not taken it off for three days and nights lest I should disturb that exquisite pose. Ladies, princes, queens, ecclesiastical processions go by in vain: I do not remove it. That angel of the hat is something to mount

Taken shortly after his marriage. The pose is quite natural; he refused to obey any photographer.

Frances.

Overroads, Beaconsfield, the home of Gilbert and Frances
Chesterton between 1909 and 1922.

Warwick Gardens, 1911. Brother Cecil is in the back row.
Gilbert is seated center with Frances to his left.

Dr Johnson was Gilbert's favourite costume. Frances was not as confident or happy in fancy dress.

guard over. As Swinburne says – "Not twice on earth do the gods do this."

The Blogg family did not maintain its happy state. Gertrude, clever and articulate, full of argument and sense, was knocked from her bicycle by a bus and horribly injured. She lived for a few days, but was never expected to pull through. Frances was Gertrude's closest friend; they were intimate companions and shared most secrets of their love journeys together. Gertrude probably gave Frances her last talk of advice and reassurance before Gilbert proposed. There had been so much sharing, and now it all seemed so pointless. Frances had long been of a weak physical disposition and this blow hit her harder than anything else before. Her mental condition was also subject to swings – she would suffer from depression throughout her life – and the death of such a near soul almost destroyed her. She went to Italy soon after the funeral in an attempt to escape the pain and recapture the balance in her life which had seemed so easy a few months earlier. Gilbert was concerned not just for the loss of a future sister-in-law and present friend, but because of the change it had produced in Frances. He was made aware for the first time of the tragic dimension to his fiancée's character. It shocked him. Here was no mere mourning for a sister, more a breakdown of spirit and faith. His own inexperience with death and his father's antipathy to illness and dying made it all the more difficult for a confused young man, quite out of his depth.

The funeral was viciously sad. Gilbert attempted to break the circle of suffering by sending a wreath of scarlet and orange flowers, with the attached inscription: "He that maketh His angels spirits and His ministers a flame of fire." They stood out beautifully amongst the universally white blooms, but to little avail. He began to write to Frances, unsure of how much humour he should include. He was worried and frightened, often shaken, when he considered the doubt now cast over his future, but adamant that he would not give up his love without a struggle.

... I am black but comely at this moment: because the cyclostyle has blacked me. Fear not. I shall wash myself. But I think it my duty to render an accurate account of my physical appearance every time I write: and shall be glad of any advice and assistance ...

I have been reading Lewis Carroll's remains, mostly Logic, and have much pleasure in enlivening you with the following hilarious query: "Can a Hypothetical, whose protasis is false, be legitimate? Are two Hypothetical of the forms, If A, then B, and If A then not B compatible?" I should think a Hypothetical could be, if it tried hard ...

To return to the Cyclostyle. I like the Cyclostyle ink; it is so inky. I do not think there is anyone who takes quite such a fierce pleasure in things being themselves as I do. The startling wetness of water excites and intoxicates me: the fieriness of fire, the steeliness of steel, the unutterable muddiness of mud. It is just the same with people .... When we call a man "manly" or a woman "womanly" we touch the deepest philosophy.

I will not ask you to forgive this rambling levity. I, for one, have sworn, I do not hesitate to say it, by the sword of God that has struck us, and before the beautiful face of the dead, that the first joke that occurred to me I would make, the first nonsense poem I thought of I would write, that I would begin again at once with a heavy heart at times, as to other duties, to the duty of being perfectly silly, perfectly extravagant, perfectly trivial, and as far as possible, amusing.

He concluded

I have sworn that Gertrude should not feel, wherever she is, that the comedy has gone out of our theatre. This, I am well aware, will be misunderstood. But I have long grasped that whatever we do we are misunderstood — small blame to other people; for, we know ourselves, our best motives are things we could neither explain nor defend. And I would rather hurt those who can shout than her who is silent. You might tell me what you feel about this: but I am myself absolutely convinced that gaiety that is the bubble of love, does not annoy me: the old round of stories, laughter, family ceremonies, seems to me far less really inappropriate than a single amount of forced silence or unmanly shame . . .

His letter had only the smallest of impacts. Frances could see only blackness ahead of her, she was in the midst of a serious depression. Gilbert discussed the agony of his fiancée with his family – he received precious little advice from that quarter – and Frances's mother. Should he leave her to live out her grief, or rush to her aid? The first option was not even to be considered, not when the sufferer was his greatest love. It was difficult enough being apart from Frances at all; practically impossible to know that she was in shock, was at times hopeless, and may not be able to face a future with a person so loved that if he died she would once again find her life smashed. He wrote again on 11th July

I have made a discovery: or I should say seen a vision. I saw it between two cups of black coffee in a Gallic restaurant in Soho: but I could not express it if I tried.
    But this was one thing that it said – that all good things are one thing. There is no conflict between the gravestone of Gertrude and a comic-opera tune played by Mildred Wain. But there is everlasting conflict between the gravestone of Gertrude and the obscene pomposity of the hired mute: and there is everlasting conflict between the comic-opera tune and any mean or vulgar words to which it may be set. These, which man hath joined together, God shall most surely sunder. That is what I am feeling . . . . now every hour of the day. All good things are one thing. Sunsets, schools of philosophy, babies, constellations, cathedrals, operas, mountains, horses, poems – all these are merely disguises. One thing is always walking among us in fancy-dress, in the grey cloak of the church or the green cloak of the meadow. He is always behind, His form makes the folds fall so superbly. And that is what the savage old Hebrews, alone among the nations, guessed, and why their rude tribal god has been erected on the ruins of all polytheistic

civilisations. For the Greeks and Norsemen and Romans
saw the superficial wars of nature and made the sun one
god, the sea another, the wind a third. They were not
thrilled, as some rude Israelite was, one night in the
wastes, alone, by the sudden blazing idea of all being the
same God: an idea worthy of a detective story.

More than anything else the death of Gertrude tested
Frances's faith. Gertrude had been happy, engaged to be
married, God-fearing, loving. Frances saw her as a much
better person than herself, so why should such a fate befall
her? She was not in a state of doubt, more one of despair. This
may be the supreme plan, with that she could come to terms;
but if it was, did she feel encouraged and strengthened by that
plan? It was rather like C.S. Lewis felt when his wife Joy died
of cancer. He did not question the existence of God, there
could be no dispute there. Rather, he wondered what God's
purpose was: could it be God the vivisectionist, looking down
on a planet of feeble creatures and experimenting with their
lives and emotions? Lewis lived through his grief, as Frances
was to do.

She began to search for deeper justification in the Scrip-
tures, and was comforted by the aspect of supplication which
is so common in the lives of the disciples, as well as that of
Christ. If Gertrude's death was God's will, that must be
accepted; God is all good or he isn't the real God at all. She
told Gilbert that she was feeling the warmth of comfort, and
that she now realised that "It is good for us to be here." He
was delighted at her breakthrough, and proud of her resolute
stance. He replied to her

> ... I am so glad to hear you say ... that, in your own
> words "it is good for us to be here" – where you are at
> present. The same remark, if I remember right, was made
> on the mountain of the Transfiguration. It has always
> been one of my unclerical sermons to myself, that that
> remark which Peter made on seeing the vision of a single
> hour, ought to be made by us all, in contemplating every

panoramic change in the long Vision we call life – other things superficially, but this always in our depths. "It is good for us to be here – it is good for us to be here," repeating itself eternally. And if, after many joys and festivals and frivolities, it should be our fate to have to look on while one of us, in a most awful sense of the words, is "transfigured before our eyes": shining with the whiteness of death – at least, I think, we cannot easily fancy ourselves wishing not to be at our post. Not I, certainly. It was good for me to be there.

Gradually she recovered her will, and focused on her future happiness with Gilbert. What hadn't destroyed her had made her stronger. Their relationship blossomed after Frances's recovery, and the trauma spurred Gilbert into a more industrious frame of mind. If his future wife could be liable to such fits of depression – as she was to be – the least he could do was to make her feel financially secure.

He had had little of his work published during the past year, with only a few poems appearing in print; they usually paid hardly anything at all, sometimes exactly nothing at all. Possibilities for selling work appeared to be brighter when the *Speaker,* which Gilbert had made contact with in the past, was put into the hands of some young, sophisticated men recently down from Oxford who were both friends of Oldershaw and eager for new talent and writing. The new vibrant owners of the journal took the *Speaker* on a hard turn to the Left, leaving a proportion of its readership behind as it established itself as being solidly anti-Imperialist and a mouthpiece for the radical wing of the Liberal Party. As the Second Boer War was in its bloody and disastrous early stages the angry young men of the *Speaker* had plenty to write about. And so did Gilbert.

The men who composed the ruling group on the board of the journal were fine examples of the reforming middle class of the period. Determined and well-informed in their ideas, they nevertheless represented a moribund political stance, that of the radical in the age of the socialist. Their belief in change from above, in a tampering with the results of capitalism rather than the causes of it, was not to last through the First World War, and was to see its own end looming as the first Labour members of Parliament were elected to the House of Commons. J.L. Hammond, Francis Hirst, F.Y. Eccles and Philip Comyns Carr made up the nucleus of the team, with Oldershaw and Bentley also playing their part. John Simon was another who worked for the *Speaker,* but abandoned the magazine when it began obviously to alienate the powers that be in the Liberal Party hierarchy; he was set on an ambitious political and legal career, and achieved both. The atmosphere and flavour of the *Speaker* and its staff appealed to Gilbert. "This group was just then enabled to achieve a very important work; which will probably be not without an ultimate effect on history," he wrote. "It managed to buy the old . . . . weekly paper . . . and run it with an admirable spirit and courage in a rather new mood of Radicalism. . . ." "Its editor was Mr J.L. Hammond, who was afterwards, with his wife, to do so great an historical service as the author of studies on the English Labourer in the last few centuries. He certainly was the last man in the world to be accused of a smug materialism or a merely tame love of peace. No indignation could have been at once more fiery and more delicate, in the sense of discriminating. And I knew that he also understood the truth, when I heard him say the words which so many would have misunderstood: 'Imperialism is worse than Jingoism. A Jingo is a noisy fellow, who may happen to make a noise on the right side. But the Imperialist is the direct enemy of liberty.' That was exactly what I meant; the Boers might be making a noise (with Mauser rifles) but I thought it was a noise on the right side."

For all of its supposed liberalism and defence of the small against the large, the *Speaker* was not without the nastier prejudices of its era, and demonstrated such feelings in a ludicrous rejection of Gilbert's work. He wrote a piece for them, and was confident that it would be accepted and published by a grateful editor – "the first of the New Speaker, is coming out soon," he wrote Frances, "and may contain some-

thing of mine . . ." The editor did not disagree with his sentiments or style, but his race; it was thought that Gilbert was
Jewish, because his handwriting looked to be "that of a Jew."
F.Y. Eccles, a somewhat absurd man with pretensions far
above his abilities, had overheard some of the infantile theories circulating concerning Jewish traits and their physical
manifestations, and somehow had discerned a Semitic form in
Gilbert's writing and signature – one can only imagine that it
was written from right to left in the Hebraic manner! Further,
he refused to read anything more from the then unknown
writer, in spite of the protestations from Oldershaw and
Bentley, and would only turn away material from what he
referred to as their "Jew friend."

The reasons for this reluctance to print anything from a
Jewish writer are as clear as they are unpleasant. Anti-
Semitism as a philosophy, as opposed to a gutter hatred, was
taking root in Europe at this time, gaining as much credence
on the political left as on the political right; sections of the
former seeing a Jew in the middle of each and every capitalist
undertaking, even larger parts of the latter believing that
revolution world-wide was a Jewish concern. In the case of
the *Speaker* and its obsession with the South African war the
problem was one of for whom the war was being fought. In
the eyes of the young anti-Imperialists the might of the British
Empire had been turned against a powerless breed of Dutch
farmers – who were later to introduce and implement apart-
heid – due to the vested interests and needs of foreign bankers
and businessmen, many of whom were thought to be Jewish.
Some of them were Jewish, just as most of them happened to
be gentiles. On this pretext Gilbert, who they continued to
believe was Jewish, must be a biased commentator and must
not be allowed access to their media. It was a thin covering of
twisted logic disguising a larger racism, a much deeper resentment and intolerance. How ironic that Gilbert would himself
later be accused of anti-Semitism.

A hostile response from a contributor so treated would be
expected, understood, by all. There is no record of any such
anger from Gilbert, not even of any particular disappoint-

ment. The callous dismissal merely gave fuel to his efforts, and strengthened his determination to make both his and Frances's living as a professional writer. The coming years were to transform him from a talented youth to a respected author; it was as though all the experience, pain and joy were a training ground for just this.

V

Gilbert Chesterton: Journalist

F riendship was tested to its limits when Bentley, who had been contributing on a regular basis to the *Speaker,* was asked by the editorial staff to join the magazine as a full-time writer. He agreed. A tremendous strain is placed upon any partnership when one of the pair achieves a position where advancement is in his gift; does he help out someone who is known to be his friend, thus risking accusations of nepotism, or possibly dissolve an important friendship out of fear of ridicule? Bentley sung Gilbert's praises in the offices of the *Speaker,* and constantly pushed the case for his long-time ally. Eventually these efforts were to merit a reward, but by the time they did Gilbert was already established as a writer in demand. Bentley was a good friend; he was also an astute young man with dreams of grandeur. To his credit Gilbert never once applied any pressure, content to accept what may come by natural means, not influenced by his pleas.

It was another and more recent friend, Ernest Hodder Williams, who opened the door for Gilbert's writings. Their first meeting had taken place at University College, and the bonds had built up both spontaneously and quickly. Hodder Williams's family owned the *Bookman,* a small circulation but highly respected magazine which took freelance work and encouraged younger writers. Gilbert described these early articles as an act of "letting me loose in the literary world," and wrote to Frances that ". . . I am developing into a sort of art critic, under the persistent delusion which possesses the Editor of the *Bookman.* And I think an article attacking the theories that every sane man has held about classic art for a thousand years would be the sort of thing I should enjoy writing. You will come back next week probably just in time to see my first experiment in art criticism in the *Bookman*. The two reviews do not join on well together having been written separately. Otherwise I think they will do."

Frances came back to no review in the *Bookman,* because Gilbert's review was held over – more disappointing and upsetting to Miss Blogg than to the author. It appeared in the next issue, unfortunately uncredited. Ironically Hodder Williams had written to him when he sent the book to be reviewed, a work on Nicolas Poussin, stating that "The next issue of the Bookman will run to some 30,000 copies so I think you will like to have your name appear in it." He also asked for a review which would be "thoroughly critical both of the book and of Poussin's work." A dubious request, hardly advertising the merits of literary commentary at the end of the nineteenth century. Gilbert rarely delivered what was asked of him, but he always delivered quality and quantity.

When paganism was re-throned at the Renaissance, it proved itself for the first time a religion by the sign that only its own worshippers could slay it. It has taken them three centuries, but they have thrashed it threadbare. Just as poets invoked Mars and Venus, for every trivial flirtation, so Poussin and his school multiplied nymphs and satyrs with the recurrence of an endless wall-paper, till a bacchanal has become as respectable as a bishop and the god of love is too vulgar for a valentine . . . . This is the root of the strange feeling of sadness evoked by the groups and landscapes of Poussin. We are looking at one of the dead loves of the world. Never were men born so much out of the time as the modern neo-pagans. For this is the second death of the gods – a death after resurrection. And when a ghost dies, it dies eternally.

The review was received with cries of enthusiasm by editor and readers alike. This was cultivated and mature criticism of the highest form, and from a writer so young and inexperienced it made a deep impression. Letters to the *Bookman* enquired as to who the reviewer was, and why the piece was unsigned. Frances's family were impressed only to a degree, Frances was proud and hopeful, Gilbert thought he could have done better.

The *Bookman* did not pay very well. Gilbert, a financial infant, would not even have asked for payment if he had not been advised and persuaded. His father had experienced the demands of business in his younger days, and although a reluctant man-of-the-world he did understand the pressures of married life and monetary security. He took charge of his son's affairs for a period. Gilbert wrote to Frances about the issue, beginning in his usual manner with affairs more weighty and pertinent to him.

> A rush of the Boers on Natal, strategically quite possibly successful, is anticipated by politicians. The rising of the sun tomorrow morning is predicted by astronomers. My father again is engaged in the critical correspondence with Fisher Unwin, at least it has begun by T.F.U. stating his proposal terms – a rise of 5/- from October, another rise possible but undefined in January, 10 per cent royalty for the Paris book and expenses for a fortnight in Paris. These, as I got my father to heartily agree, are vitiated to the bone as terms by the absence of any assurance that I shall not have to write "Paris," for which I am really paid nothing, outside the hours of work for which I am paid 25/-. In short, the net result would be that instead of gaining more liberty to rise in the literary world, I should be selling the small liberty of rising that I have now for five more shillings. This my father is declining and asking for a better settlement. The diplomacy is worrying, yet I enjoy it: I feel like Mr Chamberlain on the eve of the war. I would stop with T.F.U. for £100 a year – but not for less. Which means, I think, that I shall not stop at all.

The details of financial negotiation were unimportant to Gilbert when held up to the shining delights of his private and social life at the time. Debating was continuing in Bedford

Park, Frances was almost out of her depression and his reputation as a writer was increasing beyond the confines of his own set. He was becoming the toast of Bedford Park amongst the intellectuals and thinkers, perceived as an orator of unique gifts; something unheard of for someone of his years. He found the admiration on display at the debates and organised discussions difficult to resist.

As well as the I.D.K. and infrequent old boy meetings of the Junior Debating Club there was a thriving society which met elsewhere in Bedford Park, at the villa home of the artist Archie Macgregor. Macgregor was a local celebrity, the leader of a much admired little club in the area which was known for its lavish entertainments, light-hearted banter and sense of humour. Gilbert was invited to attend a debate at the sumptuous Macgregor house in April 1900, and as the meeting was expected to continue until late into the night – they usually did – the Blogg family suggested he stayed at Bath Road; Frances was away at the time, otherwise the proposition would have been out of the question. Gilbert accepted the invitation most readily, Macgregor meetings possessed a strong social cachet. The two men always got on, in spite of their differences. Macgregor, the friend of Yeats and committed atheist, was a charismatic man, graceful in defeat as well as victory. "There could be no more virile or valiant type . . . than my old friend Archie Macgregor . . ."

They discussed the Boer War, and the evils of Imperialism. The importance of the evening was the presence in the same room of the two men who were to form the closest literary alliance of their generation. This was the first time that Gilbert saw and heard Hilaire Belloc, and Belloc heard him. They did not meet, but they listened and were conquered. He instantly wrote to Frances, unable to contain his news.

> You hate political speeches therefore you would not have hated Belloc's. The moment he began to speak one felt lifted out of the stuffy fumes of forty-times repeated arguments into really thoughtful and noble and original reflections on history and character. When I tell you that he talked about (1) the English aristocracy (2) the effects

of agricultural depression on their morality (3) his dog (4) the battle of Sadowa (5) the Puritan Revolution in England (6) the luxury of the Roman Antonines (7) a particular friend of his who had by an infamous job received a political post he was utterly unfit for (8) the comic papers of Australia (9) the mortal sins in the Roman Catholic Church – you may have some conception of the amount of his space that was left for the motion before the house. It lasted half-an-hour and I thought it was five minutes.

Gilbert was just under twenty-six years old at this time, Belloc was almost thirty. One was looking for a mentor, a teacher to look to as a guide and guard, the other was constantly prepared to let fly with advice and stricture – often strident, sometimes ridiculous, always convincing and brilliant. The first meeting took place in a small French eating-house in Soho, where Gilbert had arranged to meet Lucian Oldershaw. The Gallic restaurants of the period in Soho were atmospheric little venues, jealously and defensively patronised by a select few, who could indulge in fine food and cheap wine in surroundings which hardly differed from the best of family-owned provincial restaurants in France; many of the proprietors' families had emigrated from France as Huguenot refugees in the seventeenth and eighteenth centuries and come to cosmopolitan Soho. Here meals could not be rushed, but taken with time, discussion and alcohol. The encounter lasted for hours, and when the two men stumbled out into the dark of Gerrard Street it was not only the wine which made them feel heady and content

... I went to meet my friend, who entered the place followed by a sturdy man with a stiff straw hat of the period tilted over his eyes, which emphasised the peculiar length and strength of his chin. He had a high-shouldered way of wearing a coat so that it looked like a heavy overcoat, and instantly reminded me of the pictures of Napoleon; and, for some vague reason, especially of the pictures of Napoleon on horseback. But his eyes, not

111

without anxiety, had that curious distant keenness that is seen in the eyes of sailors; and there was something about his walk that has even been compared to a sailor's roll. Long afterwards the words found their way into verse which expressed a certain consciousness of the combination, and of the blend of nations in his blood .... He sat down heavily on one of the benches and began to talk at once about some controversy or other; I gathered that the question was whether it could be reasonably maintained that King John was the best English King ...

For this was Hilaire Belloc, already famous as an orator at Oxford, where he was always pitted against another brilliant speaker, named F.E. Smith. Belloc was supposed to represent Radicalism and Smith Toryism; but the contrast between them was more vital, and would have survived the reversing of the labels. Indeed the two characters and careers might stand as a study and problem in the meaning of failure and success.

As Belloc went on talking, he every now and then volleyed out very provocative parentheses on the subject of religion. He said that an important Californian lawyer was coming to England to call on his family, and had put up a great candle to St Christopher praying that he might be able to make the voyage. He declared that he, Belloc, was going to put up an even bigger candle in the hope that the visitor would not make the voyage. "People say what's the good of doing that?" he observed explosively. "I don't know what good it does. I know it's a thing that's done. Then they say it can't do any good – and there you have Dogma at once." All this amused me very much, but I was already conscious of a curious undercurrent of sympathy with him, which many of those who were equally amused did not feel. And when, on that night and many subsequent nights, we came to talking about the war, I found that the sub-conscious sympathy had something of a real significance. I have had occasion to say, somewhere or other, that I am an Anti-Vivisectionist and an Anti-Anti-Vivisectionist. Something of the same mystery united our minds; we were both Pro-Boers who hated Pro-Boers. Perhaps it would be truer to say that we hated a certain number of unimaginative, unhistorical anti-militarists who were too pedantic to call themselves Pro-Boers. Perhaps it would be truer still to say that it was they who hated us. But anyhow that was the first link in the alliance . . . . It was from that dingy little Soho café, as from a cave of witchcraft, that there emerged the quadruped, the twinformed monster Mr Shaw has nicknamed the Chesterbelloc.

Hilaire Belloc (Gilbert always addressed him as "Hilary," in the English fashion, which Belloc seemed to prefer from his friend. Nobody else used this form of his name, either through fear or ignorance; Gilbert maintained that his choice was the correct one) had been born in La Celle St Cloud, near to Paris, in 1870. It was a momentous and tragic year to come into the world as a Frenchman; the year Napoleon III fell, the Prussian military machine smashed the myth of French superiority and a generation of French youth was decimated by foreign and civil wars. In some ways it is difficult to imagine Belloc being born at any other time: upheaval and strife were constant courtiers to Belloc, he reciprocated by chasing them. His father was half-Irish and half-French, his mother was an English woman from the then booming industrial city of Birmingham, power-base of the Chamberlain family. His mother, Bessie Parkes, was a convert to Catholicism.

Belloc's father died when he was a child, and his mother moved to England to an uncle's house in Westminster; when the uncle died the house was left to Madame Belloc, together with an inheritance sufficient to keep the family in comfortable circumstances for the forseeable future. Bessie Belloc was a woman who did not take advice easily and was not content to live on what she had been given; she gambled the bulk of the inheritance on the London Stock Exchange, refused to withdraw her investment when matters looked bleak, and consequently lost a sum of money which would have seen her son into adulthood, and had taken her uncle a lifetime to accumulate. She still found it difficult to admit her errors in the money-making attempt, a characteristic which her son would take from his mother and develop.

They moved to a cottage in Arundel in Sussex – cheaper and away from condemning tongues – and Hilaire began his formal education at Newman's Oratory in Birmingham. After leaving school he drifted, unsure as to whether he was English or French, a farmer or a journalist, a radical or a conservative. And then he met an Irish–American girl by the name of Elodie Hogan. She was charming and vulnerable, had agonised for some time over whether to enter a convent or not and was under severe pressure from her mother. Belloc expressed his love. Mrs Hogan discovered the state of his finances – there weren't any – and took her daughter back to the United States. He sold all that he had to pay for a journey to San Francisco, and implored her once again to marry him. She thought she may have a vocation for marriage, but there was also the calling to celibacy. Her mother had no such doubts. Belloc left for England, in despair.

When in London Belloc was a countryman; when in Sussex he was a city dweller; in France he became an Englishman, and in Britain he was a French-born, French-speaking patriot of France. Belloc was never content with being "ordinary." To satisfy his new-found status he moved to France and joined the army as an artillery recruit. Images of Bonaparte may have motivated him, but the realities were less glorious. His French was heavily accented; others in the regiment thought him a strange man, even ridiculous. He was middle class and English educated, they were mostly rural, poorly educated French labourers and unemployed Parisians. His competence as a fighting man was average at its best. He returned to England once again.

As was the case with so many young men from good backgrounds who found themselves with time on their hands, Belloc decided to go up to Oxford and continue his studies. He had been a noted scholar at the Oratory, and gained a First in History at Balliol College. In between his reading and writing he walked – covering miles in staggeringly fast times –

and drank to excess. He was known and respected at Oxford, if not always liked.

An unhealthy note of persecution was strongly placed in Belloc's mind from an early age, something bordering on the paranoiac; he almost certainly suffered from mental illness later in life. He saw plots and plans everywhere, from Jewish world conspiracy ideas, to Prussian influence from one end of the world to the other. It was indicative of this fantasy that when he was refused a fellowship at Oxford in 1896 he blamed his rejection not on any lack of ability or character fault which he might have demonstrated to those dons who chose new fellows, but on an anti-Catholic bias inside the Oxford University power structure. He would continue to desire a fellowship, but would from now on harbour a loathing for any academic who did not prove himself first. It was an absurd suspicion.

In California Elodie Hogan had left the convent, and was now seriously ill. Her mother, the most difficult obstacle to Belloc's marriage plans, had died at almost the same time. He borrowed money for a ticket to the United States, and kept himself in food and comforts while he was there by giving lectures. He found Elodie Hogan a much easier woman to propose to this time, and they were soon married. Children followed, there were to be five, and Belloc found a peaceful lull in his life which he had never thought possible. He applied to other colleges for a fellowship, and was turned down by each one. He lectured again, both in Britain and in America; with a family to support this would not be sufficient. So he wrote, at first without notice, and then with a colossal impact. *The Bad Child's Book of Beasts* sold over 4000 copies within three months of publication, and made Belloc a well-known and well-paid author. It is a book which has retained its popularity over the decades, and is read by people who would not think of looking at some of his more adult, cutting and offensive works. It consists of a collection of rhymes, all peculiarly Bellocian. Nor did he forget the villains of his story

The Whale that wanders round the Pole
Is not a table fish.

> You cannot bake or boil him whole
>   Nor serve him in a dish;
> But you may cut his blubber up
>   And melt it down for oil.
> And so replace the colza clean
>   (A product of the soil).
> These facts should all be noted down
>   And ruminated on,
> By every boy in Oxford town
>   Who wants to be a Don.

He was spoken of in the same breath as Edward Lear, a major writer of nonsense and humour, often disguised in marvellously horrible visions. Belloc took to the literary life of London with enthusiasm, buying a house at 104 Cheyne Walk, and contributing to magazines and newspapers. In 1899 his biography of Danton appeared, establishing him as an author of historical studies as well as light poetry. In it he outlined his theories on the French Revolution, which was "a reversion to the normal – a sudden and violent return to those conditions which are the necessary bases of health in any political community, which are clearly apparent in every primitive society, and from which Europe had been estranged by an increasing complexity and a spirit of routine," and his concrete beliefs in the "absolute sovereignty in the case of the State, absolute ownership in the case of the individual."

Hence it was an experienced, older and wiser man who befriended Gilbert on that cool evening. He could and did speak as a traveller, a soldier, a man of the Church, a man of the fields, an author and a lover. Gilbert had never appeared so boyish and in awe; he would try to emulate this lion of a character, this hero as well as friend.

On the Good Friday of 1900 Gilbert replied to a letter from Frances, in which she asked how he was, what he was doing, where was he going. He answered her in the fashion she had come to love

As you have tabulated your questions with such alarming precision, I must really endeavour to answer them categorically.

(1) How am I? I am in excellent health. I have an opaque cold in my head, cough tempestuously and am very deaf. But these things I count as mere specks showing up the general blaze of salubrity. I am getting steadily better and I don't mind how slowly . . .

(2) Am I going away at Easter? The sarcastic might think it a characteristic answer, but I can only reply that I had banished the matter from my mind, a vague problem of the remote future until you asked it: but since this is Easter and we are not gone away I suppose we are not going away.

He then describes the place of their next meeting, a conference he is to have with a publisher and whether a review he wrote had appeared or not. Frances had also raised the subject of his appearance once again.

Does my hair want cutting? My hair seems pretty happy. You are the only person who seems to have any fixed theory on this. For all I know it may be at that fugitive perfection which has moved you to enthusiasm. Three minutes after this perfection, I understand, a horrible degeneration sets in: the hair becomes too long, the figure disreputable and profligate: and the individual is unrecognised by all his friends. It is he that wants cutting then, not his hair.

His work came as low as point no. 9 in the letter, and he had good news.

I have got a really important job in reviewing – the Life of Ruskin for the Speaker. As I have precisely 73 theories about Ruskin it will be brilliant and condensed. I am also reviewing the Life of the Kendals, a book on the Renascence and one on Correggio for the Bookman . . . . Really and truly I see no reason why we should not be married in April if not before. I have been making some calcula-

117

tions ... and as far as I can see we could live in the country on quite a small amount of regular literary work ...

The reviews duly appeared in the *Speaker* and the *Bookman,* as did a poem entitled "An Election Echo." He was now contributing regularly to both journals, reviewing books and submitting his own pieces on any subject which he chose. No amount of articles could equal Gilbert's pleasure at the appearance of his first book, in his case books. In 1900 *Greybeards At Play* and *The Wild Knight and Other Poems* were published. The first, *Greybeards,* had been spoken about by Gilbert, family and friends for months now, and a publisher had seemed assured. But Mr Nutt, who appears constantly in Gilbert's letters to Frances at the time, withdrew from the proposition. Gilbert does not refer to this setback in his *Autobiography,* nor does he mention the book at all. He was not pleased with it, and understood the scant critical attention paid to it. Nevertheless it did strike a chord with some people, who did not agree with him that "to publish a book of my nonsense verse seems to me exactly like summoning the whole of the people of Kensington to see me smoke cigarettes." It were as though he did not want the book to be published, ignoring the pleas of friends and admitting to Frances "Alas! I have not been to Nutt. There are good excuses, but they are not the real ones ..." It was illustrated by Gilbert, with his drawings taking up more of the book than his verse; perhaps with reason. There are noticeable flavours of Bentley in *Greybeards at Play,* and predictions of greater things to come

> I am the tiger's confidant,
>   And never mention names:
> The lion drops the formal "Sir,"
>   And lets me call him James.

And

> I love to bask in sunny fields,
>   And when that hope is vain,

118

> I go and bask in Baker Street,
> All in the pouring rain.

The man who finally published the book was Rex Brimley Johnson, the fiancé of Gertrude Blogg. Through the death of Gertrude, Gilbert had been drawn closer to Brimley Johnson, and a fond, if not loving, friendship had developed. Gilbert also offered his second book, *The Wild Knight,* to the young publisher, but for some reason he turned this one down. He could not have so acted due to the poor response to Gilbert's first book – they were offered almost simultaneously, and it was obvious to the most untrained eye that the second volume was far superior – but he may have come to the decision out of a desire to distance himself from the Blogg family because of his understandable grief. He would publish more of Gilbert's work later.

The Wild Knight was offered to Grant Richards, and was published on 20th November 1900. The financial backing for the project, however, came from Gilbert's father. The book consisted of a series of short poems written during the past ten years, and contained at least two pieces which would always be remembered. "The Donkey," that perennial favourite, with its poignant ending

> Fools! For I also had my hour;
> One far fierce hour and sweet;
> There was a shout about my ears,
> And palms before my feet.

The other, "By the Babe Unborn," was particularly liked by the critics. It is an imaginative, hopeful dream-poem of the potentials of life from the view of one not yet brought into the world

> They should not hear a word from me
> Of selfishness or scorn
> If only I could find the door,
> If only I were born.

119

The book was sent to Rudyard Kipling by Rex Brimley Johnson, who had met the author through Gertrude. Kipling was an admirable correspondent and, as he had already come into contact with some of Gilbert's work, he was prepared to offer criticism as well as praise

> Many thanks for the Wild Knight. Of course I knew some of the poems before, notably The Donkey which stuck in my mind at the time I read it.
> I agree with you that there is any amount of promise in the work – and I think marriage will teach him a good deal too. It will be curious to see how he'll develop in a few years. We all begin with arranging and elaborating all the Heavens and Hells and stars and tragedies we can lay our poetic hands on – Later we see folk – just common people under the heavens.
> Meantime I wish him all the happiness that there can be and for yourself such comfort as men say time brings after loss. It's apt to be a weary while coming but one goes the right way to get it if one interests oneself in the happenings of other folk. Even though the sight of this happiness is like a knife turning in a wound.
> [He added a postscript.] Merely as a matter of loathsome detail, Chesterton has a bad attack of "aureoles." They are spotted all over the book. I think everyone is bound in each book to employ unconsciously some pet word but that was Rossetti's.
> Likewise I notice "wan waste" and many "wans" and things that "catch and cling." He is too good not to be jolted out of that. What do you say to a severe course of Walt Whitman – or will marriage make him see people?

Others detected a strong influence of Whitman already in his work – hardly surprising in view of Whitman's impression on him in earlier years – and more than a touch of Browning. There was little of this in the title poem of the book, a tired story of journeys towards God, sins and Satan and ultimate redemption. Its origins lay clearly in Gilbert's troubled years, and it was a poem which he did not like to remember in middle age; not so much for its autobiographical revelations as for its lack of quality and stylistic faults.

The reviews were mostly glowing, some from the most unexpected of sources. Mr Eccles of the *Speaker,* the self-appointed authority on Jewish handwriting, commented on *The Wild Knight* for his magazine

> Mr Chesterton is a poet whose sincerity is, so to speak, in the first degree; who speaks directly, from soul to soul, of the things that preoccupy all men, who applies a spontaneous and cultivated lyrical talent not to the adornment of given themes, but to the representation of the world he sees, divines and desires.

Sales of the book were disappointing, at least from Edward Chesterton's point of view. Gilbert was delighted with any royalties at all, still unsure as to why intelligent men and women would pay good money for a bound collection of his writings. They also paid good money for magazines and newspapers containing his pieces, which he explained to Frances in March, 1901.

"... The following, however, are grounds on which I believe everything will turn out right this year. It is arithmetic. The Speaker has hitherto paid me £70 a year, that is £6 a month." His success elsewhere and the promptings of Bentley and Oldershaw had finally convinced the staff of that magazine that he was too great an offer to be turned down. "It has now raised it to £10 a month, which makes £120 a year. Moreover they encourage me to write as much as I like in the paper, so that assuming that I do something extra (poem, note, leader) twice a month or every other number, which I can easily do, that brings us to nearly £150 a year. So much for the Speaker. Now for the Daily News, both certainties and probabilities." The probabilities were that he had been strongly recommended for the post of literary editor of the paper, paying at least £200 a year; the certainties concerned a series of articles which he had been commissioned to write, earning him some £144 a year. When all of the figures were added up, with the odd payment from the *Bookman* supplementing his income, his annual income amounted to approximately £400. Belloc felt confident that the *Pilot* would ask Gilbert to write for them, and other sources suggested that the *Echo* would employ him as reviewer. "I can keep ten poems and twenty theories in my head at once. But I can only think of one practical thing at a time," he wrote. In his opinion, it was time they got married. To his mother he raised his estimated earnings to something approaching £470, and then broached the subject which was dearest to his heart

> There is something . . . that is distressing me a great deal. I believe I said about a year ago that I hoped to get married in a year, if I had money enough. I fancy you took it rather as a joke: I was not so certain about it myself then. I have however been coming very seriously to the conclusion that if I pull off one more affair – a favourable arrangement with Reynolds' Newspaper, whose editor wants to see me at the end of this week, I shall, unless you disapprove, make a dash for it this year . . . Believe me, my dearest mother, I am not considering this affair wildly or ignorantly: I have been doing nothing but sums in my head for the last months. [He discussed the details of his income, and thought that he could afford] . . . a very cheap flat, even a workman's flat if necessary, have a woman in to do the laborious daily work and for the rest wait on ourselves, as many people I know do in cheap flats. Moreover, journalism has its ups as well as downs, and I, I can fairly say, am on the upward wave. Without vanity and in a purely businesslike spirit I may say that my work is talked about a great deal. [And discussing the various journals which had taken him on] I know the clockwork of these papers and among one set of them I might almost say that I am becoming the fashion.

Books, articles and speeches had turned Gilbert into "the fashion" in London, as had his blossoming character. Because of his youth, the fact that many of his articles had been uncredited and only later attributed to him, and that he adopted the habit of signing himself "G.K.C." at the end of his letters, reviews and commentaries rather than his full name, introduced a sense of the mysterious to him. Some suggested that there was no such person behind these initials, merely a committee of writers or a well-known journalist hiding behind a *nom de plume.* His literary fame in the early stages of his career owed much to a pungent, precise article written for the *Speaker* of 26th May, entitled "A Defence of Patriotism." It would later be published in a book of articles from the *Speaker* and the *Daily News* under the title *The Defendant.* The phrase on every editor's lips after the piece appeared was as typical a product of Gilbert's thinking as anything he wrote throughout his career: "My country, right or wrong," is a thing that no patriot would think of saying except in a desperate case. It is like saying, "My mother, drunk or sober."

He denounced the extreme Imperialists as being interested in only the trivial, unimportant features of Britain and British society, and totally ignoring what it was that made the country virtuous and strong. The greatness of Britain was in front of every British subject, within seeing and feeling distance, not in far away colonies and obscure wars with settler and native peoples. He concluded the analysis thus

> We have deliberately neglected this great heritage of high national sentiments. We have made our public schools the strongest walls against a whisper of the honour of England. And we have had our punishment in this strange and perverted fact that, while a unifying vision of patriotism can ennoble bands of brutal savages or dingy burghers, and be the best thing in their lives, we who are – the world being judge – humane, honest, and serious individually, have a patriotism that is the worst thing in ours.

And

> What have we done, and where have we wandered, we that have produced sages who could have spoken with Socrates and poets who could walk with Dante, that we

123

should talk as if we have never done anything more intelligent than found colonies and kick niggers? We are the children of light, and it is we that sit in darkness. If we are judged, it will not be for the merely intellectual transgression of failing to appreciate other nations, but for the supreme spiritual transgression of failing to appreciate ourselves.

Reputation founded, financial security assured and his mother at least partly satisfied, Gilbert and Frances set a date for their wedding, 28th June 1901 at the Kensington parish church, St Mary Abbots, and a mutual friend, Conrad Noel, would marry them. Between them the couple had a multitude of friends and acquaintances, all of whom seemed to be sending wedding gifts. "I feel like the young man in the Gospel," said Gilbert, "sorrowful, because I have great possessions." Lucian Oldershaw, the best man, was surprised at how calm the groom appeared to be. It was not so much calmness as Gilbert's ability to ignore the bustle and panic of affairs around him and simply switch off; a valuable attribute on occasion, disastrously irresponsible at other times. Gilbert managed to arrive on time at his wedding – something which surprised most of those present who knew him well – but found that he was not wearing a tie. Rhoda Bastable, a bridesmaid, sent her brother running into the High Street to purchase one; he arrived back at the church, tie in hand, only moments before Frances entered. When Gilbert knelt down during the ceremony the price tag on the sole of one of his new shoes became clearly visible; there was nothing to be done, so his mother and friends simply giggled to themselves, accepting the ludicrously inevitable. Other than this all went smoothly, though it was noted that the tall, large Gilbert and his petite wife did not quite fit into the category of perfect couple, at least in the physical context. Emotionally they seemed to combine as well as young man and wife could, accepting each other's faults, praising each other's qualities. It was sincere love, and sincere commitment.

Oldershaw drove off to Liverpool Street station with the newlyweds' luggage to place it on the train to Ipswich; they were to spend one night there, on their journey eastwards to the Norfolk Broads. Gilbert once said that the only way to be sure of catching a train is to miss the one before it. He did not, however, put this self-advice into practice on his wedding day, and the Ipswich train, containing almost all of his and his wife's luggage, went off without the Chestertons. The reasons for their delay were not logical, or even reasonable; but then Gilbert always distrusted the conventional understanding of logic and reason. He felt obliged to halt his progress to Liverpool Street to take his new wife to a dairy bar in Kensington High Street. "I had always drunk a glass of milk there when walking with my mother in my infancy. And it seemed to me a fitting ceremonial to unite the two great relations of a man's life," he was later to say in his defence. The couple could still have made their destination on time, but for his insistence that they then stop off at a firearms shop to enable him to purchase a revolver and some bullets; "with the general notion of protecting my wife from the pirates doubtless infesting the Norfolk Broads, to which we were bound; where, after all, there are still a suspiciously large number of families with Danish names."

They were forced to take the slow train to Ipswich, a vapid trek to a city of limited charm. Once there they were taken to the White Horse Inn, and seeing that his wife was tired and pale Gilbert sat down with her and poured his love a glass of wine. He then recommended that she lie down for a time, the day had been exhausting; he would go for a walk. He became lost. After aimless wanderings he asked for directions from a passer-by – not a marauding Dane – and strolled back to the Inn. There he found Frances, nervous and timid, as would be expected from a new bride of her day. The moment of their first time alone, in a bedroom, with God and society's blessing, had been a long time in coming; Gilbert had certainly procrastinated during the last twelve hours. He was nervous, unsure, and prepared for difficulties.

What happened next is, of course, a matter of speculation. What has been passed on is an account from Ada Chesterton, Gilbert's sister-in-law, which she claimed to have been given by her husband, Cecil. As has been said earlier, she is a hostile witness.

He was fathoms deep in love, and in that first transcendent moment of their honeymoon when far beyond time and space they found themselves utterly, incomparably alone, he must have heard the sun and the moon and the stars singing together. And then the whole went crash. The woman he worshipped shrank from his touch and screamed when he embraced her. A less sensitive or more experienced man would have regarded the whole affair as distressing but by no means irremediable, but he was haunted by the fear that his brutality and lust had frightened the woman he would have died to protect. He dared not even contemplate a repetition. He went to Cecil, quivering with self reproach and condemnation. His young brother took a completely rationalistic view of the contretemps, and suggested that some citadels must be taken by storm while others yield only to a long siege. Anyway he insisted that nothing had happened that couldn't be put right. They could both be happy and have lots of children. But the mischief had been done. Gilbert hated himself for what had happened and Frances couldn't resign herself to the physical realities of marriage. Temperamentally ascetic, physically sick from spinal disease, the experience must have shocked her profoundly. Her tragedy was that desiring children she shrank from sex. The final adjustment between them seems never to have been made, and Gilbert in a vital hour was condemned to a pseudo-monastic life in which he lived with a woman but never enjoyed one. For there was that about the Chestertons which would not let them be unfaithful. It was a family idiosyncrasy – apart from religion, belief or social tradition. Once married, they were dedicate for life. The story of the wedding night was ancient history when I heard it from Cecil, but the effect still survived. Even fidelity exacts its price, and as the years went on, physically speaking, Gilbert ran to seed . . .

It is a disturbing, unsavoury report, and contains elements of truth. For Ada Chesterton to describe fidelity as an "idiosyncrasy" implies that it is not the norm; yet in the early

1900s, the pre-permissive decades, faithfulness within the marriage bed, even if that bed was used only for sleeping upon, was considered standard. As to Gilbert putting on weight and declining in physical health, he was clearly heading towards gross obesity before he met Frances – the trends were apparent by his twenty-first birthday – and it was not his wife but his massive appetite, which his wife gently tried to reduce through words of wisdom and diet, which was the cause.

It is probable that the marriage night was an embarrassing and humiliating débâcle. They would both have been virgins, and failures on honeymoon nights, both then and now, are not unknown. Gilbert would not have been able to go to his brother for any experienced advice – Cecil was as naïve as he – and Frances is unlikely to have received anything more than the thinnest of encouragement from her mother and sister. Ada Chesterton's accusation that the entire marriage was without sex is impossible to prove or disprove. They were childless; a result of Frances's physical vulnerability and weakness. When it was discovered that children would not be forthcoming Frances decided to undergo a painful, dangerous operation to remedy the problem. It failed. But would a woman who had not had intercourse with her husband go through such an operation? It seems certain that the Chestertons were a normal, if sometimes reluctant, married couple. Gilbert's disinclination to discuss sexuality did cast a fog of rumour over his opinions, and his writings reveal a certain immaturity in this area. His faithfulness – there was and never has been any evidence that he made use of mistresses or prostitutes – only serves to enhance his character.

The best verdict on this part of their marriage may be in Gilbert's written opinions on women, most notably in *What's Wrong With The World,* written in 1910. "In all the old flowery and pastoral love-songs," he wrote, "you will find a perpetual reproach against woman in the matter of her coldness; ceaseless and stale similies compare her eyes to northern stars, her heart to ice, her bosom to snow . . . . I think those old cavalier poets who wrote about the coldness of Chloe had hold of a psychological truth missed in nearly all the realistic novels of today." He went on to describe how contemporary writers thought women to be emotional. "But in truth the old and frigid form is much nearer to the vital fact. Most men, if they spoke with any sincerity, would agree that the most terrible quality in women was not so much being emotional as being unemotional. There is an awful armour of ice which may be the legitimate protection of a more delicate physical organism; but whatever be the psychological explanation there can surely be no question of the fact. The instinctive cry of the female in anger is noli me tangere . . . . The proper name for the thing is modesty; but as we live in an age of prejudice and must not call things by their right names, we will yield to a more modern nomenclature and call it dignity. Whatever else it is, it is the thing which a thousand poets and a million lovers have called the coldness of Chloe."

The rest of the honeymoon was a complete success. Their love was strong enough to overcome the painful newness of intimacy. Both wished the time together to be longer, and Gilbert put his regret, and joy, on to paper

> Between the perfect wedding day
>   And that fierce future proud, and furled,
> I only stole six days – six days
>   Enough for God to make the world.

They did not return to any permanent home, Gilbert had yet to find one which would suit, but to the house of a friend of the Blogg family, in beautiful Edwardes Square, very close to the Chesterton residence. The rent they paid was absurdly high for their meagre income. After three months of luxurious, but misleadingly affluent, living they moved to a smaller, more realistic, abode. Their time in Edwardes Square was happy. Bentley remembered the gatherings at the rented house, "with its garden of old trees and its general air of Georgian peace. I remember too," he wrote, "the splendid flaming frescoes, done in vivid crayons, of knights and heroes and divinities with which G.K.C. embellished the outside wall at the back, beneath a sheltering portico. I have often wondered whether the landlord charged for them as dilapidations at the end of the tenancy." It would seem that Gilbert's habit of drawing on walls had not ceased with marriage; on one occasion he requested an extraordinarily long pencil to enable him to draw on the ceiling when he was in bed, and told friends that the best form of wallpaper would be brown paper, being the easiest to write upon.

Because the house was so near to the family home in Warwick Gardens it was easy for Gilbert and his new wife to walk over for tea, and sympathy. Frances often enjoyed the trips, but would have preferred a less intense relationship with her in-laws. Food and drink were only part of the reason for Gilbert's visits to his father's house; the main reason was his brother Cecil. They had been virtually inseparable since boyhood, best friends and the best of enemies. It was remembered that Gilbert's wedding reception was one of the few times when the two brothers did not argue, albeit with respect and good nature. Cecil was a tough, robust boy, capable of provoking strong feelings of like and dislike at a remarkably early age. He enjoyed dominating, and at times found it essential. If Gilbert could be the wittier debater, Cecil could provide the cutting edge, the final blow which Gilbert seldom found himself able to deliver – due to compassion rather than ineptitude.

An early letter from Cecil to Gilbert demonstrates the precocious nature of the youth.

I have been bathing in rather rough weather lately . . . . It is almost impossible to stand up against a big wave when it is breaking and the sensation of being thrown violently on a pebbly beach is not pleasant. As, however, I can now swim pretty well it does not affect me as much as it did . . . . The Imperial Parliament is getting a little livelier thanks mainly to Timothy Healey and Doctor Tanner. The former is playing a clever and rather amusing game against the Government and indirectly against his own colleagues. He is trying to make himself popular in Ireland by showing himself the most active in the House. Did you see Dr Tanner's Bull? "Let them," he said, "not allow a golden moment to slide. Let them reinstate the

129

evicted tenants first and do something for the Irish labourers at the same time." Yours, C.E. Chesterton.

As Cecil matured his sense of righteousness increased, transforming him from a strong-willed little boy into a young man of intolerant views, completely confident that he was correct on any and every issue he decided to take up; in this he was not unlike Hilaire Belloc, with whom he would become firm friends. Cecil had his heart set on Fleet Street, and also on Ada Jones, who also often visited Warwick Gardens. She was a natural partner for Cecil, and one of the few people capable of standing up to one of his frontal attacks, and returning the fire. She was a successful journalist, and had started in the trade as a teenager. In the late 1890s and early 1900s Fleet Street was so male-dominated and structured that any woman working in or near it would find life very difficult indeed. The road had been hard and humiliating, but Ada Jones had established herself as a reporter and columnist, writing short stories and contributing superior fiction to various women's magazines. She wrote under the pen-name of John Keith Prothero – a large circle of friends called her Keith to her face – and she was as striking a woman to look at as she was to read and hear.

It took Cecil seventeen years of courting before he married Ada Jones, and at times he found the strain difficult to bear. Gilbert got to know her well through that time, as did his wife, and came to like her. She reciprocated the feeling, but could never comprehend the lack of drive in Frances, something she discerned as a failure in character rather than a quality of contentment. When he first met her Gilbert was impressed by the "Queen of Fleet Street . . . a free-lance or the Joan of Arc of free-lances." They disagreed most of the time, and knew each other's ways and means in thought and argument. There was a tacit intellectual regard between Ada and Gilbert, and from Gilbert a note of admiration

She always had a hundred irons in the fire; though only one of her fires is now so big as to be a bonfire and a beacon. Everyone has heard of the Cecil Houses, in which homeless women find that real hospitality, human and humorous, which was incredibly absent from the previous priggish philanthropy; and nearly everyone has read about their origin, in her own outstanding book which records her own astounding adventure. She went out without a penny to live among the penniless; and brought back our only authoritative account of such a life .... She has sympathy with Communists, as I have, and perhaps points of agreement I have not. But I know that she stands, first, for the privacy of the poor who are allowed no privacy. She fights after all, as I do, for the private property of those who have none.

It marked a sort of sublimination of the Fleet Street spirit in my sister-in-law that, within healthy limits, she not only could do everything, but she would do anything .... It was of her that the story was told that, having driven whole teams of plotters and counter-plotters successfully through a serious Scottish newspaper, she was pursuing one of the side-plots for a few chapters, when she received a telegram from the editor, "You have left your hero and heroine tied up in a cavern under the Thames for a week, and they are not married."

Ada Jones, Gilbert, Cecil and, often along for the ride, Frances would spend at least one evening a week at a debating meeting, searching out the worthwhile societies and arriving at their doors together. Debating was a craze which grabbed middle-class London and some of the larger provincial cities in the years leading up to the First World War, and a plethora of junior, senior and university groups were formed; alongside these were the would-be parliaments, which undergo periodic re-births every few years, which model themselves on the Westminster Assembly and debate policies and politics along party lines. Frances had lost some of her enthusiasm for these affairs, their charm and appeal had limitations for a young woman in her first year of marriage. She was the fourth member of the group, and always felt as much.

The move to their own home in Battersea came as a relief. Overstrand Mansions was to be their lasting and last London home. It was not what either had been used to, being a medium-sized block of flats with a fine view but lacking any particularly attractive features. The annual rent was £80, a solid but affordable payment for a middle-class couple. Belloc immortalised the figure in a poem, which was pinned up on the wall of the new Chesterton residence

> Frances and Gilbert have a little flat
> At eighty pounds a year and cheap at that
> Where Frances who is Gilbert's only wife
> Leads an unhappy and complaining life:
> While Gilbert who is Frances's only man
> Puts up with it as gamely as he can.

Belloc's bitter-sweet sense of humour was taken with good feeling by Frances; Gilbert adored it. He was to be a regular guest at the Battersea flat, and the Chestertons enjoyed his company. He did not always give good notice of his visits

It will annoy you a good deal to hear that I am in town tomorrow Wednesday evening and that I shall appear at your Apartment at 10.45 or 10.30 at earliest. P.M.! You are only just returned. You are hardly settled down. It is an intolerable nuisance. You heartily wish I had not mentioned it. Well, you see that (arrow pointing to "Telegrams, Coolham, Sussex"), if you wire there before One you can put me off, but if you do I shall melt your keys, both the exterior one which forms the body or form of the matter and the interior one which is the mystical content thereof. Also if you put me off I shall not have you down here ever to see the Oak Room, the Tapestry Room, the Green Room, etc.

It did not take long for Overstrand Mansions to take on some of the character of past lodgings. Father O'Connor, later to be the model for Father Brown, remembered sending a prize Wensleydale cheese to the Chesterton apartment for Christmas; they were "at home to callers," and it did not last for very long. When he visited Gilbert and Frances he saw "Max Beerbohm's cartoon of Belloc converting Chesterton from the errors of Calvinism. The conversion was almost complete, the pint pot being nearly empty. A special dedication in Max's hand I do not remember verbatim, but it was a paragraph in the Chestertonian manner to the effect that scoffing was true worship, and the Yah! of the rude boy in the street is but an act of reverence, being the first syllable of the Unutterable Name!" Father O'Connor also travelled with Gilbert from Battersea to a dinner in the West End, and was amused but not surprised when Frances called her husband back to check whether he was wearing a clean collar. He wasn't.

The reminder board inside the flat was invariably dripping with pinned notes to aid Gilbert's appalling memory; they were usually ignored. The unfortunate object was headed "Lest we forget!" Of the other people in the block, most were of a similar class and background, with artists and civil servants making up the majority of residents, and would-be politicians and authors also contributing their share. Another writer, Rann Kennedy, occupied the flat directly below the Chestertons'; Kennedy was a playwright with a middling reputation, and an ability to match. They met when passing one another on the stairs one day; there were no lifts. "Gilbert would walk up very slowly, writing an article on his cuff," recalled Mr Kennedy. On one occasion Gilbert slowed down even more and said, "Isn't it jolly out in the park there?" Kennedy responded, "Yes, it is lovely, have you just been there?" When they met again, on the next day, Kennedy said to Gilbert, "Did you notice when we saluted yesterday we both greeted each other in a choriambus and a hypermetric?" Friendship was instantaneous, and became close.

Also in the block were the Saxon Mills family, who also became friends. "We were very poor in those days," said Mrs Saxon Mills. "When we were short, they used to feed us. When they were short, we used to feed them." Mr Saxon Mills was a political opponent of Gilbert's, but only in the most civilised of senses. When they shared a taxi it was decided that Saxon Mills would pay for the journey to their destination, Gilbert would pay the return. One day Saxon Mills paid three shillings and sixpence to the driver. Gilbert exclaimed "Well, I won't be outdone by an old Tariff Reformer," and promptly gave the driver seven shillings and sixpence. The cabbie, it seemed, was not political. The building was conducive to friendship and sharing, with an atmosphere of a club or school. Gilbert took to it immediately, and Frances enjoyed the company and the friendliness. None of the neighbours worried about groups of slightly drunken men returning to the Chesterton rooms at a late hour, and when they sat down to consume huge quantities of meat and cheese and eggs they kept as quiet as they could. Frances pretended that they were succeeding in their endeavours.

The Defendant, Gilbert's third volume, was published just before he moved to Battersea. It was clearly the most successful and most recognised of his books to date. It consisted of sixteen essays, most of them previously published in the *Speaker.* An introductory piece entitled "In Defence of a New Edition" was added to the second edition in 1903. The subjects defended, for each essay involved a defence of something, ranged from skeletons to baby-worship, planets to china shepherdesses. It failed to impress some critics but to most the wit and penetration on display marked the author out as a notable talent. He began his "A Defence of Nonsense" in a way which was to become familiar to his readers, offering alternatives and laying the ground for the paradox to come

There are two equal and eternal ways of looking at this twilight world of ours: we may see it as the twilight of evening or the twilight of morning; we may think of anything, down to a fallen acorn, as a descendant or as an ancestor. There are times when we are almost crushed, not so much with the load of the evil as with the load of the goodness of humanity, when we feel that we are nothing but the inheritors of a humiliating splendour. But there are other times when everything seems primitive, when the ancient stars are only sparks blown from a boy's bonfire, when the whole earth seems so young and experimental that even the white hair of the aged, in the fine biblical phrase, is like almond-trees that blossom, like the white hawthorn grown in May . . . .

For all of its praise from press and public the book did not make the amount of money which was expected. It was not a serious problem, because Gilbert's journalism was cutting a deep groove in the magazine and newspaper world, ensuring him outlets and raising the price of his work. Each time a book was published, no matter how little money it actually gained for its author, editors in London would see Gilbert in a brighter light and be willing to raise his payments. He felt more secure, more able to experiment in his contributions.

Gilbert would be blessed throughout his working life with having two books published in quick-fire succession. It provoked resentment in some quarters, and created the impression in others that such a rapid author could not be a serious author; for the most part it made Gilbert seem a ubiquitous character, always on somebody's lips, always in the review pages as a subject or a commentator. Shortly after *The Defendant* Gilbert's fourth book, *Twelve Types,* was issued. It too was a collection of articles from the *Speaker* and *Daily News,* but this time was on the theme of biography. He discussed Scott, St Francis, Tolstoy, Savonarola, Charlotte Bronte, William Morris, Pope, Byron, Stevenson, Charles II, Carlyle and Rostand. Most of the studies contained some point which outraged historians, for Gilbert was never one to check his facts or worry about the accuracy of his memory. The joy, the genius, of the essays was in their sharpness, their ability to cut through the centuries and myths and get straight to the point. On Sir Walter Scott: "The whole of the best and finest work of the modern novelist (such as the work of Mr Henry James) is primarily concerned with that delicate and fascinating speech which burrows deeper and deeper like a mole; but we have wholly forgotten that speech which mounts higher and higher like a wave and falls in a crashing peroration."

Admirers now said that half of London was reading G.K.C., while the other half was asking "Who is G.K.C?" It was of course an exaggeration. Literary London was intrigued however; not the least Max Beerbohm. Henry Maximillian Beerbohm, later Sir Max, was the leading satirist and caricature artist in Britain, if not the world. Although he constantly denied it, he was almost certainly of Jewish stock,

135

out of Lithuania. He had attended Charterhouse and Merton College, Oxford, finding acceptance and welcome in places where others of his background would have met tangible hostility. In 1898 he had become drama critic of the *Saturday Review,* following George Bernard Shaw in that position. His reviews were published in book form, as were collections of his essays and drawings. He was very much the elegant man-about-town, an individual to know.

The fact was that Beerbohm wanted to know Gilbert. He wrote to him from the Savile Club in May 1902

> I have seldom wished to meet anyone in particular; but you I should very much like to meet. I need not explain who I am for the name at the end of this note is one which you have more than once admitted, rather sternly, into your writings. By way of personal and private introduction, I may say that my mother was a friend of your grandmother, Mrs Grosjean, and also of your mother. As I have said, I should like to meet you. On the other hand, it is quite possible that you have no reciprocal anxiety to meet me. In this case, nothing could be easier than for you to say that you are very busy, or unwell, or going out of town, and so are not able – much as you would have liked – to lunch with me here either next Wednesday or Saturday at 1.30.
>
> I am, whether you come or not, yours admiringly,
>
> Max Beerbohm

> P.S. I am quite different from my writings (and so, I daresay, are you from yours) so that we should not necessarily fail to hit it off. I, in the flesh, am modest, full of common sense, very genial and rather dull. What you are remains to be seen – or not to be seen by me, according to your decision.

Nobody could have turned down such an offer, hardly Gilbert. He did indeed know of Beerbohm, and did not like all of what he knew. He shared the opinion of so many others that this gifted man "exhibited the cheek of a guttersnipe in the garb of a dandy." After the lunch his verdict was different.

The reputation for having a larger than life ego, for being impudent and ambitious, disappeared after the first moments of their meeting. "Max was and is a remarkably humble man," Gilbert wrote. "I have never known him, by a single phrase or intonation, claim to know more or judge better than he does; or indeed half so much or so well as he does. Most men spread themselves a little in conversation, and have their unreal victories and vanities; but he seems to me more moderate and realistic about himself than anything else . . ." So began a long-term friendship and respect, mutually given, mutually received.

Gilbert immortalised his opinions of his new friend in verse

> And Max's queer crystalline sense
> Lit, like a sea beneath a sea,
> Shines through a shameless impudence
> As shameless a humility.
> Or Belloc somewhat rudely roared
> But all above him when he spoke
> The immortal battle trumpets broke
> And Europe was a single sword.

It was Max Beerbohm who was dining with Gilbert when he received the request from Macmillan the publishers for a biography of Robert Browning. Beerbohm was enthusiastic – he was about most things with which he was vaguely connected – and encouraged the unsure young author to accept the project. The book was to be one of the "English Men of Letters" series, and would be the largest, most important undertaking of Gilbert's life as a writer. He would be in illustrious company: Anthony Trollope had written the book on Thackeray for the series, J.A. Froude had been responsible for Bunyan and Viscount Morley for Edmund Burke. He was extremely young to be awarded such an honour; he was only twenty-nine when the book appeared, and he was not a natural biographer.

Most of his research took place in the British Museum Reading Room, a location with which he was very much in love, and involved copious amounts of reading. Reading was not enough; this was pleasure to Gilbert, and more was required of him. His note taking was flimsy and volatile, of a sporadic nature and relied entirely on what particular theme of Browning appealed to him on any particular day. There was no realistic pattern of work, no idea as to how the chapters would connect or combine. With carelessness and a touch of arrogance, he steadfastly refused to check his remembered quotations from Browning, and this resulted in a highly inaccurate manuscript.

Concentration was not a problem, concentration on one subject was. He became a familiar and eccentric figure in the Reading Room, which is noted for its collection of "characters," with his strange ways and long hours. A story which may be apocryphal concerns him reading late into the evening at the British Museum. He found that he had no money, and as he was hungry and thirsty he set about remedying the situation. He drew a picture of a little man trembling with hunger, passed it around the desks nearest to him, and when he had received enough funds promptly walked off to the nearest pub. It is difficult to imagine the busy scholar donating money to such an obviously well-fed young man.

When the Browning manuscript was handed in it caused no end of trouble both to Gilbert and to the publishers. Stephen Gwynn, a junior editor at Macmillan's, had promoted the idea of Gilbert writing the Browning biography, and had to face the consequences: "Old Mr Craik, the Senior Partner, sent for me and I found him in white fury, with Chesterton's proofs corrected in pencil; or rather not corrected; there were still thirteen errors uncorrected on one page; mostly in quotations from Browning. A selection from a Scottish ballad had been quoted from memory and three of the four lines were wrong. I wrote to Chesterton saying that the firm thought the book was going to 'disgrace' them. His reply was like the trumpeting of a crushed elephant. But the book was a huge success."

Gilbert himself was always scrupulously honest in explaining his attitude to biography in general, and Browning in particular. He claimed not to have written "a book of Browning; but . . . a book on love, liberty, poetry, my own views of

God and religion (highly developed), and various theories of my own about optimism and pessimism and the hope of the world; a book in which the name of Browning was introduced from time to time, I might almost say with considerable art, or at any rate with some decent appearance of regularity."

His biographies would increase in popularity and importance, and his attitude towards accuracy would remain constant. Sometimes the mistakes caused confusion and chaos, more often than not they delighted readers and were treated as gems of insight which had to be taken with just a little salt. The success of the book carved an indelible place for its author. Reviews were mostly sanguine, with those of outright excitement outnumbering the hardened attacks. It was partly a book by Gilbert on Browning, partly, as he said, a book by Gilbert on Chesterton. Such a division is evident from the first page of the book: "His work has the mystery which belongs to the complex; his life the much greater mystery which belongs to the simple. He was clever enough to understand his own character; consequently we may be excused if that part of him which was hidden from him is partly hidden from us. The subtle man is always immeasurably easier to understand than the natural man; for the subtle man keeps a diary of his moods, he practises the art of self-analysis and self-revelation, and can tell us how he came to feel this or to say that. . . ."

One of the admirers of *Robert Browning* was someone who was to become as close a friend as Belloc, perhaps even closer. Maurice Baring was one of the banking family of that name, a tall, bald-headed man with a streak of madness and an unquenchable appetite for story-telling and stories. He was a noted linguist, and used that skill in the service of the British diplomatic service. He specialised in Russia and the Russians, and many of the poems and short stories he wrote were influenced by the Slavonic temperament. He wrote dozens of novels, plays and articles, but hardly any of them have survived as published works to the present day. In his Westminster house Gilbert, Belloc and others of their set would gather and drink and discuss until the hours before dawn. Expense was not a problem, and neither was the necessity to rise early next morning for work. It was a bohemian life-style which attracted Gilbert immediately – the romance of the night, the influence of the good wines and the stimulating and intimate company. He was never formally invited into the Baring–Belloc party scene, but neither man could later remember a time when he wasn't an integral part of it.

The food and drink took its toll. It is possible for human beings to consume amounts of food far in excess of their needs and only put on ten or fifteen pounds. Serious obesity comes about when the so-called "take-off" point is reached, and instead of only a fraction of the superfluous food being retained, the bulk of it is. This means that even the smallest meal will put on weight, until the body is disciplined back into its previous state. The "take-off" point for Gilbert occurred around the year 1903, when his fatness was recognised by all who knew him, and taken as truth by those who didn't. His beer intake was extreme, and his exercise meagre; the occasional walk or a country stroll. Bernard Shaw described him as "a young Man Mountain," and "a large abounding gigantically cherubic person who is not only large in body . . . but seems to be growing larger as you look at him." Gilbert was aware of the increase in his size, Frances was often concerned about it.

> I was as light as a penny to spend,
>   I was thin as an arrow to cleave,
> I could stand on a fishing-rod's end,
>   With composure, though on the *qui vive,*
>   But from Time, all a-flying to thieve
> The suns and the moons of the year,
>   A different shape I receive;
> The shape is decidedly queer.

By his thirtieth year the image of G.K. Chesterton had been fully created, with only the Catholicism of his later years still outstanding. Some of it was his natural self, much of it was not even the stuff of truth. That he accused people in argument of "being sober" is based on a single statement, and was not a regular Chestertonian refrain. That he was absent-minded was certainly the case, but not as forgetful as he would have had posterity believe. He would often leave his home with the wrong shoes on or without a tie, sometimes forgetting where he was meant to be going when he did manage to dress correctly.

His ability to get lost was part accident, part intention. It was a delight of his life, and an aspect of his love for London, to simply wander from his front door and take no notice of his surroundings or the direction in which he was travelling until the streets appeared to be new to him, and adventure was a possibility. "There are two ways of getting home," he wrote in *The Everlasting Man,* "and one of them is to stay there. The other is to walk round the whole world till we come back to the same place. . . ." The latter was his choice. He favoured the night, and his walks could last for hours. The novelty was the extraordinary in the seemingly ordinary; battle and glory behind a garden wall, secrets and societies just beyond the front door of a suburban dwelling. Getting lost was a recreation.

His eating habits were constantly the subject of jokes and tales. On one afternoon he was served two poached eggs in a teashop. As gesticulation was an essential part of his conversation, it did not take long before his wild movements knocked the plate from the table and into his lap. His friend noticed the accident, but Gilbert did not; and proceeded to order another helping, informing the giggling waitress that he had misplaced the first. His diet was heavily based around meat and vegetables, with a particular penchant for desserts and cakes. He was addicted to childhood temptations, devouring sticky buns and chocolate concoctions. He could drink milk by the pint. He was not an ugly eater, but was a rapid one; and it was common for him to spill food and drink, both down his front and on to the floor.

Most of the mythology about Gilbert had its origins in Fleet Street. His brother wrote as to how he would begin a conversation with anyone who happened to be about, in bar or pub. The stranger might be flattered by the attentions, or quite put out. "He talks," said Cecil, "especially in argument, with powerful voice and gesture. He laughs at his own jokes loudly and with quite unaffected enjoyment . . . . He will take a cab halfway up a street, keep it waiting an hour or so, and then drive halfway down the street again." He was in love with the cab as a means of transport, and was aware that its future had been darkened by engines and the modern need for as much speed as possible. The horse-drawn hansom was an elegant way to move around London, and with its two-seat capacity was admirably fitted to Gilbert's frame. He was a legend in the esoteric community of the cabbie, and they tolerated his keeping them waiting and not knowing where he wanted to go, certain that the tip would be generous and the conversation, when possible, vibrant.

Fleet Street was his domain, and he was as much a part of it as the El Vino and Cheshire Cheese watering holes which he frequented. Kenneth Baker, now a cabinet minister, remembers a family story concerning a relative walking up Fleet Street on a beautiful summer's day. She passed an alleyway and saw a man sitting on the ground begging. A side door opened and Gilbert Chesterton came out. He saw the man, looked for a moment, and then turned his pockets completely inside out, emptying the contents into the lap of the amazed beggar.

Ada Chesterton was often present at the Fleet Street marathons of Gilbert and his friends and wrote

He revelled in the movement, the humour, the humanity of Fleet Street, the infinite variety of companionship, the sharp-edged brains and debating ability. It was a masculine period of hard thinking and hard drinking, a recrudescence of the Old Grub Street, with G.K. as the presiding figure . . . . The Fleet Street El Vino was one of Gilbert's favourite haunts, with the George and the Bodega. It was a jolly place, and in those days sported many and noble barrels. Under the shelter of a vast cask of sherry, on the corner of an old mahogany table, G.K. would reel off hundreds of words and talk in a glowing flow of epigram and paradox. It became a custom to look in round about six in the hope of finding him. Those who arrived early sat at G.K.'s table, the others pushed in where they could . . . . Belloc might rush in like a nor'-easter, and expound the universe, insisting that some particular manifestation, political, social or psychological, could only happen at three places in the world, all of them widely and wildly apart . . . . Maurice Baring, the most modest and distinguished of special correspondents, exquisite poet, famous for his Russian studies, would drift along . . . . Sometimes the tavern party broke up early, but often we stayed on until closing time, which in that Arcadian era was twelve midnight, or midway in the evening we would adjourn to the other side of the Street, to Peel's or the Cheshire Cheese for sandwiches. G.K. generally walked on such occasions. When alone, however, he always took a hansom, even if it were only from the Daily News office to the Telegraph, a hundred yards across the road . . . . This was his method also of settling the score of his own drinks and those of his friends. The barman had to help himself. If, as might happen, his pockets were found empty, it would not matter, every pub within the radius of Fleet Street knew the big figure, recognised the chuckling laugh and would have given credit for so long as it was wanted.

His public speaking was always of the highest quality, and he was one of the best platform speakers of the age. Those who witnessed his oratory remembered a genial approach, with a great deal of swaying, humming and laughing. He would sometimes drawl, and his digression was legendary. The rate of his demand caused problems. Again, Ada Chesterton wrote of an evening in the El Vino, when he suddenly exclaimed, "I'm supposed to be speaking to the Literary Society at Bletchley – I should be speaking now . . ." He mused a moment on the clock, which pointed to the hour of seven, ordered another glass of port and then with an effort heaved himself up . . . . His absent-mindedness on the platform also had a following. One follower and acquaintance recalls Gilbert turning to face the audience with his fly buttons undone, and his size making the lapse in memory completely obvious. He turned around as though nothing had happened, there was a moment of silence, and then he faced the meeting once again and proceeded to give his lecture, buttons done up, as if nothing had happened.

One anecdote of his dressing habits has been told and re-told so often by Chestertonians down the years that there are now a dozen varieties of the theme. It occurred when he was staying with Conrad Noel at Paddington Green. He was to speak at a Literary Society, and was required to wear formal dress. He went into the bedroom to get ready, and came out wearing a dress coat which was so ill-fitting that it showed his braces, the arms being so short that his wrists were uncovered. When Conrad Noel went into the same room to put on his suit of clothes, he found a suit which could have covered him twice over. The explanation was fairly straightforward – they had picked up the wrong suits from the bed – but while Conrad Noel simply changed his costume and went out, Gilbert insisted that some sort of miracle had happened, the tiny suit was his own, and went out in it.

At home his style of entertaining was of the most generous kind. The Chesterton flat was opened up to guests, though they would often find that their host was late in getting home, and that Frances had to make do; explanations were entirely unnecessary. "Our Fleet Street contingent behaved with great propriety," wrote Ada Chesterton, "remaining in the draw-ingroom until, late in the evening, catching G.K.'s beckoning eye we followed him into the cosy little kitchen where mounds of sausages were eaten and pints of beer consumed and the talk grew better and better. Gilbert's symbol of hospitality was always sausages and beer." She may well have written "drunker and drunker," as the evenings at the Chesterton flat were invariably alcoholically supported. It became a point of pride amongst the Chesterton-Belloc set to drink heavily, and sometimes become drunk. It was both a sign of membership and friendship, and a defiant gesture aimed at the puritanical young things who were so influential at the time in politics and literature, calling for a renaissance in muscular Christian abstention. Gilbert could, and would, write under the influence of alcohol, with no visible difficulties or impairments to his thought and clarity.

There also began the habit of costume parties, with Gilbert

favouring the dress of Dr Johnson. He enjoyed being photo-graphed in eighteenth-century garb, and would express his preference for the Age of Enlightenment. During one such dinner Cecil came dressed as Liberty Wilkes, a character he resembled both physically – Wilkes was often parodied be-cause of his ugly looks – and in character; critics would describe them both as trouble-makers and egoists. Gilbert's other fancy dress for parties was as a character out of *The Pickwick Papers,* and on such evenings stories and drinking were, of course, demanded. His life was more full, more developed and more satisfying than ever before. He was still searching, for a cause and for a belief, to love and to write about. They would come.

VI

A Little Suffolk Priest and a Little London Suburb

E ngland and the English were always Gilbert's most special loves, and he preferred a holiday in the British Isles to the most exotic trip abroad. The climate suited his bulk, and the eccentric ways of the people matched his own peculiarities. The north was a regular vacation spot, with Yorkshire and its magnificent moors occupying a place of particular fondness for the Chesterton couple. The clean air and bracing winds of the area helped Frances's vulnerable physical state, or at least made her feel stronger and more able to cope. He wrote

> When I brought Frances away here, she was hit so heavily with a sort of wasting fatigue, that I really wanted to find out whether the doctors were right in thinking it only fatigue or whether (by one hellish chance out of a hundred) it might be the beginning of some real illness. I am pretty well convinced now, thank God, that the doctors are right and it is only nervous exhaustion. But – I would not write this to anyone else, but you combine so unusually in your own single personality the characters of (1) priest (2) human being (3) man of science (4) man of the world (5) man of the other world (6) old friend (7) new friend, not to mention Irishman and picture dealer, that I don't mind suggesting the truth to you. Frances has just come out of what looked bad enough to be an illness and is just going to plunge into one of her recurrent problems of pain and depressions. The two may be just a bit too much for her and I want to be with her every night for a few days – there's an Irish

146

bull for you! One of the mysteries of Marriage (which must be a Sacrament and an extraordinary one) is that a man evidently useless like me can yet become at certain instants indispensable. And the further oddity (which I invite you to explain on mystical grounds) is that he never feels so small as when he really knows that he is necessary. You may understand this scrawl; I doubt if anyone else would.

The man he was writing to was Father John O'Connor, Parish Priest, later a Privy Chamberlain to Pope Pius XI, and the model and inspiration for a fictional detective named Father Brown. Their initial meeting was in some ways inevitable: Gilbert was often in Yorkshire, O'Connor was based at St Anne's Church in Keighley and knew of and admired Gilbert's work; they had much in common. Nature abhors a vacuum, faith and friendship cannot tolerate two kindred spirits not joining in friendship. In 1903 and 1904 the Chestertons spent some time in West Yorkshire, Gilbert lectured and they enjoyed a holiday. They were based near to Ilkley, a spa town of some beauty on the River Wharfe, with a population then of over 13,000. They frequently lodged with the Steinthal family, and through them made the acquaintance of O'Connor. As with Max Beerbohm, Gilbert was approached with a view to friendship. In February 1903 Father O'Connor wrote to him that he was a "Catholic priest, and though I may not find you quite orthodox in details, I first wish to thank you very heartily, or shall I say, to thank God for having gifted you with the spirituality which alone makes literature immortal, as I think."

As to their first meeting, there are differences of opinion. In his book *Father Brown on Chesterton,* O'Connor writes: ". . . We met at Keighley in the spring of 1904, at the house of Mr Herbert Hugill, who was a much older Chesterton fan than I was . . . . There we agreed to walk over the moor to Ilkley, where Chesterton was spending a short holiday, and I was his willing guide. The actual conditions for both of us were as near the ideal as makes no difference: he was on holiday, having delivered his lecture to the Keighley intelligentsia, and I was in possession of the heart's desire, which was to talk with him. March was awaking and blowing the hair out of her eyes, and our bit of moorland is among the finest in Yorkshire, especially when white clouds race across the blue . . ."

He went on to explain that he had been introduced to Gilbert's work through *The Defendant,* and that as they marched over the northern English countryside both O'Connor and Gilbert recounted anecdotes and opinions. They reached the subject of confession ". . . If everyone frequented the Sacrament of penance as much as mere pious authors urge, it would soon kill off all the confessors, but the modern practice keeps the track smooth, open, and safe. If people went to confess only great crimes, the C.I.D. might begin to haunt our churches after a murder or a burglary, and this would lead to heavier complications."

The conversation became smothered in digression, occasionally reaching points of mutual concern and remaining on a single point just long enough for a dialogue to take place. "We even got on to the burning of heretics," O'Connor recalls. "Neither of us could bear to look on it as practical politics; neither of us could bear to apply a hot flat-iron to the soles of their feet, as I once in an hospital, pretending to be the visiting doctor, recommended very loudly for a woman who was shamming epilepsy; but Chesterton was already convinced that something drastic was necessary for bad cases which could and did occur . . ." They shouted to make themselves heard in the wind, sang songs together and gorged on each other's company. O'Connor's recollection of the beginnings of friendship are as authentic as any, and Gilbert agreed with most of the account in his *Autobiography*

Father John O'Connor of Bradford . . . . is not shabby, but rather neat . . . . he is not clumsy, but very delicate and dexterous; he not only is but looks amusing and amused. He is a sensitive and quick-witted Irishman, with the profound irony and some of the potential irritability of his race. My Father Brown was deliberately described as a Suffolk dumpling from East Anglia. That,

148

and the rest of his description, was a deliberate disguise
for the purpose of detective fiction . . . . But for all that,
there is a very real sense in which Father O'Connor was
the intellectual inspiration of these stories; and of much
more important things as well . . . . I had gone to give a
lecture at Keighley on the high moors of the West Riding,
and stayed the night with a leading citizen of that little
industrial town; who had assembled a group of local
friends such as could be conceived, I suppose, as likely to
be patient with lecturers; including the curate of the
Roman Catholic Church; a small man with a smooth
face and a demure but elvish expression. I was struck by
the tact and humour with which he mingled with his very
Yorkshire and very Protestant company; and I soon
found out that they had, in their bluff way, already
learned to appreciate him as something of a character.
Somebody gave me a very amusing account of how two
gigantic Yorkshire farmers, of that district, had been
deputed to go the rounds of various religious centres, and
how they wavered, with nameless terrors, before entering the little presbytery of the little priest. With many
sinkings of heart, they seem to have come finally to the
conclusion that he would hardly do them any serious
harm; and that if he did, they could send for the police.
They really thought, I suppose, that he had his house
fitted up with all the torture engines of the Spanish Inquisition. But even these farmers, I was told, had since
accepted him as a neighbour, and as the evening wore on
his neighbours decidedly encouraged his considerable
powers of entertainment. He expanded, and was soon in
the middle of reciting that great and heart-searching
dramatic lyric which is entitled "My Boots are Tight." I
liked him very much . . .

I mentioned to the priest in conversation that I proposed to support in print a certain proposal, it matters
not what, in connection with some rather sordid social
questions of vice and crime. On this particular point he
thought I was in error, or rather in ignorance; as indeed I
was. And, merely as a necessary duty to prevent me from
falling into a mare's nest, he told me certain facts he

knew about perverted practices which I certainly shall
not set down or discuss here. I have confessed on an
earlier page that in my own youth I had imagined for
myself any amount of iniquity; and it was a curious
experience to find that this quiet and pleasant celibate
had plumbed those abysses far deeper than I. I had not
imagined that the world could hold such horrors. If he
had been a professional novelist throwing such filth
broadcast on all the bookstalls for boys and babies to
pick up, of course he would have been a great creative
artist and a herald of the Dawn. As he was only stating
them reluctantly, in strict privacy, as a practical necessity, he was, of course, a typical Jesuit whispering poi-
sonous secrets in my ear. When we returned to the house
we found it full of visitors, and fell into special conversation with two hearty and healthy young Cambridge
under-graduates . . . . I never knew a man who could turn
with more ease than he from one topic to another, or
who had more unexpected stores of information, often
purely technical information, upon all . . .

The description of their first meeting concludes with

Next morning he and I walked over Keighley Gate, the
great wall of the moors that separates Keighley from
Wharfedale, for I was visiting friends in Ilkley; and after
a few hours' talk on the moors, it was a new friend whom
I introduced to my old friends at my journey's end. He
stayed to lunch, he stayed to tea; he stayed to dinner; I
am not sure that, under their pressing hospitality, he did
not stay the night . . .

They had so much in common, as well as so much to teach
and learn from each other. The relationship often seemed to
be on the edge of falling into a master-pupil partnership, with
Gilbert sitting at the feet of this sage-like figure, with the
apparent quality and ability of a worldly philosopher. This
never happened. Gilbert had enough to reciprocate; O'Connor was willing to listen and be informed and entertained.
Father Brown would not materialise for some time, but the

bond between the two men would strengthen, Frances would also become a follower and friend, and they would have their lives broadened and enriched by the friendship. O'Connor was not possessive of Gilbert, as some celibate priests are towards their close friends, even when it appeared that Gilbert wanted to be possessed.

In some ways Father O'Connor acted as a safety valve for Gilbert, a channel where new ideas or half-formed theories could be tested, and if found to be dangerous or unhealthy, be promptly dismissed or challenged. The respect between them was fundamental to their friendship, as was the confidentiality which surrounded much of their dialogue; a consequence of this is that we are left with only the more bland of their letters and the most meagre records of their talks. The relationship was at its centre a journey; of discovery, faith, style and enlightenment. The journey included the appearance of Father Brown, but even without the unique fictional character it was a magnificent example of two men in platonic love.

Gilbert was always anxious to inform Father O'Connor of his forthcoming publications, and often discussed the initial thoughts which resulted in a book or article. Such was the case with his biography of G.F. Watts, published in March 1904. Gilbert was always at his best when writing about his heroes, and the painter George Frederick Watts had been a source of hope and inspiration since the lonely, desperate days of art school and isolation. The book was not particularly well publicised or promoted by its publishers at the time, and subsequently became one of Gilbert's more obscure achievements. Since reprinted, as a study of art, an artist and a man, it is a poignant reminder of how much can be said and explained in only a few pages. Watts was still living when the book appeared, a fact which Gilbert dealt with early on in his biography

It will appear to many a somewhat grotesque matter to talk about a period in which most of us were born and which has only been dead a year or two, as if it were a primal Babylonian empire of which only a few columns are left crumbling in the desert. And yet such is, in spirit, the fact. There is no more remarkable psychological element in history than the way in which a period can suddenly become unintelligible . . . . To the early Victorian period we have in a moment lost the key: the Crystal Palace is the temple of a forgotten creed. The thing always happens sharply: a whisper runs through the salons, Mr Max Beerbohm waves a wand and a whole generation of great men and great achievement suddenly looks mildewed and unmeaning. We see precisely the same thing in that other great reaction towards art and the vanities, the Restoration of Charles II. In that hour both the great schools of faith and valour which had seemed either angels or devils to all men: the dreams of Strafford and the great High Churchmen on the one hand; the Moslem frenzy of the English Commons, the worship of the English law upon the other; both seemed ridiculous. The new Cavalier despised the old Cavalier even more than he despised the Roundhead . . .

All the grand sweeps and understandings of history, analysis and meaning were present in the book, enough so to provoke an invitation that Gilbert should be nominated for the Chair of English Literature at Birmingham University. Unlike his friend Hilaire Belloc he had no academic pretensions, and much to the bewilderment and chagrin of his supporters in Birmingham he rejected the flattering request with polite apologies. If the biography of G.F. Watts produced an enthusiastic audience, his next book placed him firmly amongst the leading handful of English writers of his era, and still enjoys constant publication and a healthy readership. It is possibly his finest book, certainly his most ambitious and successful of his early years. As with so many of his projects, the surface plot and meaning of the book had little to do with its actual content. It was the product of years of daydreaming and attempted stories in notebooks and diaries, and included a philosophy of what was, and what was possible, which says more about Gilbert than most of his directly autobiographical writings. *The Napoleon of Notting Hill* is a fantasy set in the future – not an unusual device in

152

literature – and as with other books which have employed such a style it gives warnings and interpretations about contemporary society, asking the reader to think what might happen if certain trends continue, and to draw conclusions from one man's vision. It manages to be both optimistic and pessimistic, never pointing out the potential gloom without also highlighting the ways out.

In Gilbert's tale of things to come the nation is ruled by a king who is chosen out of the ranks of the civil service by a perverse form of democracy: when an individual's name is chosen, he has to serve his time as monarch, however unsuitable he may be. Auberon Quin, the man who finds himself King at the beginning of *Notting Hill,* is an eccentric character who tells unintelligible jokes and outrages his companions with his behaviour and odd manners. E.C. Bentley, reviewing the book for the *Bystander,* described the story as that of "a cynically humorous Autocrat of England who, a century hence, has the idea of reviving in the swarming parochial divisions of London the old mediaeval pomps and prides of municipal patriotism. Thus, King Auberon endows Notting Hill, West Kensington, Hammersmith, Bayswater, and all the other recognised neighbourhoods (including Battersea) with town charters, coats of arms, and mottoes, together with funny privileges and immemorial rights, invented on the spur of the moment. Also, it is the story of a splendid visionary, Adam Wayne, who alone of all men takes the King's freak quite seriously, and as provost of Notting Hill, infects all his fellow Notting Hillers with his own ardour – the story, in fact, of the triumph of a spiritual idea over the multitude of common-minded men, a possibility of which Mr Chesterton is, to his great honour, one of the resolute maintainers."

The influences on the book are as clear as they are powerful. His childhood adventures along the streets of West London were centred around the areas mentioned in *Notting Hill,* those streets where his often lonely, sometimes bewildered imagination came to grips with romantic dreams of battles and chivalry. He would pass small corner shops in the morning as they opened their doors to trade and the sunshine, and pass by them again as they closed up for the evening. It seemed an insular, satisfying life, embodying so much of what Gilbert's home and country represented; he was attracted by the self-contained smallness of urban villages, and would rush to their defence whenever so called upon. That Notting Hill stands firm for its ancient rights in the book and is prepared to fight for them to the last man is an extension of Gilbert's longing for a time when local honour required, demanded, stout support; if indeed that era ever existed. *The Napoleon of Notting Hill* was the setting down of a wistful, wishful fantasy.

The story of the commissioning of the book is as indicative of its author as the writing itself. "I was 'broke' – only ten shillings in my pocket," wrote Gilbert. "Leaving my worried wife, I went down Fleet Street, got a shave, and then ordered for myself, at the Cheshire Cheese, an enormous luncheon of my favourite dishes and a bottle of wine. It took my all, but I could then go to my publishers fortified. I told them I wanted to write a book and outlined the story of Napoleon of Notting Hill. But I must have twenty pounds, I said, before I begin. 'We will send it to you on Monday.' 'If you want the book,' I replied, 'you will have to give it to me today as I am disappearing to write it.' They gave it."

Conflict dominates *Notting Hill,* as it would do most of Gilbert's novels; between religion and atheism, modern and traditional, native and alien, light and dark. The struggle, and blurring, of the serious and the humorous arise again and again, never as strongly as in the men of Notting Hill fighting and dying for what their absurd king had begun simply as a glorified joke. The reader is not told what to think, what to conclude from the story; the cynical and the stridently dedicated are given their moments of triumph. Adam Wayne, the young lion of belief, is nearest to the hero in the book, explaining to his monarch at the end that he understands the antagonism between the causes, and that when "dark and dreary days come, you and I are necessary, the pure fanatic, the pure satirist. We have between us remedied a great wrong. We have lifted the modern cities into that poetry which every one who knows mankind knows to be immeasurably more common than the common place. But in healthy people there is no war between us. We are but the two lobes of the brain of a ploughman. Laughter and love are everywhere. The cathedrals, built in the ages that loved God, are full of blasphemous grotesques. The mother laughs continually at the child, the lover laughs continually at the lover, the wife at the husband, the friend at the friend. Auberon Quin, we have been too long separated; let us go out together . . ."

The success of *Notting Hill* made reputation more than money. Gilbert was writing and speaking enough for three authors, but still finding it difficult to keep his fees in his wallet or pockets for any period of time; he was generous, and he was frequently irresponsible with cash. With the larger-than-life energy which characterised his earlier years he set about earning more money in the only way he knew, by working harder. In 1905 he published two books, both major achievements. *The Club of Queer Trades* contained a number of stories, with illustrations by the author, which had either appeared before or ran along a theme which Gilbert had previously explored. There are shades of Father Brown in the tales, all journeys into outlandish mystery and puzzles of the most obscure kind. The link between each tale is the "Club" in question, with each member of the institution having to prove that he earns his living by a "queer trade." He leaps from a character who decides to communicate in a new sign language, to someone who lives in a tree-house, to a professional victim who hires himself out in order to lose witty arguments. It was a perfect vehicle for the Chestertonian mind, set free to range as far as it wanted and needed. Critics, and even some admirers, were disappointed with the book; it is one of the few volumes by Gilbert which has probably increased in popularity over the decades.

Heretics followed soon after, and reassured all of those who were upset by Gilbert's wanderings into detective fiction. It was published on 6th June by John Lane, to immediate praise and immediate offence. It was by its very nature a contemporary book, looking at literary people. Rudyard Kipling, Bernard Shaw, and H.G. Wells were three of the people analysed and criticised, also Lowes Dickinson, George Moore and Joseph McCabe, but most of those discussed are now obscure and forgotten and therefore inevitably a great deal of its passion and cutting edge has been lost. He wrote

> Nothing more strangely indicates an enormous and silent evil of modern society than the extraordinary use which is made nowadays of the word "orthodox." In former days the heretic was proud of not being a heretic. It was the kingdoms of the world and the police and the judges who were heretics. He was orthodox. He had no pride in having rebelled against them; they had rebelled against him. The armies with their cruel security, the kings with their cold faces, the decorous processes of State, the reasonable processes of law – all of these like sheep had gone astray. The man was proud of being orthodox, was proud of being right. If he stood alone in a howling wilderness he was more than a man; he was a church. He was the centre of the universe; it was round him that the stars swung. All the tortures torn out of forgotten hells could not make him admit that he was heretical. But a few modern phrases have made him boast of it. He says, with a conscious laugh, "I suppose I am very heretical," and looks round for applause. The word "heresy" not only means no longer being wrong; it practically means being clear-headed and courageous. The word "orthodoxy" not only no longer means being right; it practically means being wrong. All this can mean one thing, and one thing only. It means that people care less for whether they are philosophically right. For obviously a man ought to confess himself crazy before he confesses himself heretical. The Bohemian, with a red tie, ought to pique himself on his orthodoxy. The dynamiter, laying a bomb, ought to feel that, whatever else he is, at least he is orthodox.

The spirit of right-thinking which Gilbert promulgated in *Heretics* was the result of years of theorising and debate. In criticising other writers of the period he was not making personal attacks, but pulling at the structure of modernity which had been established in the early years of the century. The book advocated a return to fundamentals, and in that sense was truly radical; only by returning to the roots, looking again at our beliefs and changing accordingly can we achieve an equitable society. Each of the individuals discussed embodied something which was wrong with Edwardian Britain. Gilbert had been waiting to write the book most of his adult life, the public had been waiting for such a book for just as long.

H.G. Wells was the most able and advanced proponent of the "new" world, of scientific progress; his antipathy to religion was constantly publicised and cleverly supported. He and Gilbert found friendship difficult – Wells had the greater problem – and the chapter on the Wellsian heresy began with a blast rather than a caress: "We ought to see far enough into a hypocrite to see even his sincerity." On the character of Wells himself he wrote of "a man of genius" and "scientific humility." It was still an intense assault on the comfortable preconceptions of a generation of reformers, the like of which had not been seen before and, more importantly, was not at all expected.

Joseph McCabe was a man who has many imitators today. A former priest, after leaving the Church he decided to attack all that he had claimed and sworn to believe. McCabe had made Gilbert one of his main targets, launching attacks upon him and taking issue with most of his writings. McCabe was treated with the utmost courtesy in *Heretics,* but behind the polite phrases was an angry diatribe; he was the physical culmination of most of the ills which Gilbert perceived in the modern world. "Humanity stands at a solemn parting of the ways," stated McCabe. "Towards some unknown goal it presses through the ages, impelled by an over-mastering desire of happiness. Today it hesitates, light-heartedly enough, but every serious thinker knows how momentous the decision may be. It is, apparently, deserting the path of religion and entering the path of secularism . . ." It was not the sort of statement which could go unanswered, at least in Gilbert's eyes. He was particularly sensitive to McCabe's attack on his use of humour and wit. "To sum up the whole matter very simply" he wrote, "if Mr McCabe asks me why I import frivolity into a discussion of the nature of man, I answer, because frivolity is a part of the nature of man. If he asks me why I introduce what he calls paradoxes into a philosophical problem, I answer, because all philosophical problems tend to become paradoxical. If he objects to my treatment of life riotously, I reply that life is a riot . . ."

In his chapter on Bernard Shaw — a lifelong friend and admirer — he showed sympathy if not full agreement. Kipling was vulgar and ridiculous in his colonial mentality, Ibsen a man of ambivalence and doubt. Style and content impressed all, from the Prime Minister and highest bishops of the Anglican and Roman Catholic churches, to a wave of students and young scholars who embraced this new thinking as the vanguard of a totally new and liberating form. Gilbert was not sure how to handle the acclaim, always mildly uncomfortable with praise and flattery. His usual solution was to laugh at the enthusiastic critics, and laugh even louder at the unkind ones. He was now drinking heavily, becoming increasingly absent-minded and working far too hard. Still financial security and stability eluded him. That changed at the end of 1905 when Sir Bruce Ingram, editor of the *Illustrated London News,* began his search for a successor to L.F. Austin as the author of the "Our Notebook" column. "The article runs to about 2,000 words and takes the form of a light discussion on matters of the moment" wrote Sir Bruce, "and it is treated without political bias. I feel that no-one is better fitted than yourself to do the work and I shall be extremely glad if your other engagements permit you to take it up. The remuneration would be at the rate of £350 per annum, but I should propose that in the first instance the agreement should be for six months. In the event of your acceptance I shall send you further particulars as to the time for copy. I do not know that the remuneration is very dazzling, but I thought perhaps that you might have sufficient interest in this ancient journal to induce you to become a regular. If so, I should feel extremely honoured."

Such a gracious invitation, and such a timely offer of a regular income, was accepted immediately. Gilbert was to write the column for over thirty years, contributing some 1600 articles. They lacked the cutting edge of some of his other short pieces – politics and religion were not included in his subjects – but were precisely what a journal such as the *Illustrated London News* required; clever, beautifully written and able to appeal to a broad range of reader. He became as essential to the magazine as its title.

In January 1922, squeezed in between an article on submarines, a piece on the dangers of fishing and "A Week's Shooting Trip in the Jungles of Nepal," he wrote

A daily paper recently published a leading article on the good old subject of the good old days. Of course, it was devoted to the defence of the present against the past, for this practice also is by this time tolerably old. As a result, those who discuss the good old days and how bad they were, are a little vague about how old they are.

And in one of the last *Illustrated London News* articles before his death

The time has come to protest against certain very grave perils in the cinema and the popular films. I do not mean the peril of immoral films, but the peril of moral ones . . .

It was a shining two years for Gilbert, full of works being published, friends being made and a theology being shaped. The death of Frances's brother, Knollys, interrupted the happiness. The wretched young man had been in a state of depression since Gertrude's death. He had attempted to find ways out of his illness, eventually discovering a certain peace inside the Roman Catholic Church. Hence the shock at his suicide, by drowning. Frances reacted badly to the event, rejecting Gilbert's support and sinking into a black period of grief and guilt herself. It was to lead to her asking, insisting, that she and Gilbert abandon the Fleet Street scene to which she was becoming increasingly hostile.

Gilbert found solace, as usual, in his work. His love affair with Charles Dickens had intensified, culminating in his biography of the man and his writings in the summer of 1906. Shaw was quick to comment: "As I am a supersaturated Dickensite, I pounced on your book and read it, as Wegg read Gibbon and other authors, right slap through. . . ." Once again, Gilbert viewed his subject in the context of his time, exhibiting a unique ability for empathy. It was not the presentation of the facts of Dickens's life which impressed readers, so much as the portrayal of his character and writings which shone out of the book. Nor did Gilbert abstain from writing about himself in the biography, just as he had done with Browning. Writing of Dickens's remarkable popularity he said

There is one aspect of Charles Dickens which must be of interest even to that subterranean race which does not admire his books. Even if we are not interested in Dickens as a great event in English literature, we must still be interested in him as a great event in English history . . . . If he had not his place with Fielding and Thackeray, he would still have his place with Wat Tyler and Wilkes; for the man led a mob. He did what no English statesman, perhaps, has really done; he called out the people. He was popular in a sense of which we moderns have not even a notion. In that sense there is no popularity now. There are no popular authors today. We call such authors as Mr Guy Boothby or Mr William Le Queux popular authors. [Their current obscurity proves his point.] But this is popularity altogether in a weaker sense; not only in quantity, but in quality. The old popularity was positive; the new is negative. There is a great deal of difference between the eager man who wants to read a book, and the tired man who wants a book to read. A man reading a Le Queux mystery wants to get to the end of it. A man reading the Dickens novel wished that it might never end. Men read a Dickens story six times because they know it so well. If a man can read a Le Queux story six times it is only because he can forget it six times. In short, the Dickens novel was popular, not because it was an unreal world, but because it was a real world; a world in which the soul could live. The modern "shocker" at its very best is an interlude in life. But in the days when Dickens's work was coming out in serial, people talked as if real life were itself the interlude between one issue of "Pickwick" and another.

He could have made the comparison, in his own terms, between Dickens and any number of writers of the early twentieth century. It was pointed out that the book about a nineteenth-century novelist, travel writer and reformer was as much a critique of modern literature and values as it was a biography. The comment pleased Gilbert; he had not intended it to be anything but such an achievement. There were few criticisms of his analysis of Dickensian characters, described by him as all being "great fools."

There is the same difference between a great fool and a small fool as there is between a great poet and a small poet. The great fool is a being who is above wisdom rather than below it .... A man can be entirely great while he is entirely foolish. We see this in the epic heroes, such as Achilles. Nay, a man can be entirely great because he is entirely foolish. We see this in all the great comic characters of all the great comic writers of whom Dickens was the last. Bottom the Weaver is great because he is foolish; Mr Toots is great because he is foolish. The thing I mean can be observed, for instance, in innumerable actual characters. Which of us has not known, for instance, a great rustic? – a character so incurably characteristic that he seemed to break through all canons about cleverness or stupidity; we do not know whether he is an enormous idiot or an enormous philosopher; we know only that he is enormous, like a hill. These great, grotesque characters are almost entirely to be found where Dickens found them – among the poorer classes. The gentry only attain this greatness by going slightly mad ...

After describing the different types of characters which Dickens invented and brought to vibrant life he discussed the staggering number of such individuals. "The whole point of Dickens is that he not only made them, but made them by

161

myriads; that he stamped his foot, and armies came out of the earth." He used the character of Mr Toots, "a good example of the real work of Dickens," and dwelt on the "grotesque greatness" of the man.

> Toots is a type that we all know as well as we know chimney-pots. And of all conceivable human figures he is apparently the most futile and the most dull. He is the blockhead who hangs on at a private school, overgrown and underdeveloped. He is always backward in his lessons, but forward in certain cheap ways of the world; he can smoke before he can spell. Toots is a perfect and pungent picture of the wretched youth. Toots has, as this youth always has, a little money of his own; enough to waste in a semi-dissipation he does not enjoy, and in a gaping regard for sports in which he could not possibly excel. Toots has, as this youth always has, bits of surreptitious finery, in his case the incomparable ring. In Toots, above all, is exactly rendered the central and most startling contradiction; the contrast between a jauntiness and a certain impudence of the attire, with the profound shame and sheepishness of the visage and the character ...

For all the favourable reviews there was one constant theme of criticism: Gilbert was still a careless biographer, refusing to check his references and relying on a memory which was more susceptible than most to a vivid imagination. He was almost proud of some of the errors in his factual books which so outraged the traditional teachers and critics of his age, refusing to change them or apologise – in his mind there was nothing for which to apologise. He had waxed lyrical about Dickens and the postcard, and was not particularly upset when one reviewer stated that the first postcard in Britain was seen some three months after the great man's death. On one issue he was touched, and was prepared to act upon it. Dicken's daughter, Kate Perugini, wrote two letters to Gilbert, praising his biography of her father and congratulating him on its success. She did however take issue with his statement that Dickens had married the wrong sister in the

In his mid-fifties in cloak and hat. Frances had developed the image, Gilbert exploited it.

His toy theatre models. He made them and played with them
until his late middle age.

Gilbert loved the eighteenth century! His angry look is deceiving;
it is simply a myopic stare.

With Andre Maurois, on board ship.

Shaw, Belloc and Gilbert before the 1927 debate at Kingsway Hall.

Top Meadow. The house Gilbert designed and built, and in which he died.

Devils, demons and knights in shining armour. This drawing is an exercise book scribble of Gilbert's early adult years.

Hogarth family, and that he was in fact in love with all the sisters.

"My mother had no sister at that time with whom it was possible to fall in love," she wrote. "Or, no doubt, my father, being young and quite likely very impressionable, might have done so. As it was, he sincerely loved my mother, or thought he did, which came to the same thing, for he married her and, as you know, they did not live happy ever after, although I fancy they had several years of very great happiness indeed before my poor father found out his mistake, and before my poor mother suffered from this discovery. They were both to be pitied." She also informed Gilbert that as at the time of her parents' marriage her mother was the eldest of the Hogarth sisters and the other girls were aged fifteen and younger it was hardly likely that Dickens had any romantic feelings towards them. As to the suggestion that the family would have to listen to Dickens's laments and abusive tantrums she wrote, "In my father's unhappiness there were no railings. When he was really sorrowful he was very quiet, and depression with him never took the form of petulance. For in his unhappy moods he was singularly gentle and thoughtful for those around him."

Gilbert was a feeling man, moved to tears at times, always vulnerable to a story of grief or loss. The letters from Mrs Perugini genuinely upset him, and he was anxious to put matters right. The lady lived in Victoria Road in Kensington, and Gilbert lost no time in visiting and explaining himself. He was contrite, grateful, and would amend his statements in all future editions of the Dickens biography. Such was Gilbert's sorrow at the pain caused this delightful lady that she herself became worried about his own state of mind, and wrote to Frances explaining that the protest was only made on behalf of her mother: "From my own knowledge of her I feel sure that at the time she was engaged to my father she was a very winning and affectionate creature, and although the marriage, like many other marriages, turned out a dismal failure, I am also convinced that my dear father gained much from her refining influence and that of her family, and perhaps would never have been quite what he became without that influence."

163

The postscript to this incident is indicative of Gilbert's character. Here he was, sincerely upset and willing to do virtually anything to correct his mistake. It would have been relatively simple for him to inform his publishers of his wishes and make the relevant corrections for subsequent editions of the book, and subsequent editions there most certainly would be. No corrections were made, all his statements remained in the biography of Charles Dickens for posterity. Why? Malice and deceit were not the reasons; only over the death of a loved person would he ever show anything resembling bitterness and lack of charity, and the telling of a lie was as unnatural to Gilbert as the act of going on a diet. His memory was frequently poor, he was a very busy man and there were many other pressures on him at the time of the Dickens book. The central explanation lies elsewhere. After a brief time he came to the conclusion that corrections and apologies didn't matter. The victim would not harbour a grudge, Dickens was long dead. He was to exhibit this form of unintending insensitivity throughout his life, and most of his allegedly anti-Semitic comments in later years were the result not of racism, but of too humorous an attitude towards other people's feelings, demanding of them as thick a skin as he himself possessed.

His growing faith was a major factor in enlarging his sense of conscience and concern for others. His reading and thinking had taken him in the direction of orthodox Christianity for some years, and his friendship with Father O'Connor – though O'Connor scrupulously avoided any attempts at conversion – opened up the door to Roman Catholicism. He was perceived quite early on as a defender of the Church in all of its many shapes, and this was acknowledged by enemies as well as friends. One opponent who had taken issue with Gilbert as soon as he had encountered him was Robert Blatchford, editor of the *Clarion* and, according to Gilbert, "an old soldier with brown Italian eyes and a walrus moustache, and full of the very sentiments that soldiers have and Socialists generally have not." The confrontation between the two men and the two beliefs had begun in 1903 when Blatchford and his allies had written an atheistic manifesto

entitled "God and My Neighbour." Gilbert comments upon
Blatchford and his writings in the *Daily News*

> The problem is what is normal in man or, to put it more
> simply, what is human in him. Now, there are some who
> maintain, like Mr Blatchford, that the religious experi-
> ence of the ages was abnormal, a youthful morbidity, a
> nightmare from which he is gradually waking. There are
> others like myself who think that on the contrary it is the
> modern rationalist civilisation which is abnormal, a loss
> of ancient human powers of perception of ecstasy in the
> feverish cynicism of cities and empire. We maintain that
> man is not only part of God, but that God is part of man;
> a thing essential, like sex. We say that (in the light of
> actual history) if you cut off the supernatural what re-
> mains is the unnatural. We say that it is in believing ages
> that you get men living in the open and dancing and
> telling tales by the fire. We say that it is in ages of
> unbelief, that you get emperors dressing up as women,
> and gladiators, or minor poets wearing green carnations
> and praising unnamable things. We say that, taking ages
> as a whole, the wildest fantasies of superstition are noth-
> ing to the fantasies of rationalism . . .

Blatchford replied by putting four questions to Gilbert.
"Are you a Christian?" he asked. Gilbert: "Certainly."
"What do you mean by the word Christianity?" Gilbert: "A
belief that a certain human being whom we call Christ stood
to a certain superhuman being whom we call God in a certain
unique transcendental relationship which we call sonship."
"What do you believe?" Gilbert: "A considerable number of
things. That Mr Blatchford is an honest man, for instance.
And (but less firmly) that there is a place called Japan. If he
means what do I believe in religious matters, I believe the
above statement (answer 2) and a large number of other
mystical dogmas, ranging from the mystical dogma that man
is the image of God to the mystical dogma that all men are
equal and that babies should not be strangled." "Why do you
believe it?" Gilbert: "Because I perceive life to be logical and

workable with these beliefs and illogical and unworkable without them."

The dispute was by now interesting other people, provoking letters and taking up a great deal of time. Each time an attack was defended and parried another thrust would follow. Did not the believers realise, the new thinkers argued, that Christianity inspired manic depression, the black asceticism which had caused so much damage? Not so, replied Gilbert, and the "very oddity and completeness of these men's surrender make it look very much as if there were really something actual and solid in the thing for which they sold themselves. They gave up all pleasures for one pleasure. They gave up all human experiences for the sake of one superhuman experience . . ." The response was not attacked; another attack was conceived. What of the torture, cruelty and intolerance which had followed devout Christian belief? "Men commit crimes not only for bad things, far more often for good things," wrote Gilbert. "For no bad things can be desired quite so passionately and persistently as good things can be desired, and only very exceptional men desire very bad and unnatural things." It did not satisfy Blatchford, and not for that matter many of the observers of the debate.

He pursued the point, introducing the example of the French Revolution

> . . . And if the slow and polite preaching of rational fraternity in a rational age ended in the massacres of September, what an a fortiori is here! What would be likely to be the effect of the sudden dropping into a dreadfully evil century of a dreadfully perfect truth? What would happen if a world baser than the world of Sade were confronted with a gospel purer than the gospel of Rousseau?
>
> The mere flinging of the polished pebble of Republican Idealism into the artificial lake of eighteenth-century Europe produced a splash that seemed to splash the heavens, and a storm that drowned ten thousand men. What would happen if a star from heaven really fell into the slimy and bloody pool of a hopeless and decaying

humanity? Men swept a city with a guillotine, a continent with a sabre, because Liberty, Equality, and Frater-
nity were too precious to be lost. What if Christianity
was yet more maddening because it was yet more precious?

But why should we labour the point when One who
knew human nature as it can really be learnt, from fisher-
men and women and natural people, saw from his quiet
village the track of his truth across history, and, in saying
that He came to bring not peace but a sword, set up
eternally His colossal realism against the eternal senti-
mentality of the Secularist?

Blatchford was dying, but would not lie down. His attacks
became less intense, less striking and difficult to answer. He
fired his final shot with an accusation that the Jewish people's
God was a mere manifestation of the Jewish people's need, at
a time when they were under the iron and agonising rule of
either an Egyptian or a Roman empire. This was a God of
ancient Judea and Israel, not a God of the world that was, and
was to be. What was the sense in believing in a parochial over-
being? The tribalism of the ancient Hebrews, Blatchford
claimed, negated the universal theme of the Christian God;
and the conditions of the time and state of ancient Israel
made ridiculous any claims that scripture should apply to
twentieth-century Britain or even fourteenth-century Europe.
Gilbert was anxious to reply to this particular point, it being
an argument he had considered seriously in the past, and
come to strong conclusions

This is an excellent example of one of the things that if I
were conducting a detailed campaign I should use as an
argument for the validity of Biblical experience. For if
there really are some other and higher beings than ourselves, and if they, in some strange way, at some emotional crisis, really revealed themselves to rude poets or
dreamers in very simple times, that these rude people
should regard revelation as local, and connect it with the
particular hill or river where it happened, seems to be
exactly what any reasonable human being would expect.

167

It has a far more credible look than if they had talked cosmic philosophy from the beginning. If they had, I should have suspected "priestcraft" and forgeries and third-century Gnosticism.

If there be such a being as God, and He can speak to a child, and if God spoke to a child in the garden, the child would, of course, say that God lived in a garden. I should not think it less likely to be true for that. If the child said: "God is everywhere; an impalpable essence pervading and supporting all constituents of the Cosmos alike" – if, I say the infant addressed me in the above terms I should think he was much more likely to have been with the governess than with God.

So if Moses had said God was an Infinite Energy, I should be certain he had seen nothing extraordinary. As he said he was a Burning Bush, I think it very likely that he did see something extraordinary. For whatever be the Divine Secret, and whether or no it has (as all peoples have believed) sometimes broken bounds and surged into our world, at least it lies on the side furthest away from pedants and their definitions, and nearest to the silver souls of quiet people, to the beauty of bushes, and the love of one's native place.

Thus, then, in our last instance (out of hundreds that might be taken), we conclude in the same way. When the learned sceptic says: "The visions of the Old Testament were local, and rustic, and grotesque," we shall answer: "Of course. They were genuine."

The Blatchford affair had a twin effect on Gilbert's reputation. For all the acclaim he received from the religious communities in Britain, North America and Europe, he was completely misunderstood by the bulk of secular opinion, which was beginning to regard any committed form of theology as something extreme, alien and undesirable. It was not something which would, or could, have concerned him; such apparent suffering for the cause delighted him no end. The damage inflicted was in society's perception of him as a man to be taken seriously, but not too seriously, and that opinion has followed Gilbert down to the modern day, contributing to his relatively low standing as a modern novelist and philosopher. There is little doubt that if his cause had been socialism or the pursuit of a permissive age he would now be known and read by a far larger audience. The literate world of Edwardian England was just as irreligious as the contemporary world, with a stronger pressure from the positively anti-religious sectors in the country. Gilbert was polarising his readers between those who saw him as their champion and those who thought him a gifted, fundamentally wrong and extreme eccentric. Gilbert considered his writings against Blatchford were eminently moderate

It was not a question of some abstract theological thesis, like the definition of the Trinity or the dogmas of Election or Effectual Grace. I was not yet so far gone in orthodoxy as to be so theological as all that. What I was defending seemed to me a plain matter of ordinary human morals. Indeed it seemed to me to raise the question of the very possibility of any morals. It was the question of Responsibility, sometimes called the question of Free Will, which Mr Blatchford had attacked in a series of vigorous and even violent proclamations of Determinism; all apparently founded on having read a little book or pamphlet by Professor Haeckel. The question had a great many amusing or arresting aspects . . . . It was the secularists who drove me to theological ethics, by themselves destroying any sane or rational possibility of secular ethics. I might myself have been a secularist, so long as it meant that I could be merely responsible to secular society . . .

Nor was the unfortunate Mr Blatchford the only subject of Gilbert's vehement writings. Darwinism, in both its biological and social manifestations, was a phenomenon which he detested, and was willing to comment upon whenever the opportunity arose. It was not merely Darwin himself and his theories which outraged the traditional Christian writer, but the floodgates of cynicism and modern thought which were opened following the publication of Darwin's ideas. Gilbert's longing for an age when men knew what they believed and

169

believed what they knew – or pretended to – often led him along paths of irrational thought. When he dressed as Dr Johnson and lamented the passing of that man's age, he lapsed into the fault of anachronism; the notion that there was a watershed in British history separating middle English decency and the stout yeomanry who loved their God and their country on one side, and the darker men of false prophets and dangerous politics on the other, was clearly absurd. Nevertheless, he did believe that the world was on a dangerous slope towards something still unimaginable, and that the concept of evolution was one of the root problems. In a satire upon a famous poem by Thomas Hood he wrote his own entitled "Race-Memory, by a dazed Darwinian"

> I remember, I remember,
>   Long before I was born,
> The tree-tops where my racial self
>   Went dancing round at morn.
>
> Green wavering archipelagos,
>   Great gusty bursts of blue,
> In my race-memory I recall
>   (Or I am told to do).
>
> In that green-turreted Monkeyville
>   (So I have often heard)
> It seemed as if a Blue Baboon
>   Might soar like a Blue Bird.
>
> Low crawling Fundamentalists
>   Glared up through the green mist,
> I hung upon my tail in heaven
>   A Firmamentalist.

And concluded with

> The past was bestial ignorance:
>   But I feel a little funky,
> To think I'm further off from heaven
>   Than when I was a monkey.

It was not Gilbert at his best. He had read Darwin, and knew that the monkey obsession which so many critics of evolution had, who had not made themselves familiar with Darwin's writings, was heavily out of proportion; Darwin had much more to say than a few suggestions about the relationship between man and ape. Gilbert had chosen the role of champion of tradition, and to an extent that position had been thrust upon him. The result was the same. He was now the shining knight of orthodoxy, looked to for support and protection from that long silent group who considered themselves the majority, and knew themselves to be both correct and voiceless.

VII

The Man Who Was Orthodox

Gilbert's second novel, a work which he was unsure of and not satisfied with, appeared in the February of 1908. Sub-titled "A Nightmare," as *The Man Who Was Thursday* it received more recognition than any of his previous writings. He dedicated it to Edmund Clerihew Bentley, with an introductory poem

> A cloud was on the mind of men,
>   And wailing went the weather,
> Yea, a sick cloud upon the soul
>   When we were boys together.
> Science announced nonentity
>   And art admired decay;
> The world was old and ended:
>   But you and I were gay;
> Round us in antic order
>   Crippled vices came —
> Lust that had lost its laughter,
>   Fear that had lost its shame.
> Like the white lock of Whistler,
>   That lit our aimless gloom,
> Men showed their own white feather
>   As proudly as a plume.
> Life was a fly that faded,
>   And death a drone that stung;
> The world was very old indeed
>   When you and I were young.
> They twisted even decent sin
>   To shapes not to be named:
> Men were ashamed of honour;
>   But we were not ashamed.

Weak if we were and foolish
  Not thus we failed, not thus;
When that black Baal blocked the heavens
  He had no hymns from us.
Children we were – our forts of sand
  Were even as weak as we,
High as they went we piled them up
  To break that bitter sea.
Fools as we were in motley,
  All jangling and absurd,
When all church bells were silent
  Our cap and bells were heard.

Not all unhelped we held the fort,
  Our tiny flags unfurled;
Some giants laboured in that cloud
  To lift it from the world.
I find again the book we found,
  I feel the hour that flings
Far out of fish-shaped Paumanok
  Some cry of cleaner things;
And the Green Carnation withered,
  As in forest fires that pass,
Roared in the wind of all the world
  Ten million leaves of grass;
Or sane and sweet and sudden as
  A bird sings in the rain –
Truth out of Tusitala spoke
  And pleasure out of pain.
Yea, cool and clear and sudden as
  A bird sings in the grey.
Dunedin to Samoa spoke,
  And darkness unto day.
But we were young; we lived to see
  God break their bitter charms
God and the good Republic
  Come riding back in arms;
We have seen the City of Mansoul,
  Even as it rocked, relieved –
Blessed are they who did not see,
  But being blind, believed.

This is a tale of those old fears,
    Even of those emptied hells,
And none but you shall understand
    The true thing that it tells —
Of what colossal gods of shame
    Could cow men and yet crash,
Of what huge devils hid the stars,
    Yet fell at a pistol flash.
The doubts that were so plain to chase,
    So dreadful to withstand —
Oh, who shall understand but you;
    Yea, who shall understand?
The doubts that drove us through the night
    As we two talked amain,
And day had broken on the streets
    E'er it broke upon the brain.
Between us, by the peace of God,
    Such truth can now be told;
Yea, there is strength in striking root,
    And good in growing old.
We have found common things at last,
    And marriage and a creed,
And I may safely write it now,
    And you may safely read.

The intent of the novel was set down quite clearly in the poem: an attack upon the misconceptions of fashionable decadence, a defence of the values which Gilbert, his friends and — so he thought — his God cherished so dearly. He employs the character of Gabriel Syme, a romantic young poet who is also an undercover agent working for the British police. Syme's experiences throughout the book are based in the twilight area of the nightmare, and we are never sure where reality and dream mingle or become one. Syme passes himself off as an anarchist, defeating a real anarchist poet at his own game of distorted honour and bluff. As he walks through a haunting area of London, which is Bedford Park by all appearances, he learns more of an anarchist plot and the extent of the world conspiracy. The hub of the crime is the Central Anarchist Council, consisting of seven members each named after a day of the week. By extreme demonstrations of courage and a calm wit Syme joins their ranks. He meets all the council members, discovering that they are undercover agents working for the police, mistrusting each other until the disguises are lifted. Only one member, the President, Sunday, is loyal and true to his cause. He is more than a man, more than a monster

> The form it took was a childish and yet hateful fancy. As he walked across the inner room towards the balcony, the large face of Sunday grew larger and larger; and Syme was gripped with a fear that when he was quite close the face would be too big to be possible, and that he would scream aloud. He remembered that as a child he would not look at the mask of Memnon in the British Museum, because it was a face, and so large.

When the surreptitious detectives join together and chase President Sunday they undergo a series of outlandish adventures, eventually tracking the man who represents so much evil to his own garden. When confronted face-to-face their sworn enemy is exposed as the Chief of Police who originally gave them their orders, explaining why he was always hidden in darkness when he addressed his men. He is questioned, but will only reply "I am the Sabbath. I am the peace of God."

Syme, the only character with any depth in the book, responds to Sunday's actions and to the appearance at the end of the novel of the real anarchist poet who he had hoodwinked earlier, with a fit of revelation; he shakes from head to foot

> "I see everything," he cried, "everything that there is. Why does each thing on the earth war against each other thing? Why does each small thing in the world have to fight against the world itself? Why does a fly have to fight the whole universe? Why does a dandelion have to fight the whole universe? For the same reason that I had to be alone in the dreadful Council of the Days. So that each thing that obeys law may have the glory and isolation of the anarchist. So that each man fighting for order may be

175

as brave and good a man as the dynamiter. So that the real lie of Satan may be flung back in the face of this blasphemer, so that by tears and torture we may earn the right to say to this man, "You lie!" No agonies can be too great to buy the right to say to this accuser, "We also have suffered."

"It is not true that we have never been broken. We have been broken upon the wheel. It is not true that we have never descended from these thrones. We have descended into hell. We were complaining of unforgettable miseries even at the very moment when this man entered insolently to accuse us of happiness. I repel the slander; we have not been happy. I can answer for every one of the great guards of Law whom he has accused. At least – – "

He had turned his eyes so as to see suddenly the great face of Sunday, which wore a strange smile.

"Have you," he cried in a dreadful voice, "have you ever suffered?"

As he gazed, the great face grew to an awful size, grew larger than the colossal mask of Memnon, which had made him scream as a child. It grew larger and larger, filling the whole sky; then everything went black. Only in the blackness before it entirely destroyed his brain he seemed to hear a distant voice saying a commonplace text that he had heard somewhere, "Can ye drink of the cup that I drink of?"

Gilbert's use of dream symbolism was a new departure for him, without doubt having its roots in the painful years of his lonely period, when his sleep as well as his waking hours were filled with nightmare visions which seemed never to leave him. He was to play down some of the theological meaning in the book, anxious that the story and the moral should stand on their own merits. He wrote that the tale was of a nightmare of things, "not as they are, but as they seemed to the half-pessimist of the '90s . . ." In an interview published many years later, when *The Man Who Was Thursday* was adapted for the stage, he spoke of an ordinary detective tale and the tearing away of menacing masks.

Associated with that merely fantastic notion was the one that there is actually a lot of good to be discovered in unlikely places, and that we who are fighting each other may be all fighting on the right side. I think it is quite true that it is just as well we do not, while the fight is on, know all about each other; the soul must be solitary, or there would be no place for courage.

A rather amusing thing was said by Father Knox on this point. He said that he should have regarded the book as entirely pantheist and as preaching that there was good in everything if it had not been for the introduction of the one real anarchist and pessimist. But he was prepared to wager that if the book survives for a hundred years – which it won't – they will say that the real anarchist was put in afterwards by the priests.

But, though I was more foggy about ethical and theological matters than I am now, I was quite clear on that issue; that there was a final adversary, and that you might find a man resolutely turned away from goodness.

People have asked me whom I meant by Sunday. Well, I think, on the whole, and allowing for the fact that he is a person in a tale – I think you can take him to stand for Nature as distinguished from God. Huge, boisterous, full of vitality, dancing with a hundred legs, bright with the glare of the sun, and at first sight, somewhat regardless of us and our desires ...

It was a book which Gilbert underestimated, believing that if any of his writings would still be being read and discussed in the future it most certainly would not be this one. His reasons were many; not least that it revealed a little too much of the fears and anxieties he underwent as a younger man. He had more faith in his essays. Few of them are read today for anything more than a glimpse of a clever literary style or witty debating points. They deserve far more analysis than that. Shortly after *The Man Who Was Thursday* a collection of pieces from the *Illustrated London News* was published under the title *All Things Considered*. Compared to the book which preceded it this volume of essays made a limited impression, but it is a lasting testimony to the Chestertonian ability to grasp relevance and present argument. In it he explored the contrast between the French and the English, the city of Oxford and its attractions, the delights of Christmas, spiritualism and a host of diverse subjects. One essay, "Patriotism and Sport," has a particular pertinence today, in a world of fighting football fans running and screaming at each other under their respective flags; and nations banned from international sporting gatherings because of political belief and hypocrisy. In it he considered the notion of "Anglo-Saxon superiority," dismissing it with "No quite genuine Englishman ever did believe in it." He continued

> The typical Jingoes who have admired their countrymen too much for being conquerors will, doubtless, despise their countrymen too much for being conquered. But the Englishman with any feeling for England will know that athletic failures do not prove that England is weak, any more than athletic successes proved that England was strong. The truth is that athletics, like all other things, especially modern, are insanely individualistic. The Englishmen who win are exceptional even among men. English athletes represent England just about as much as Mr Barnum's freaks represent America. There are so few of such people in the whole world that it is almost a toss-up whether they are found in this or that country.

He also argued that all communities, all races, possess athletic abilities. He used as an example, interestingly enough, the Jewish people

> Or, to take another case: it is, broadly speaking, true that the Jews are, as a race, pacific, intellectual, indifferent to war, like the Indians, or, perhaps, contemptuous of war, like the Chinese: nevertheless, of the very good prize-fighters, one or two have been Jews.

In actual fact most of the British, and a large number of the world boxing champions of this period were Jewish, and the observation revealed how startled Gilbert was to learn that there may be a dent in the stereo-type of the Edwardian Jew as

178

a cowardly man interested only in finance and ambition. Gilbert had been informed about a tough Jewish working class in the East End of London clawing its way out of the ghetto by eighteen-hour working days and the immediate success of the boxing ring, but he found it difficult to believe. The best he could do was to acknowledge that "one or two" Jewish fighters were good.

In *Orthodoxy,* which appeared in September 1908, he set out to "answer a challenge." Following the publication of *Heretics* some critics had asked Gilbert for a defence of his own views as well as an attack on other people's. Not one to ignore a challenge, he wrote what is essentially a history of his own education as a thinker and believer, what Maisie Ward described as "Chesterton's own history of his mind." Gilbert's primary aim was to satisfy himself in terms of exploring his faith and confirming it on paper; if he could answer his critics with the same action so much the better. He was not prepared at this stage to identify himself with Roman Catholicism, indeed he did not consider himself a Roman Catholic, but instead defended what he constantly referred to as "Orthodox Christianity." He explained his reasons as follows

To show that a faith or a philosophy is true from every standpoint would be too big an undertaking even for a much bigger book than this; it is necessary to follow one path of argument; and this is the path that I here propose to follow. I wish to set forth my faith as particularly answering this double spiritual need, the need for that mixture of the familiar and the unfamiliar which Christendom has rightly named romance. For the very word "romance" has in it the mystery and ancient meaning of Rome. Any one setting out to dispute anything ought always to begin by saying what he does not dispute. Beyond stating what he proposes to prove he should always state what he does not propose to prove. The thing I do not propose to prove, the thing I propose to take as common ground between myself and any average reader, is this desirability of an active and imaginative life, picturesque and full of a poetical curiosity, a life such as western man at any rate always seems to have desired. If a man says that extinction is better than variety and adventure, then he is not one of the ordinary people to whom I am talking. If a man prefers nothing I can give him nothing. But nearly all people I have ever met in this western society in which I live would agree to the general proposition that we need this life of practical romance; the combination of something that is strange with something that is secure. We need so to view the world as to combine an idea of wonder and an idea of welcome. We need to be happy in this wonderland without once being merely comfortable. It is this achievement of any creed that I shall chiefly pursue in these pages.

His thesis was that modern thinkers were attempting to restructure the way in which people thought, as well what they thought. Not only did they challenge the definition of sin, but that sin was a reality at all. As well as the sure existence of evil, there was also the certain existence of good; and Gilbert was a man who, untypically for a Christian of his period, was always more interested in the Resurrection than the Crucifixion. Miracles, magic and Christian charity were real and living; so was moderation. In a prediction of the horrible polarisation of the world which would occur in the 1930s he called for a return to Orthodox Christianity as the only safe means of keeping to a moderate course in a universe of hot extremism. He concluded the book with the argument that Orthodoxy not only ensured moderation and truth, but also simple joy. Joy, happiness, was to Gilbert what conformity was to other theologians; it took on the importance of a virtual sacrament to him. "Man is more himself, man is more manlike" he wrote, "when joy is the fundamental thing in him, and grief the superficial."

Gilbert now was as content and joyous as ever he was to be in his life. Not so Frances. She had asked Gilbert about leaving London for months, and was able to bring a subtle pressure to bear on him with practised ease. They agreed to leave the city and find a permanent home elsewhere. How they found their house was recounted in his *Autobiography*

I remember that we strolled out one day, for a sort of second honeymoon, and went upon a journey into the void, a voyage deliberately objectless. I saw a passing omnibus labelled "Hanwell," and, feeling this to be an appropriate omen, we boarded it and left it somewhere at a stray station, which I entered and asked the man in the ticket-office where the next train went to. He uttered the pedantic reply: "Where do you want to go to?" And I uttered the profound and philosophical rejoinder, "Wherever the next train goes to."

The train went to Slough, and when the couple arrived there they began walking in any direction which their feet took them.

And in that fashion we passed through the large and quiet cross-roads of a sort of village, and stayed at an inn called the White Hart. We asked the name of the place and were told that it was called Beconsfield (I mean of course that it was called Beconsfield and not Beaconsfield), and we said to each other: "This is the sort of place where some day we will make our home."

He lived in the town for the rest of his life, becoming as much a part of the area as Benjamin Disraeli (Lord Beaconsfield) and Edmund Burke, who had lived there in the eighteenth century. He saw it turn from a village into a virtual suburb.

It would be truer to say that the two things in some sense still exist side by side; and the popular instinct has recognised the division by actually talking about the Old Town and the New Town. I once planned a massive and exhaustive sociological work, in several volumes, which was to be called "The Two Barbers of Beaconsfield," and based entirely upon the talk of the two excellent citizens to whom I went to get shaved. For those two shops do indeed belong to two different civilisations. The hairdresser of the New Town belongs to the new world and has the spotlessness of the specialist; the other has what may be called the ambidexterity of the peasant, shaving (so to speak) with one hand while he stuffs squirrels or sells tobacco with the other. The latter tells me from his own recollection what happened in Old Beaconsfield; the former, or his assistants, tell me from the Daily Mail what has not happened in a wider world . . .

They moved in the summer of 1909, and rented a small house known as Overroads. Up until the 1930s Beaconsfield was still semi-rural, and from the windows of their new home the Chestertons could see fields and light farm-land for miles. By the time Gilbert died no such view existed. That was nothing to the urbanisation which has taken place in the last twenty years, but some of the charm and mystery of that house, and Top Meadow, their second home in the area, still remains. In spite of the short distance between London and Beaconsfield – twenty-five miles – there is still an overwhelming feeling of being outside of and away from the business of London; detachment and solitude fill the air. It was this which so outraged his friends: being in Beaconsfield, how could he remain a companion, leader and amuser of the Fleet Street irregulars? Both Belloc and Cecil were hurt and angry, criticising Gilbert, and especially Frances. Their response was selfish to the extreme, and smacked of a complete misunderstanding and ignorance of the ties and loyalties of married life. Gilbert's concept of marriage was equally unusual: he was content for his wife to take complete charge of finances, organisation, planning of meals and meetings, and the day-to-day running of the house. At times the arrangement became pathetic, with Gilbert being awarded pocket money, due to his irresponsible attitude towards his earnings and outgoings. His friends resented the new administration, and stored up most of their wrath for Frances. Here began the belief that she was a moody, possessive woman who took Gilbert away from London, friends and work. On the last point the contrary is true, and more work was completed in Beaconsfield than in busy London. Frances did have her moods, but her simple and understandable desires were to make Gilbert more of a husband and less of a man-about-town, and to ensure that his

health and state of mind were kept in a fine condition. That
meant less huge meals in the middle of the night and far fewer
drinking sessions which began in the morning and ended in
the evening. She loved her husband, and for this was blamed
and attacked by a generation of bullish, mildly misogynistic
men who never in their married lives came close to achieving
such devotion and care.

There were regrets from Gilbert; London was more than a
city to him, it was parent, inspiration and safety. His journeys
back to Kensington and Fleet Street were frequent and busy,
but always short stays rather than prolonged sojourns. He
wrote a poem about the London he left behind, and the
flavour of lament is pungent

> When I came back to Fleet Street,
> Through a sunset nook at night,
> And saw the old Green Dragon
> With the windows all alight,
> And hailed the old Green Dragon
> And the Cock I used to know
> Where all good fellows were my friends
> A little while ago;
>
> I had been long in meadows,
> And the trees took hold of me,
> And the still towns in the beech-woods,
> Where men were meant to be.
> But old things held; the laughter,
> The long unnatural night,
> And all the truth they talk in hell,
> And all the lies they write.
>
> The men in debt that drank of old
> Still drink in debt today;
> Chained to the rich by ruin,
> Cheerful in chains, as then
> When old unbroken Pickwick walked
> Among the broken men . . .
> All that I loved and hated,
> All that I shunned and knew . . .

It took time for Gilbert to establish himself in Beaconsfield, to come to terms with the more parochial humour and talk of the country dwellers. He was shocked initially by how provincial the local people were, and how limited and limiting his style of life would have to be. He turned to routine for support, relying on the regularity of his days to sustain him.

Most of the anecdotes concerning him in the early years in Buckinghamshire are mundane, even a little pathetic. They are of small events and small matters, and Gilbert was not a man who was meant to deal in small things. His befriending of the local children was a charming insight into his character. As the years passed by in Beaconsfield Gilbert and his home became regular entries in every local child's calendar. He would entertain them, individually and in groups. The games he conceived for them were refreshing and sometimes worrying to the conservative parents. Various people, often adults, would be asked to adopt certain strange and outrageous positions, and the children would be asked to explain how such poses came about. On one occasion the mother of Monsignor Bartlett – the senior priest today at one of London's Catholic churches – was said to be "dancing on a table with a rose in her mouth outside a notorious Paris Left Bank restaurant"; hardly a likely circumstance. The children would scream with delight at such games, dancing around the huge Gilbert as though he were a never-ending source of fun and amusement.

Nor was it only children who appreciated the humour, and the absurdities, of Gilbert. When he stated that "If a thing is worth doing, it is worth doing badly," or that he would like to die by driving over a cliff in the last horse-drawn cab in London, his readers and supporters both enjoyed and understood him. During the First World War a society lady would ask him why he "wasn't out at the front?" "If you go round to my side Madam," he replied, "you will see that I am." He was always willing to laugh at his own failings. His susceptibility to alcohol was parodied, in disguise, in the poem "Wine and Water"

Old Noah he had an ostrich farm and fowls
   on the largest scale,

He ate his egg with a ladle in an egg-cup big as a pail,
And the soup he took was Elephant Soup
    and the fish he took was Whale,
But they all were small to the cellar he took
    when he set out to sail,
And Noah he often said to his wife when he sat
    down to dine,
"I don't care where the water goes if it doesn't get
    into the wine."

Gilbert's love for children grew as he realised that it was most unlikely that he would ever be a father. As he came to terms with that painful reality he devoted his energies towards other people's offspring, seldom demonstrating any feelings of sorrow. His sword-stick, never far from his side, fascinated the small people. Seeing their eyes widen when they realised that inside the decorated cane was a hidden weapon, he would expose the blade and lunge at nearby bushes or flowers. Games of cowboys and Indians would be organised, and Gilbert would enthuse as much as the wildest child. When arrows flew and charges were made at Fort Apache the ring-leader was invariably a large, tall, sweating gentleman with ink on his cuffs. Animals began to fill the house. Scottish terriers were favourites of Frances and Gilbert, given the names of Quoodle and Winkle; the cat was awarded the title Perky. Friends came to stay, but detected a coldness in Frances which turned them away. Gilbert was lonely, and found it impossible to explain this to his wife. Walking in the country and playing with the local children was not sufficient for such a gregarious and energetic man. Once again he turned to work, employing as a secretary Nellie Allport. Her work load was enormous, simply taking dictation. Gilbert was also writing in his own hand. The result was a total output which staggered even other busy and industrious writers. Articles, essays, introductions to other works, contributions to debates and speeches occupied his working day. When he wasn't writing for payment or commission he wrote and drew for his own recreation, or to help plan future projects which often failed to materialise. Before he left for Beaconsfield he had been working on his *George Bernard Shaw,* a very personal book about a very personal subject. "Most people either say that they agree with Bernard Shaw or that they do not understand him" he wrote, "I am the only person who understands him, and I do not agree with him." In September his understanding of other matters was demonstrated with the publication of *Tremendous Trifles,* a collection of essays and articles which had previously appeared in the *Daily News.* The famous "What I Found In My Pocket" was reproduced in the book

> I have only once in my life picked a pocket, and then (perhaps through some absent-mindedness) I picked my own. My act can really with some reason be so described. For in taking things out of my own pocket I had at least one of the more tense and quivering emotions of the thief; I had a complete ignorance and a profound curiosity as to what I should find there. Perhaps it would be the exaggeration of eulogy to call me a tidy person. But I can always pretty satisfactorily account for all my possessions. I can always tell where they are, and what I have done with them, so long as I can keep them out of my pockets. If once anything slips into those unknown abysses, I wave it a sad Virgilian farewell. I suppose that the things that I have dropped into my pockets are still there; the same presumption applies to the things that I have dropped into the sea. But I regard the riches stored in both these bottomless chasms with the same reverent ignorance. They tell us that on the last day the sea will give up its dead; and I suppose that on the same occasion long strings and strings of extraordinary things will come running out of my pockets. But I have quite forgotten what any of them are; and there is really nothing (excepting the money) that I shall be at all surprised at finding among them.

What's Wrong With The World followed shortly afterwards, in which Gilbert outlined his political and social beliefs, many of them clearly moulded or at least influenced by Cecil Chesterton and Hilaire Belloc. Women and the liberation movement received a strong attack, the evils of Calvinism were held up to criticism, and the development of his later Distributist ideas can be seen throughout the volume. Gilbert was taking a greater political interest in the years leading up to and following his departure from London, falling under the spell of those around him who were keenly political animals. His beliefs had ranged from liberal conservatism to conservative liberalism, and his brief period as a would-be socialist was an aberration; he was moved by the sufferings of the poor, but nothing else in the state socialist credo attracted him. Political issues began to enter his writings, and he was increasingly of the opinion that religious orthodoxy was not enough. Politically he was a child, in a world of strident adults. Here was such a magnificent vacuum, such a source of potential support for the cause which captured it; he would not hold out for long.

Returning to biography, his *William Blake* appeared in 1910. The extent of Gilbert's other commitments showed in the book, it was written in a hurry and without sufficient consideration. He admitted to not understanding his subject a great deal of the time, and critics pointed out this defect. *Alarms and Discursions,* another anthology of essays, was more of a success, with its highly praised pieces on "Cheese," "The Nightmare," "The Long Bow," and "The Anarchist," all familiar themes in his writings. There were throughout Gilbert's life fallow periods, when it appeared that he was taking time to prepare himself for a massive burst of energy and creation. This was just such a time. A beacon of the forthcoming genius was lit with *The Ball and the Cross,* a stylised novel concerning the struggle of two men, one atheist and one Catholic, to fight a duel; and the revelation that real evil is something greater and more powerful than mere mortal disagreement and wrong-thinking. The book incorporated several of his established ideas – faith, chivalry, the defence of the sword, honour, humanity – and, at least according to the most recent introduction to it, "is the best novel . . . . ever made out of an argument."

The special triumph for Gilbert was the publication in July 1911 of *The Innocence of Father Brown.* The first Father

Brown story, "The Blue Cross," had appeared in September 1910 in the *Storyteller* magazine, and is still considered by many to be the best in the canon. It introduces its hero, a diminutive Catholic priest, and the king of criminals, Flambeau. It also gave readers a glimpse of things to come, with chases over London fields and plots revealing flashes of genius from Father Brown, and touches of pure evil from his opponents. Gilbert did not think particularly highly of his new creation, but to others it appeared that a new Sherlock Holmes had arrived. Nor was the character the preserve of a Catholic readership; non-Catholics were fascinated by the mysteries and wit of this Roman man of God, at a time when to those outside the Catholic Church Catholicism was still a religion of dark corners and secret practices.

Father Brown matured as a character in the course of the first book, as did Gilbert as a writer of detective stories. Though the first tale retains its popularity, the construction of the later mysteries is technically superior. Flambeau, who was becoming far too attractive to both writer and readers, repents in the fourth story and by the time of the fifth is on the side of Father Brown, as a private detective. The fifth tale, "The Invisible Man," is a fine example of what the Father Brown stories represented. In a beautifully described London setting a millionaire receives death letters. The man's home is watched, but nobody is seen to enter. Yet the letters continue to appear. The explanation? The postman is in fact the culprit in disguise. Everyday people and things are in reality capable of being the most extraordinary. Father Brown, as a reflection of Gilbert's imagination, noticed and relished the strange within the normal; a postman may be "invisible" to most people, but to the inquisitive eye there is much to see. "The little Suffolk dumpling from East Anglia" would maintain Gilbert's lifestyle, earning him enough money to be able to indulge in less lucrative affairs, including giving lectures to enthusiastic but often impoverished clubs and societies. It was during one lecture journey that Gilbert telegraphed his wife "Am at Market Harborough. Where ought I to be?" Her answer? "Home." It would always be her response.

Travel presented him with the opportunity to indulge in

some of his finest offerings of description. He was a gifted setter of scenes, letting his imagination take control of his pen. Sometimes this involved a lot of hard work for his editors, having to come to terms with long, rambling journeys into dark forests which smothered the actual story. With the Father Brown stories this rarely happened. His use of language was beautiful, sometimes captivating. He began the first story as follows

> Between the silver ribbon of morning and the green glittering ribbon of sea, the boat touched Harwich and let loose a swarm of folk like flies, among whom the man we must follow was by no means conspicuous – nor wished to be. There was nothing notable about him, except a slight contrast between the holiday gaiety of his clothes and the official gravity of his face. His clothes included a slight, pale grey jacket, a white waistcoat, and a silver straw hat with a grey-blue ribbon. His lean face was dark by contrast, and ended in a curt black beard that looked Spanish and suggested an Elizabethan ruff. He was smoking a cigarette with the seriousness of an idler. There was nothing about him to indicate the fact that the grey jacket covered a loaded revolver, that the white waistcoat covered a police card, or that the straw hat covered one of the most powerful intellects in Europe. For this was Valentin himself, the head of the Paris police and the most famous investigator of the world; and he was coming from Brussels to London to make the greatest arrest of the century.

His public debates had established a large following amongst the public, the most popular being together with George Bernard Shaw. The intellectual quality of their discussions was of the highest; just as entertaining was the evident friendship which the two exhibited. Spectators knew that the smoke of animosity would never obscure the points made by them. both men were reaching the peak of their reputations, Gilbert's becoming international at the end of August with *The Ballad of the White Horse*. This was a work which had taken Gilbert the longest time, a pet project which he had laboured over with love. It was the story of King Alfred's defeat of the Danes at the battle of Ethandune, also the story of England and its nature. From the jaws of defeat, victory. It was the story of the Peninsular War, of Balaclava, the Dunkirk to come; the story of a people who take time to awake, but as long to sleep again once roused. He had been driven to write the poem by a dream, which provided him with a complete stanza

> People, if you have any prayers,
>   Say prayers for me:
> And lay me under a Christian stone
> In that lost land I thought my own,
> To wait till the holy horn is blown,
>   And all poor men are free.

The theme and symbol of the white horse had interested Gilbert from the time when his father had carved him a white hobbyhorse when he was a child. The inn where he spent his honeymoon was named after such a beast, and he had been deeply moved by his first sight of the white horse cut into the chalk of the Wiltshire downs. He began the epic in 1906, and was showing early versions of it to people the following year. The facts of the battle are, true to Gilbert's previous record, inaccurate. He had the left-hand end of the Danish army fighting the left-hand end of King Alfred's forces; this was mentioned by both his family and his critics, but his only response was to laughingly agree. He knew, as did all lovers of the poem, that it was the spirit rather than the strategy of the battle which was being recounted. His initial intention however had been to maintain a standard of authenticity in the poem, and to this purpose he travelled with Frances to Glastonbury and the Somerset areas where King Alfred had hidden and later taken up arms. His dedication revealed the purpose and background to the poem

> Therefore I bring these rhymes to you
> Who brought the cross to me . . .
> Do you remember when we went

Under a dragon moon,
And 'mid volcanic tints of night
Walked where they fought the unknown fight
And saw black trees on the battle-height,
Black thorn on Ethandune? . . .
Take these; in memory of the hour
We strayed a space from home
And saw the smoke-hued hamlets, quaint
With Westland king and Westland saint,
And watched the western glory faint
Along the road to Frome.

The Danes are depicted with a true horror and terror as they invaded and conquered England. Nobody was willing to take on these hellish, granite armies, until Alfred, inspired by a vision of the Virgin Mary, raised the banner of England and Christ. The battle is bloody, the losses are great. It seems that the day is lost, but no. Smashed and tired, the English are called by their King once again to charge their enemies, and they do so. The Danes are pushed back, and Wessex is saved. Gilbert was faithful enough to history to describe the event as only a partial victory – the north of England was still held by the enemy – but it was a victory indeed. It moved readers to patriotic tears, touched a nerve in the pre-First World War days when Germany seemed to be ever on the rise.

During another war with a far more barbaric Germany *The Times* quoted the poem, feeling that nothing else was necessary in its leader article than the lines

I tell you naught for your comfort,
   Yea, naught for your desire,
Save that the sky grows darker yet
   And the sea rises higher.

Night shall be thrice night over you,
   And heaven an iron cope.
Do you have joy without a cause,
   Yea, faith without a hope?

His next prose work was *Manalive,* an optimistic tale of one Innocent Smith and his endeavours to make the world a

191

better, happier place. He has adventures with other women, lives in other houses; but all the women turn out to be his wife, all the various houses his own home. It is a charming tale, if drawn out and in dire need of a strong editor. *The Victorian Age in Literature* was a study not so much of nineteenth-century writers and writing, but of Gilbert's attitude towards nineteenth-century writers and writing. "Macaulay took it for granted" he wrote, "that common sense required some kind of theology, while Huxley took it for granted that common sense meant having none. Macaulay never talked about his religion: but Huxley was always talking about the religion he hadn't got." There are some painfully vapid and uninteresting passages in the book, usually when he is discussing the writers he liked as opposed to those he disliked; he always found sharp criticism easier than flattering praise. The one-liners and succinct descriptions are memorable: "Matthew Arnold kept a smile of heartbroken forbearance, as of the teacher in an idiot school, that was enormously insulting." On the Oxford Movement he wrote, "it was a bow that broke when it had let loose the flashing arrow that was Newman;" of Thomas Hardy, "he became a sort of village atheist brooding and blaspheming over the village idiot;" and of John Stuart Mill that there was about him "even a sort of embarrassment; he exhibited all the wheels of his iron universe rather reluctantly, like a gentleman in trade showing ladies over his factory." It was a successful book, and has been ever since publication.

While Gilbert was working on *The Victorian Age in Literature* his friend Hilaire Belloc and brother Cecil were launching the first issue of their magazine *The Eye-Witness*. The motivation for the weekly journal was in part a genuine interest in exposing corruption in high places, in part a weighty dose of paranoia and a conspiracy theory mania. The two men had written a book entitled *The Party System* earlier, a fascinating but heavily faulted work which aimed to "support the tendency now everywhere apparent and finding expression, a tendency to expose and ridicule as it deserves, to destroy and to supplant the system under which Parliament, the governing institution of this country, has been rendered null." Belloc edited the magazine for the first year, but his attention and loyalties were seldom lasting. He was succeeded by Cecil Chesterton, a fearless and forward child, an aggressive young man and a cuttingly hard editor.

Maurice Baring, a friend of both the Chestertons and Belloc, was also involved with the project, having been closely connected with the magazine which preceded *The Eye-Witness*. Baring was now a Roman Catholic, an adult convert, and a man of deeply conservative and anti-Semitic views. He had established a close friendship with Belloc, the odd couple drinking, debating and abusing long into the night. When he detached himself from the new magazine a higher quality of writers offered their services: H.G. Wells and Bernard Shaw, both Fabian socialists, wrote articles, and Gilbert contributed some ballads. His "A Ballade of Suicide" appeared on 21st September 1911

> The gallows in my garden, people say,
> Is new and neat and adequately tall.
> I tie the noose on in a knowing way
> As one that knots his necktie for a ball;
> But just as all the neighbours – on the wall –
> Are drawing a long breath to shout "Hurray!"
> The strangest whim has seized me . . . After all
> I think I will not hang myself today.

Nor was this the only lasting poem to appear. "Lepanto," that lyrical expression of Gilbert's sense of history, also graced the pages of the magazine

> The Pope was in his chapel before day or battle broke,
> (*Don John of Austria is hidden in the smoke.*)
> The hidden room in a man's house where God sits
>   all the year,
> The secret window whence the world looks small
>   and very dear.
> He sees as in a mirror on the monstrous twilight sea
> The crescent of his cruel ships whose name is mystery;
> They fling great shadows foe-wards, making Cross
>   and Castle dark,
> They veil the plumèd lions on the galleys of St Mark . . .

Cecil Chesterton re-named the troubled journal the *New Witness,* and subsidised it with a generous loan from his father. Ada Jones, who he was still determined to marry, was asked to become assistant editor; she accepted the journalistic post, declined for the time being the offer of marital status. There were always personality clashes within the ranks of the staff at the magazine, which attracted eccentrics as well as skilled journalists. Ada Jones did not get along with the company secretary, pushed for his dismissal, and provoked a threat of litigation and very bad publicity. In spite of this humour played a part in the life of the *New Witness,* frequently too great a part. It was an inefficient organisation, a collection of individuals and opinions masquerading under the disguise of a serious, campaigning newspaper. There were some dynamic young writers on call, amongst them Arthur Ransome and Charles Scott Moncrieff; they rapidly realised that this was not the thrusting, lean journal they had been expecting. Cecil Chesterton needed a scandal, a cause to pursue. He did not need to look very far.

VIII

Marconi and the Jews

The public issue which fell so neatly into Cecil Chesterton's hands was not as important or dramatic as he believed; viewing it through the distorting telescope of history its impact on British society appears to be minimal. Yet the Marconi scandal occupied the time, thoughts and work of the Chesterton brothers to such an extent that even politically active friends believed them to be obsessed. The incident captured the imagination of Cecil first, it seemed to prove all of his ideas about a huge international conspiracy, and then took hold of Gilbert. In his *Autobiography* he had this to say

> It is the fashion to divide recent history into Pre-War and Post-War conditions. I believe it is almost as essential to divide them into the Pre-Marconi and Post-Marconi days. It was during the agitations upon that affair that the ordinary English citizen lost his invincible ignorance; or, in ordinary language, his innocence. And as I happened to play a part, secondary indeed, but definite, in the quarrel about this affair, and as in any case anything that my brother did was of considerable importance to me and my affairs, it will be well to pause for a moment upon this peculiar business; which was at the time, of course, systematically misrepresented and which is still very widely misunderstood. I think it probable that centuries will pass before it is seen clearly and in its right perspective; and that then it will be seen as one of the turning-points in the whole history of England and the world.

195

The facts, rather than the dramatic fiction, of Marconi are as follows. In the March of 1912 Sir Herbert Samuel was offered and accepted a tender from the English Marconi Wireless Telegraph Company for the construction of a chain of wireless stations throughout the British Empire, an enormous contract. Samuel was a Jewish politician in the Liberal Party, held the position of Postmaster-General and was well known for his Zionist views. This singled him out, for amongst Jewish politicians and leaders at the time there was a tendency to hide under Anglo-Saxon attitudes and to reject Zionism as "an instrument to force us back into the ghetto." Edwin Montagu, the Conservative minister, for example, took control of a Jewish anti-Zionist newspaper; inconceivable only a few years later. There was no such assimilation from Sir Herbert Samuel; he believed that he was an Englishman, a Jew, a Liberal, in that order; if anyone felt ill at ease with those attributes that was a problem for them, not for Samuel. When he accepted the Marconi contract there was a sudden and dramatic rise in the price of Marconi shares, especially since the sinking of the *Titanic* on the night of the 14th April and the subsequent public realisation of how vitally important wireless communications were, and would become. The managing director of the English Marconi Company was Godfrey Isaacs, who was also managing director of the American Marconi Company; technically an independent organisation but in reality simply another branch of the same Marconi empire. The Isaacs brothers were, of course, Jewish, and very successful. For Cecil Chesterton the idea of Jews as Jews was acceptable, the idea of Jews as successful and important men of affairs was a little harder to stomach.

Godfrey Isaacs decided to expand the American company, in which the English company had a majority shareholding, by floating a new issue of shares on the British market on 18th April. This would have been a tolerable practice, but only nine days earlier he had indicated to his brothers Harry and Rufus that it might be a wise idea to buy some of the shares, then at a price far below what even the least astute of economists would have predicted once the market opened up. Harry Isaacs bought 56,000, Rufus bought 10,000 and both Lloyd George and the Liberal Chief Whip took 1,000 shares.

When the new issue was floated on the 19th April the shares immediately jumped to £4.00, twice the price the politicians and their friends had paid for them. The three government ministers sold their shares without delay, making an easy and substantial profit. It took no time at all for rumour to circulate within the City of London, then in Westminster and Whitehall, and finally in Fleet Street. The guilty group knew people in extremely high places, and had influence far beyond the confines of government and business. The press was reluctant to print too much at first, but as more information leaked out to the public they had to make a statement. It escaped the notice of nobody that most of those involved in the scandal were Jewish.

To Cecil Chesterton it seemed that all his painful anger, all his efforts to convince others that there were secret cabals of dark men plotting dark deeds had been proved worthwhile. After severe pressure a Parliamentary Commission of Inquiry was formed, and concluded that the men involved had acted in good faith. A motion was proposed in the House of Commons which criticised their actions, but after a show of contrition from Sir Rufus Isaacs and Lloyd George it was defeated. It seemed that the matter was at an end, and that this was a generous verdict for those at the centre of the affair. There was no conspiracy, there may not have been any positive wrong-doing on the part of Rufus Isaacs, but at the very least there was a case to answer for acting without sufficient thought, and with far too little consideration for their public positions. Men in the leading firms of the City were undoubtedly carrying out similar deals on a weekly basis, but they were not ministers of the Crown.

Cecil Chesterton, of course, was not satisfied. The *Eye-Witness* had made its position clear in the joint issues of business conspiracy and the Jews – it felt that the two obstacles were by their nature linked – from an early stage. A 1911 article stated that

There exists in the midst of European civilisation a race alien to and different from the Western blood among which it must live. This race is segregated in no artificial manner yet permanently and uniquely survives intact. So far from this segregation being due to stratification or difference of abilities between higher and lower, the Jewish nation is, and has always been, eminent in the highest intellectual employment which European civilisation could find. It has on this account been accepted sometimes as a necessity, sometimes as an advantage, but always in practice as a part of the European scheme. None the less the presence of this alien element has proved sometimes an irritant, always an element of friction, and a social arrangement in which that friction should be reduced to a minimum, and the necessary or, at any rate, normal presence of the small non-European minority in our midst shall be made as innocuous as possible, is a goal practically obtainable and eminently to be desired.

The style of Hilaire Belloc is obvious. In a further piece he wrote

Now unless the Jewish race is to be absorbed and disappear in the mass of European blood and tradition surrounding it, that contrast and its consequent friction will increase in the near future until their worst fruit shall have ripened: a fruit of oppression, injustice, and enduring hatred.

To avoid that lamentable conclusion three policies are present. The first – and that still most generally held in Western Europe – is to regard the matter as solved; vaguely to suppose the absorption of the alien race as feasible, and its presence for the moment as something at once absurdly separate and yet not separate from the life of the community as innocuous. The second policy is that of exclusion. The third policy is to grant the Jew recognition and privilege.

Which of these three shows comprehension of our need and of the Jewish need, and which is the most likely to afford a standing answer to this gravest of modern questions?

Such an early obsession with the Jewish question made it an easy step for the staff and supporters of the *New Witness* to take a firm stand on Marconi. Cecil Chesterton did not have the passion of Belloc on the subject, and was more the victim of ignorance. Later, during the First World War he, as a Catholic, was given the most menial tasks to serve by a bigoted superior. The other soldier to suffer because of his faith was a Jewish man, who was given even more unsavoury tasks to perform. Cecil could not understand why the Protestant saved his most angry prejudice for the Jew rather than the Catholic. He had no idea, no real conception, of how hateful gentiles could be towards Jews, and insisted on believing anti-Semitic talk to be at best constructive criticism, at worst light-hearted teasing. Hence he had no qualms about attacking Jewish men of affairs not only for their apparent dishonesty, but also for their Jewishness. It was his duty, his job, at times his virtual recreation.

He accused Godfrey Isaacs of theft, and of gross dishonesty in other business affairs as well as Marconi. In January 1913 his magazine listed twenty bankrupt companies which Isaacs had had some connection with, and paid sandwichmen to march up and down in front of Isaacs's office with accusations against the unfortunate man written on their signs. Godfrey Isaacs could take no more. He decided to prosecute Cecil on a charge of criminal libel. As arrogant as ever, Cecil laughed at the summons and put it in a frame in the *New Witness* offices. He was warned by friends to take care; his friends were ignored. Gilbert pleaded with Cecil to back down before it was too late, to no result. The case went to the Central Criminal Court at the Old Bailey on the 27th May 1913. Gilbert was there, along with his uncle Arthur, and the writer J.M. Barrie. What they saw was the humiliation of a proud man.

The prosecution was carried out by F.E. Smith and Sir Edward Carson, the brilliant Irish Protestant lawyer who had successfully prosecuted Oscar Wilde; if he had been able to defeat the genius Wilde in open court, he would have little trouble with Cecil Chesterton. So it turned out. In the dock Cecil was slow and hesitant, seemingly out of his depth and frightened. The judge was not on his side from the very beginning, but even so his defence was a poor one. He withdrew all charges of corruption against the government ministers early on in the trial, and took back the accusation that Sir Herbert Samuel was either dishonest or dishonourable. He remained firm on the issue of Godfrey Isaacs's doubledealing. The family were beginning to panic, fearing that a prison sentence would be the verdict. The jury found him guilty, but the judge thought a £100 fine and a stern lecture would be sufficient punishment. Ridiculously egotistical to the last, Cecil and his companions perceived this as a victory, believing the light sentence to be a partial success; it is more likely that all present considered the defendant and the case too petty to merit a more harsh decision. There was cheering from the supporters of the *New Witness*, quiet satisfaction from Isaacs, and general apathy from the public.

Cecil celebrated his self-imagined triumph by being received into the Roman Catholic Church, without giving any serious explanation to friends or family. His life was not changed to any remarkable degree by the trial, he continued to imagine what he wanted, to believe what he wanted, and to print what he wanted. Gilbert, by far the more sensitive of the two brothers, was shocked by the events. He loved his brother dearly, was shattered by the insults and defeat which he had suffered in court, and was frightened for his future.

Cecil died in 1918 in a military hospital in Boulogne; a German bullet did not end his life, but sickness caused by the strains of army life, and twelve-mile marches in pouring rain. Pretence was maintained until the last, with the tributes to him in the *New Witness* cloaked in a cryptic language which left readers unsure as to the reasons for his death: "died in France of the effects of the last days of the fighting," wrote Gilbert. The death of his brother broke Gilbert, and opened up the flood-gates of any anger and hatred which existed in him. Cecil was dead, the Isaacs brothers were still alive. It was all too much to tolerate.

On 13th December 1918 in the *New Witness* he wrote an "Open Letter" to Lord Reading, previously Rufus Isaacs. For those who allege that Gilbert was an anti-Semite, and that opinion still holds sway, this communication of vitriol is evidence indeed

My Lord – I address to you a public letter as it is upon a public question: it is unlikely that I should ever trouble you with any private question; and least of all on the private question that now fills my mind. It would be impossible altogether to ignore the irony that has in the last few days brought to an end the great Marconi duel in which you and I in some sense played the part of seconds; that personal part of the matter ended when Cecil Chesterton found death in the trenches to which he had freely gone; and Godfrey Isaacs found dismissal in those very Courts to which he once successfully appealed. But believe me I do not write on any personal matter; nor do I write, strangely enough perhaps, with any personal acrimony. On the contrary, there is something in these tragedies that almost unnaturally clarifies and enlarges the mind; and I think I write partly because I may never feel so magnanimous again. It would be irrational to ask you for sympathy; but I am sincerely moved to offer it. You are far more unhappy; for your brother is still alive.

Are we to lose the War in which we have already won? That and nothing else is involved in losing full satisfaction of the national claim in Poland. [Lord Reading was a delegate to the Versailles Peace Conference, in which the question of Poland would be discussed.] Is there any man who doubts that the Jewish International is unsympathetic with that full national demand? And is there any man who doubts that you will be sympathetic with the Jewish International? No man who knows anything of the interior facts of modern Europe has the faintest doubt on either point. No man doubts when he knows, whether or not he cares. Do you seriously imagine that those who know, that those who care, are so idolatrously infatuated with Rufus Daniel Isaacs as to tolerate such risk, let alone such ruin? Are we to set up as the standing representative of England a man who is a standing joke against England? That and nothing else is involved in setting up the chief Marconi Minister as our chief Foreign Minister. It is precisely in those foreign countries with which such a minister would have to deal, that his name would be, and has been, a sort of pantomime proverb like Panama or the South Sea Bubble.

Foreigners were not threatened with fine and imprisonment for calling a spade a spade and a speculation a speculation; foreigners were not punished with a perfectly lawless law of libel for saying about public men what those very men had afterwards to admit in public. Foreigners were lookers-on who were really allowed to see most of the game, when our public saw nothing of the game; and they made not a little game of it. Are they henceforth to make game of everything that is said and done in the name of England in the affairs of Europe? Have you the serious impudence to call us Anti-Semites because we are not so extravagantly fond of one particular Jew as to endure this for him alone. No, my lord; the beauties of your character shall not so blind us to all elements of reason and self-preservation; we can still control our affections; if we are anything but Anti-Semite, we are not Pro-Semite in that peculiar and personal fashion; if we are lovers, we will not kill ourselves for love. After weighing and valuing all your virtues, the qualities of our own country take their due and proportional part in our esteem. Because of you she shall not die.

My fancy may be quite wrong; it is but one of many attempts I have made to imagine and allow for an alien psychology in this matter; and if you, and Jews far worthier than you, are wise they will not dismiss as Anti-Semitism what may well prove the last serious attempt to sympathise with Semitism. I allow for your position more than most men allow for it in the darker days that yet may come. It is utterly false to suggest that either I or a better man than I, whose work I now inherit, desired this disaster for you and yours, I wish you no such ghastly retribution. Daniel, son of Isaac, Go in peace; but go.

This makes for distasteful reading, especially in the light of the holocaust which was to follow. There is no excuse, no justification for Jew-baiting and anti-Semitism, and the dark side of Gilbert's character certainly held pockets of racism which cannot be lightly ignored. How much bigotry existed, and to what depths that feeling sunk, is a matter capable of question. For all of his hurtful, rash statements there was never a contentment with attacking people because of their race. Gilbert stung others when he was angry, and when he was following friends. He was a creation of his time and of his environment, and that meant he was exposed to anti-Semitism from an early age.

Gilbert's friend, E.C. Bentley, had written in the classic detective thriller *Trent's Last Case,* "In Paris a well-known banker walked quietly out of the Bourse and fell dead upon the broad steps among the raving crowd of Jews, a phial crushed in his hand. In Frankfurt one leapt from the Cathedral top . . . . Men stabbed and shot themselves." Bentley was painting a portrait of closely connected, sinister world finance, and his views were far from untypical. John Buchan's hero would lament the international conspiracy of the Jews and wonder what to do about it, thriller stories of the Edwardian years and the 1920s would invariably include a villain whose "origin was somewhere inside a Polish or Russian ghetto." English literature had not always been so disposed. Charles Dickens had an understanding, an empathy, for Jewish experience and suffering which left a mark on his readers. George Eliot and her *Daniel Deronda* is equally profound in its treatment of a Jewish character. This was the period of Disraeli, when the Jewish population of the country was small and often prosperous. These immigrants who had come to Britain as early as the seventeenth century, were mostly Sephardi (Eastern origin) and could be as easily ignored as they could be liked.

Between 1884 and 1905 over 250,000 Jews came to Britain. They were the victims of a series of pogroms in Poland and the Ukraine, during which government-inspired mobs would murder, rape and destroy. These were not simple riots, but horribly violent tirades. The number of Jews who were slaughtered during this period is outrageous, large enough to classify the appalling time as a mini-holocaust. The police and the army would intervene only after the damage was done, and if the Jews organised themselves for self-defence they would be arrested or executed. The people who left everything behind and came to London, Leeds, Manchester and Glasgow were mostly peasants, speaking a mixture of Russian, Yiddish, Polish and Ukrainian. They had different ways, different manners. They were frightened and proud, anxious and willing to work every hour they could to build a new life. Such large numbers could no longer be forgotten, they were now an issue. So it was that when Gilbert was a young man tens of thousands of Ashkenazi (European) Jews were living just a few miles from his home.

As a boy he had Jewish friends, and many in the Junior Debating Club were Jewish. St Paul's was, and is, a school which attracts Jewish boys. He maintained friendships with those he had met at school throughout his life, and though the defence that "some of my best friends are Jewish" is trite and absurd, Gilbert's relationships with these men were sincerely warm and reciprocated. They would not have continued to hold him in such high esteem if his real attitudes had been acrimonious. Of his school-day relationships with Jewish boys he wrote

Oddly enough, I lived to have later on the name of an Anti-Semite; whereas from my first days at school I very largely had the name of a Pro-Semite. I made many friends among the Jews, and some of these I have retained as lifelong friends; nor have our relations ever been disturbed by differences upon the political or social problem. I am glad that I began at this end; but I have not really ended any differently from the way in which I began.... I held by instinct then, as I hold by knowledge now, that the right way is to be interested in Jews as Jews; and then to bring into greater prominence the very much neglected Jewish virtues, which are the complement and sometimes even the cause of what the world feels to be Jewish faults.

After a description of his protection of a "strange swarthy little creature with a hooked nose" at school he continued with

I am not at all ashamed of having asked Aryans to have more patience with Jews or for asking Anglo-Saxons to have more patience with Jew-baiters. The whole problem of the two entangled cultures and traditions is much too deep and difficult, on both sides, to be decided upon impatiently. But I have very little patience with those who will not solve the problem, on the ground that there is no problem to solve. I cannot explain the Jews; but I certainly will not explain them away. Nor have the Jews a worse enemy than the sort of Jew sceptic who sometimes tries to explain himself away. I have seen a whole book full of alternative theories of the particular historic cause of such a delusion about a difference; that it came from mediaeval priests or was burnt into us by the Inquisition; that it was tribal theory arising out of Teutonism; that it was revolutionary envy of the few Jews who happened to be the big bankers of Capitalism; that it was Capitalist resistance to the few Jews who happened to be the chief founders of Communism. All these separate theories are false in separate ways; as in forgetting that mediaeval heresy-hunts spared Jews more and not less than Christians; or that Capitalism and Communism are so very nearly the same thing, in ethical essence, that it would not be strange if they did take leaders from the same ethnological elements . . .

I do not believe that a crowd on a race-course is poisoned by mediaeval theology; or the navvies in a Mile End pub misled by the ethnology of Gobineau or Max Fuller; nor do I believe that a mob of little boys fresh from the cricket field or tuckshop were troubled about Marxian economics or international finance. Yet all these people recognise Jews as Jews when they see them; and the schoolboys recognised them, not with any great hostility except in patches, but with the integration of instinct. What they saw was not Semites or Schismatics or capitalists or revolutionists, but foreigners; this did not prevent friendship and affection, especially in my own case; but then it never has prevented it in the case of ordinary foreigners . . .

As in most of Gilbert's writing about Jewish people, there are elements of deep understanding and sound common sense, and a ripple of gutter bigotry; he seemed to be at heart a friend of the Jews, sympathetic to their plight – but something insisted on dragging him towards prejudice. That something came in several forms: his brother Cecil, Maurice Baring, but most of all Hilaire Belloc. Belloc was an expert at playing the elder man, giving advice and hearing secular confession. "There is great psychological value in a strong affirmation" he once said, and it was exactly that which he used in his friendship with Gilbert. For his part, Gilbert would later convert to the Catholic Church for, amongst other reasons, the sake of "Authority;" the quality which Belloc possessed with such panache and confidence. Belloc found hatred an easy emotion to indulge in, and Jews ranked highly on his list of opponents. His book *The Jews,* while impressive in some of its predictions and warnings, saw the Jews as natural plotters, a strange people who could not and would not assimilate, and who would change their names so as to disguise their identity; hence easing their way into gentile society. He would blithely employ the word "Yid" in public, revelling in its shock value. He took great satisfaction in his rhyme

> At the end of Piccadilly is a place
> Of Habitation for the Jewish race.
> Awaiting their regained Jerusalem.
> These little huts, they say, suffice for them.
> Here Rothschild lives, chief of the tribe abhorr'd
> Who tried to put to death our Blessed Lord.
> But, on the third day, as the Gospel shows,
> Cheating their machinations, He arose;
> In Whose commemoration, now and then,
> We persecute these curly-headed men.

Belloc was an anti-Semite. Was Gilbert? No. The case for the prosecution first. He teased, hurt, could be insulting. In

his poems, there are references to Jews and anti-Jewish feelings to be found

> I am fond of Jews
> Jews are fond of money
> Never mind of whose.
> I am fond of Jews
> Oh, but when they lose
> Damn it all, it's funny.

And, in the same spirit, and causing the same offence

> Oh I knew a Dr Gluck
> And his nose it had a hook
> And his attitudes were anything but Aryan.
> So I gave him all the pork
> That I had upon a fork
> Because I am myself a vegetarian.

The level of paranoia amongst the Chesterton brothers and
Belloc was staggering; it was based entirely upon fear. Gilbert
was terrified that he would encounter a Jew, and not know it.
They must identify themselves as Jews, Hebrews, Semites;
otherwise, matters would go worse for them. If a Jewish
caricature approached Gilbert he would be satisfied, even
welcoming. If the Jewish individual was very English in his
manners and dress, a threat was perceived. When interviewed
by the *Jewish Chronicle* in April 1911 he attempted to explain
his position

> Oh, yes, I know they call themselves, for instance, in this
> country, Englishmen, and they are patriotic and loyal,
> and hold land and give liberally to English institutions,
> subsidise party funds, become peers and members of
> Parliament, entertain, hunt and shoot, and all the rest of
> it. Still the Jew is not an Englishman, because his nation-
> ality is not English. They are something different and in
> many ways very much better. Still, being better, they
> cannot be the same. They are allied, and rightly and
> justifiably, to their own people of their own race who are

not English even in point of citizenship – Jews in Germany, Russia, France, everywhere.

He did not realise, did not want to understand, that when European wars took place French Jews battled against and killed German Jews, in the war to come English Jews would die in trenches, killed by some of the thousands of Jews who won so many medals and so much praise in the ranks of the German army. He rejected any advice about Russian Jewish war heroes, any historical facts about Jews in Nelson's navy and Wolfe's army at Quebec. But then the image of the Jewish warrior was something else which Gilbert – far too obese and unfit to be accepted in the 1914 war – refused to come to terms with

> Our patch of glory ended; we never heard guns
>   again.
> But the squire stuck in the saddle; he was
>   foolish, as if in pain
> He leaned on a staggering lawyer, he clutched a
>   cringing Jew,
> He was stricken; it may be, after all, he was
>   stricken at Waterloo . . .

In his *A Short History of England* the subject of Edward I and the Jews was given a weighty treatment, surprising in a book which intended to cover the entire course of English history in some 240 pages

> The Jews in the middle ages were as powerful as they were unpopular. They were the capitalists of the age, the men with wealth banked ready for use. It is very tenable that in this way they were useful; it is certain that in this way they were used. The ill-usage was not indeed that suggested at random in romances, which mostly revolve on the one idea that their teeth were pulled out. Those who know this as a story about King John generally do not know the rather important fact that it was a story against King John. It is probably doubtful; it was only insisted on as exceptional; and it was, by that very insis-

tence, obviously regarded as disreputable. But the real unfairness of the Jews' position was deeper and more distressing to a sensitive and highly civilised people. They might reasonably say that Christian kings and nobles, and even Christian popes and bishops, used for Christian purposes (such as the crusades and cathedrals) the money that could only be accumulated in such mountains by a usury they inconsistently denounced as un-Christian; and then, when worse times came, gave up the Jew to the fury of the poor, whom that useful usury had ruined. That was the real case for the Jew; and no doubt he really felt himself oppressed.

Unfortunately it was the case for the Christians that they, with at least equal reason, felt him the oppressor; and that mutual charge of tyranny is the Semitic trouble in all times. It is certain that in popular sentiment, this Anti-Semitism was not excused as uncharitableness, but simply regarded as charity. Chaucer puts his curse on Hebrew cruelty into the mouth of the soft-hearted prioress, who wept when she saw a mouse in a trap; and it was when Edward, breaking the rule by which rulers had hitherto fostered their bankers' wealth, flung the alien financiers out of the land, that his people probably saw him most plainly at once as a knight errant and a tender father of his people.

An example of selective history: no mention of the infamous blood libels which plagued the Jewish community at the time, when furious and crazed mobs fired by religious superstition would murder any Jew they found; their reasons were that they believed that gentile youths were slaughtered by Jews for secret ceremonies. And the York massacre, a mass murder of English Jews in the middle ages, is entirely ignored. Again, Gilbert desired to defend the Jews, because in his personal relationships he enjoyed the company of Jewish people and admired the Jewish attitude towards education and learning; but his friends were there to put him right, to remind him of the world conspiracy. The theme permeates his books. *The Man Who Was Thursday:* " 'Its application is,' said his informant, 'that most of old Sunday's righthand men are South

African and American millionaires. That is why he has got hold of all the communications . . .' " The assumptions were that the media was controlled by Jews; there were some Jewish press barons, but only a small minority. Such things did not matter. As to South Africa, it was believed that the Boer War had been fought not for British Imperialism, but to aid the greed and self-interest of Jewish diamond merchants and financiers.

It is all discredited and infantile philosophy today, in the light of the opening of the gates at Auschwitz and Treblinka. Here lies a problem. How much do we forgive Gilbert because he wrote and thought before the holocaust, before the world was forced to see that anti-Semitism was unacceptable? Very little. There have always been, always will be, the options of conforming with evil or resisting evil. Here was an age when even allegedly radical writers like Wells and Arnold Bennett were unsympathetic towards the Jews, the fashionable set of Waugh and Mitford cutting and sardonic, the conservative generation such as Buchan and Saki positively hateful. Yet there was always room for protest, always the opportunity to stand up and be counted; and Gilbert was prepared to make himself unpopular on many other issues. It was fashionable to joke about Jewish influence and Jewish characteristics, and Gilbert gave in to the meagre temptations of a vile fashion.

In 1920 he published *The New Jerusalem,* an account of his travels in Palestine. Amongst the waves of settlers who were building a new home for the Jewish people he discovered Zionism, and wrote about it at great length, both in the book and in articles for various journals and newspapers. When he undertook a lecture tour in the United States after the book appeared, a boycott was arranged by Jewish organisations. In Omaha he said that it was as though "a kind of trail of wailing rabbis all across the continent" were following him. Hardly the type of comment to placate his critics. His book had been openly attacked in two New York synagogues, and in the Temple bel-Fifth Avenue and Seventy-Sixth Street synagogue Dr Samuel Schulmann said

The worst kind of Jew-baiting is not that of the mob, but that of the false literary prophet of the age, which subtly attempts to instil poison into the minds of those who may become leaders of the mob; it is therefore a humiliating, even if a necessary task, to dissect this latest attempt of the well-known Anti-Semite. It is necessary because as Jews and as Americans, we must protest against the attempt to transplant to our country the artifically fostered animosity against the Jew which flourishes in Europe.

Chesterton, of his own volition, undertakes to bless, if not the Jews, the Zionists, and ends by cursing them. He professes to agree with the Zionists and yet, in every line of his description of what he saw in Palestine, he bristles with suspicion, with insults, with threats, and with opposition to the Zionists' efforts. His is a book thoroughly false, and its falsity is all the more dangerous because of its attractiveness. It is false because it is pure reactionary romanticism.

On his tour of the Middle East Gilbert was anxious to come to terms with what he had heard about Zionism, and how it was transforming the Jewish people. He met Chaim Weizmann, the Zionist elder statesman and first President of Israel, and the two men appreciated each other's stature. Weizmann, who embodied a form of Jewish nationalism which did not survive past his death, discussed the possibility of turning Palestine into a Swiss-style country composed of cantons, some Arab and some Jewish. Gilbert wrote

It seems possible that there might be not only Jewish cantons in Palestine but Jewish cantons outside Palestine. Jewish colonies in suitable and selected places in adjacent parts or in many other parts of the world. They might be affiliated to some official centre in Palestine, or even in Jerusalem, where there would naturally be at least some great religious head-quarters of the scattered race and religion . . . . I think it is sophistry to say, as do some Anti-Semites, that the Jews have no more right

211

there than the Jebusites. If there are Jebusites they are Jebusites without knowing it. I think it sufficiently answered in the fine phrase of an English priest, in many ways more Anti-Semitic than I: "The people that remembers has a right." The very worst of the Jews, as well as the very best, do in some sense remember.

The tone of the book, though sometimes extremely sympathetic and even understanding, is patronising and pompous; as though Gilbert had a divine right to judge and decide on matters concerning the Jews, a people who he wished to chastise but protect, as though they were badly behaved children. The *Daily News* in November 1920 noted that "Mr Chesterton's book about his travels among the Jews will be read with all the more curiosity because he is generally regarded as an Anti-Semite . . ." When he recounts the story of a Jerusalem snow-storm his perennial ambivalence on the issue is exposed yet again

> The English soldiers cleared the snow away; the Arabs sat down satisfied or stoical with the snow blocking their own doors or loading their own roofs. But the Jews, as the story went, were at length persuaded to clear away the snow in front of them, and then demanded a handsome salary for having recovered the use of their own front doors. The story is not quite fair; and yet it is not so unfair as it seems. Any rational Anti-Semite will agree that such tales even when they are true, do not always signify an avaricious tradition in Semitism, but sometimes the healthier and more human suggestion of Bolshevism. The Jews do demand high wages, but it is not always because they are in the old sense money-grabbers . . .

"Rational Anti-Semite?" Gilbert believed that racial hatred and rational behaviour were compatible, and his Father Brown is not immune from anti-Jewish statements and descriptions. In "The Purple Wig" in *The Wisdom of Father Brown,* we are presented with a Jewish character who is "a guttersnipe who was a pettifogger and a pawnbroker not twelve years ago," and in *The Incredulity of Father Brown* we are told that "It would be nearer the truth," said Father Brown, "to say that they were the only people who weren't persecuted in the Middle Ages. If you want to satirise medi-aevalism, you could make a good case by saying that some poor Christian might be burned alive for making a mistake about the Homoiousian, while a rich Jew might walk down the street openly sneering at Christ and the Mother of God." It is a ridiculous statement, and Gilbert knew it to be. Throughout the Father Brown stories there are stinging comments about "cosmopolitans," people who "hated Jews" and descriptions of dirty, evil individuals whose gentile origins are severely in doubt. *The Ball and the Cross, The Flying Inn* and a host of essays contain equally disturbing references. And "The Song of Quoodle" is remembered by so many with its verse

> They haven't got no noses,
> They cannot even tell
> When door and darkness closes
> The park a Jew encloses,
> Where even the Law of Moses
> Will let you steal a smell

As to the defence that Gilbert, as well as Belloc and Cecil Chesterton, were Zionists and hence not anti-Semitic, this is a fatuous and ludicrously badly-informed explanation. In the early days of the campaign for a Jewish homeland it was not only Jewish nationalists and sympathisers who believed that a state of Israel was essential; for as well as the friends of the Jewish people, who saw the proposed nation as a safeguard, there were those anti-Semites who wanted the Jews expelled from Europe and America and sent to another place, any other place. The early Nazis toyed with the idea of a Jewish homeland – Madagascar was considered – before the Final Solution was conceived. Chauvinistic intellectuals of the 1920s spent a lot of time and ink on the possibility of "reset-tlement," and for a brief period felt confident that a "Jew-free Europe" could be achieved. Gilbert was less vicious, deeply

213

concerned that both for their own good and for the good of the gentile host-culture the Jews should be given a separate land; such a belief did not expunge any traces of racism from him.

Examples of regrettable postures are there for anybody to find if they search deeply enough. The case for the defence appears to be hopeless, but perhaps not. We cannot revive a long dead author and ask his opinions of a Jewish people who lost six and a half million of their race in the greatest horror the world has ever experienced; nor can we judge him by the standards of the more aware and tolerant 1980s. What can be said is that when Gilbert was left to relate to Jewish people away from the insidious influence of Belloc and brother Cecil he usually left a noble impression. His personal, social contact with Jewish people has a bearing on his wider attitudes. Margaret Halford, a Jewish friend, was scheduled to meet him and cooperate on a charitable endeavour, but was worried about the reception she would receive; would he "want to know her?" She wrote: "I'm a stiff-necked viper on the Jewish question. I wasn't really 'afraid' about my own welcome – but though I had for years been an enthralled admirer of G.K.'s, I'd have forgone the pleasure of personal friendship, if his true attitude had not become so manifest." She became a regular guest, and the warmth which she exhibited was reciprocated.

His friendship with Israel Zangwill, that most Jewish of writers, was a noted literary combination of the time. On his travels to the United States and Canada Gilbert was entertained by many Jewish people, all of whom were anxious to play host to him again. In Jerusalem his one-to-one meetings with Jewish leaders were more than friendly. The Wiener Library, the archives of anti-Semitism and holocaust history in London, regard Gilbert as a friend, not an enemy

The difference between social and philosophical anti-Semitism is something which is not fully understood. John Buchan, for example, was charming towards Jewish people he met, but undoubtedly possessed a world view of anti-Semitism. With Chesterton we've never thought of a man who was seriously anti-Semitic on either count. He was a man who played along, and for that he must pay a price; he has, and has the public reputation of anti-Semitism. He was not an enemy, and when the real testing time came along he showed what side he was on.

The Wiener Library refer to the coming to power of Hitler and the Nazi party in 1933 and the subsequent attacks on Jewish lives and liberty. Thousands of German Jews refused to believe that the country of Beethoven and Goethe would tolerate for long a gutter-level dictatorship of such cruelty. They remained in Germany, many until it was too late. A large part of the organised Left in Europe, Britain included, were willing to give Hitler time to prove himself, attracted by his opposition to capitalism; noted liberal and socialist leaders met with the German leader, anxious to come to an understanding. Opposition to the new order was not fashionable in the early days, and the people who stood up firmly against National Socialism were as righteous as they were few. Gilbert was such a man, confident from the beginnings of Hitlerism that here was a manifestation of evil. "They will find it difficult to persuade any German, let alone any European who is fond of Germany" he wrote, "that Schiller is a poet and Heine not;" and "thousands of Jews have recently been rabbled or ruined or driven from their homes, they beat and bully poor Jews in concentration camps," and "heartily as I do indeed despise the Hitlerites." He wrote an anti-Nazi pamphlet as early as 1934, pleading with the British public to take note, and take action. After his death Rabbi Wise, a major and respected figure inside the American Jewish community, paid tribute to Gilbert in a letter

Indeed I was a warm admirer of Gilbert Chesterton. Apart from his delightful art and his genius in many directions, he was, as you know, a great religionist. He as

215

Catholic, I as Jew, could not have seen eye to eye with each other, and he might have added "particularly seeing that you are cross-eyed;" but I deeply respected him. When Hitlerism came, he was one of the first to speak out with all the directness and frankness of a great un-abashed spirit. Blessing to his memory.

Harold Soref, who visited the offices of the *New Witness* as a young man – and a young Jewish man at that – detected an "atmosphere which was not pleasant, a note of hostility." There was without doubt a group of people around Gilbert who were dragging him, sometimes screaming in protest and sometimes not, along unsavoury paths. If he was guilty of one thing without any doubt, it was of being naïve, of being vulnerable. It was one thing to jest when the result would only be a childish giggle, quite another to laugh at a suffering people. He refused to mock anyone who was in jeopardy. He mellowed on many subjects as he matured, and his growing Christian spirit took him away from hatred, and was not used as an excuse for right-wing views; this cannot be said for all converts to the Catholic Church. Always conscious of his public image, both in its positive and negative aspects, he was aware of how Jewish people regarded him

In our early days Hilaire Belloc and myself were accused of being uncompromising Anti-Semites. Today, although I still think there is a Jewish problem, I am appalled by the Hitlerite atrocities. They have absolutely no reason or logic behind them. It is quite obviously the expedient of a man who has been driven to seeking a scapegoat, and has found with relief the most famous scapegoat in European history, the Jewish people. I am quite ready to believe now that Belloc and I will die defending the last Jew in Europe.

Humbert Wolfe, the Jewish poet, had attacked Gilbert for being an anti-Semite, and later bitterly regretted his attack. His tribute was as follows

Marconi and the Jews

Like a great wind after a night of thunder
He rocked the sodden marches of the soul
And ripped the mists of cowardice asunder
With laughter vivid as an aureole.
He does not need to knock against the Gate
Who every action like a prayer ascended
And beat upon the panels. Trumpets, wait
For a hushed instant. We loved him. It is ended.

IX

Trauma and Travels

Gilbert was the dramatist who never was. His novels, even his works of non-fiction, are written with a sympathy for theatre and the dramatic, and it was no surprise that in the autumn of 1913 "Magic," his first play, opened at the Little Theatre. Bernard Shaw had asked Gilbert to write a play, confident that it would be a success. It was praised by the critics but ran for only three weeks. It was a comedy, containing the now familiar theme that knowledge and love of God was a prerequisite to contentment and understanding, and that the supernatural is part of our lives, whether we desire such a thing or not. Gilbert wrote of a conjuror and a mysterious electric lamp, exploring the darker side of magic. Of the other characters, a Christian socialist, an atheist and a medical cynic all combine to live out the author's theories and arguments. Gilbert appeared at the end of the first night to minimise his part in the entire production, and emphasise that it was not the artistic quality of the play which was important, but the ideas expressed in it.

This was a frantically busy time for Gilbert. As well as the play he was completing two other books, *The Flying Inn* and *The Wisdom of Father Brown,* and contributing poems and journalism to the *New Witness*. Frances was not happy with the arrangement, fearing that journalism equalled Fleet Street, which inevitably signified yet another bout of late nights and heavy drinking. She wanted her husband to do what he did best: write books. His genuine friends told him the same thing, to remain at home and write seriously; his other companions urged him to abandon the rural temptations and make his way back to London life. He was increasingly torn, and under severe pressure. The work load was huge enough, without the constant arguments which now arose whenever the future of his career was discussed with his wife or his brother. The photographs of him at this time show a man who could no longer carry his obesity. There is a sense of melancholy in his face, a sombre thoughtfulness which was not evident in earlier days.

The Flying Inn was published by Methuen in January. In it England is governed by Moslem law, and Humphrey Pump manages to find his way round the stringent drinking laws by turning his pub into a mobile station for thirsty Englishmen. It is an extremely funny book, but does demonstrate a lack of understanding of Islam and the East which plagued Gilbert throughout his life. *The Wisdom of Father Brown* appeared a few months later. This was extremely popular and highly lucrative. It was not as brilliant and original as the first volume, but because Father Brown was now established as a public hero the book sold quickly. The profits from it enabled Gilbert to look ahead towards other projects. Some of the money went into the Chestertons' savings for Top Meadow, the proposed house adjacent to Overroads. When eating gooseberries together one summer's day Gilbert and Frances had spotted an eye-catching tree over the road. It was decided that they would build their permanent home around it. They proceeded to buy the property and land and build a studio with wood from that same tree. The Chesterton house would evolve from the studio.

Gilbert celebrated the success of his two books with a toast, to himself, by himself. He was now an isolated drinker, a far more dangerous animal than the gregarious man who finds it difficult to leave the pub. Frances had intended to take him away from drinking by keeping him in Beaconsfield, but the contrary was the case. Speculations as to whether he was an alcoholic are redundant; he may have been, but was probably not. His addiction was to quantity, quantities of anything. Any drink which was placed in front of him, any food offered, would be consumed without a second thought. His appetite was enormous. It was only a matter of time before his health suffered. In 1913 he began to experience pain in his throat,

219

which turned out to be a congestion of the larynx. His indigestion was chronic, interrupting his sleep and causing him a lot of discomfort in his waking hours. His teeth were bad, his joints were stiff and he felt more tired than he had ever been before. And there was a sluggishness about him, something Frances had refused to recognise earlier. She became frightened, writing to Father O'Connor that "Gilbert has been rather seedy too. A sharpish attack of bronchitis and now a stiff neck . . ."

On 25th November ill health forced him to abandon a lecture at Oxford half way through. He went home, was overcome, and crashed on to his bed, breaking it. Frances wrote to Father O'Connor again, informing him that "It is mostly heart trouble, but there are complications." The outbreak of the war increased the strain on him, but the fundamental cause of the breakdown was his own self-indulgence. Frances asked her friends to pray for her husband's recovery, and brought in a series of nurses to care for his every need. The collapse was almost total, both physical and mental. The body can only take so much punishment, and Gilbert's body had never been in a particularly fit state of self-defence. After an early sign of recovery he fell into a deeper decay, unable to sit up or remain alert for any time. O'Connor described his condition as "Gout all over. Brain, stomach and lungs were affected. He was ten weeks unconscious and had to be kept so. The doctor said that the shock of recognition might destroy life." Frances was concerned enough to wonder about last rites, and believed that Gilbert had come close enough to Catholic conversion to want the sacrament from a Catholic priest. "I do pray to God He will restore him to himself that we may know," she wrote. "I feel in His Mercy He will, even if death is the end of it – or the beginning shall I say?"

It was a hellish experience for Frances, not only because of her husband's agony but also because of the nature of the attacks; periods of near recovery would be followed by deeper falls, throwing her off balance and ripping into her confidence. She would come to terms with his death, and the future which that would create for her. Days later a feeling of euphoria would ensue when it appeared that her husband would regain his health. This pendulum was a dreadful one, and a lesser woman may have broken under it. By Easter it seemed that the swing had come to an end, and Gilbert was steadily if slowly heading towards full recovery. Frances appreciated the theological significance of the date of this good news. She wrote to a friend of the "resurrection of the body" and that, "Last night he said the Creed and asked me to read part of Myser's St Paul . . ."

With total seclusion, the dedicated work of a group of doctors and nurses who grew to love the wretched figure of the great writer lying on his bed, and prayers from all who knew of the attack, he did indeed begin to recover. Frances's expectations of "full recovery" were not to be fulfilled. No man could have gone through such a painful illness and return to his previous self. By the time he was conscious and out of bed Gilbert had lost stones in weight, and instead of looking fitter and more healthy, he appeared to be a man who had lost too much weight, too quickly. His body had been considerably weakened by the episode, and nobody had produced a suitable diagnosis or cure. He would have to cut down in all areas – including work – but other than that nothing was specified. By the end of May he was writing again, for the *Illustrated London News* and then for the *New Witness*. There was universal pleasure on his returning to the literary scene, with letters of congratulations and approval from all directions. His secretary, Freda Spencer, dealt with most of these. She was a delightful creature, frequently making mistakes in her business affairs for Gilbert, but always fascinating him and provoking great chuckles of laughter.

Back at work, he set about contributing to the war effort with some propaganda writing. A more important publication came in 1915; in book form his poetic efforts were called quite simply *Poems*, and were brought out by Burns and Oates. Some of his best known pieces were published separately, under the title *Wine, Water and Song*, but *Poems* contained some gems of Gilbert's writings. "Lepanto" was of course included, as was "The Secret People" and "When I Came Back to Fleet Street." "Antichrist, or the Reunion of

Christendom: an Ode" was an attack on F.E. Smith, the ambitious and gifted politician and lawyer who was later to become Lord Birkenhead, and who did such damage to Cecil Chesterton at the Old Bailey. He had rather pompously spoken out on the subject of Welsh Dis-establishment, stating that it would shock the conscience of "every Christian community in Europe." It was a ludicrous idea, and angered Gilbert with its dishonesty and political posing. He began his poem with

> Are they clinging to their crosses,
> > F.E. Smith,
> Where the Breton boat-fleet tosses,
> > Are they, Smith?
> Do they, fasting, trembling, bleeding,
> > Wait the news from this our city?
> Groaning "That's the Second Reading!"
> > Hissing "There is still Committee!"
> If the voice of Cecil falters,
> > If McKenna's point has pith,
> Do they tremble for their altars?
> > Do they, Smith?

And ended with

> It would greatly, I must own,
> > soothe me, Smith,
> If you left this theme alone,
> > Holy Smith!
> For your legal cause or civil
> > You fight well and get your fee;
> For your God or dream or devil
> > You will answer, not to me.
> Talk about the pews and steeples
> > And the Cash that goes therewith!
> But the souls of Christian peoples . . .
> > – Chuck it, Smith!

His knowledge of the war, and of military matters in general, was weak. He followed the progress of the British army's battles against the German "Barbarian" through Hilaire Belloc's articles in the magazine *Land and Water;* Belloc was, of course, an expert. At the end of 1915 Gilbert published *The Crimes of England,* a short book which blamed Britain for some of the rise of Prussian power. His fear and hatred of Protestant Prussia and the larger Germany was intense; and had been long before the 1914 war. For Gilbert and Belloc the steady increase in German influence was an international evil, especially as it was to the direct detriment of Catholic France. There was no chance of the army ever accepting Gilbert for military service, and his endeavours to join up must be viewed in their true light; the quixotic romantic, not the unworldly fool. His brother was finally taken into the military in 1916, classified as B2. After a struggle he managed to obtain a transfer to the Highland Infantry, received another classification of B1 and was able to fight for his country. Ada Jones, impressed by the dashing soldier, gave in to Cecil Chesterton's requests and agreed to marry him. They were married first in a register office, then in the beautiful, almost subterranean church of Corpus Christi in London's Maiden Lane. The wedding celebrations took place at the Cheshire Cheese.

Gilbert was busy at work on his *A Short History of England,* now employing a second secretary, a Mrs Walpole. His health was gradually better, his physical strength had mostly returned to him. He was spending more and more time working on Cecil's paper, feeling that it was his contribution to the war effort, and his sign of loyalty and gratitude to his brother, doing what Gilbert could not. It was a struggle to complete his English history, but by 1917 it was on the book-shelves. The book contained all the usual inaccuracies and faults, and all the striking wit and incisiveness which were so particular to Gilbert. Shaw wrote in the *Observer* in November, that it was impossible to review such a volume. The task was akin to writing a "comic review of Mark Twain." He continued "There is nothing worth saying left to be said of his book, because he has said it all himself: he is too good a husbandman to leave much for the gleaners. Let me therefore ask him for another chapter in his next edition. I can even give him subjects for two chapters."

It became increasingly apparent that Cecil could not edit

the *New Witness* from the western front, and in his final editorial he said "Au Revoir" to the magazine, and thanked Gilbert "who, at no little personal sacrifice, has consented to undertake the editorship in my absence, and to allow his name to appear on the front page of the paper." Frances was deeply hurt, and angry. Gilbert was the least organised of men, and the most busy. The idea of his editing a working magazine was ridiculous. As has already been noted, personality clashes on the journal were frequent and severe; Gilbert was to spend fruitless hours mediating between thin-skinned personalities and reassuring people that their efforts were indeed appreciated. Financially matters were in bad shape, and always would be. However, Thomas Beecham, a great admirer of Cecil Chesterton and a guest at his wedding party, donated large sums, and eventually became a member of the Board. Others either loaned or gave money; there was a great amount of goodwill.

Gilbert was forced to subsidise the running costs of the *New Witness* at a rate of some £200 per month, out of his personal income and savings. Frances could do nothing. It was not only the time and money being spent, wasted, which hurt her, but the fact that Ada Chesterton was now so dominant in Gilbert's life. The two women did not get on, and as Ada was taking on most of the organisational chores of the magazine she and Gilbert spent a lot of time with each other. There was no sexual jealousy – such a suggestion would have been laughed at – but the understandable resentment that a husband was working, drinking and laughing with another woman, who was hostile. It was a difficult time for the Chesterton marriage.

Gilbert was happy when writing editorials, which he approached as if they were short essays rather than journalistic leaders. He wrote in his *Autobiography* that his being an editor had seemed as likely as his being "a publisher or a banker." He was proud of the stance of the *New Witness* under him, "which was passionately patriotic and Pro-Ally but as emphatically opposed to the Jingoism of the Daily Mail." Non-Jingoist or not, the magazine announced with relish that "The Prussian devil is defeated" when the war finally came to a ghastly end. The joy of the staff of the *New Witness* was short-lived; it was announced that Cecil Chesterton was dead. Gilbert was left senseless. Ada, so recently a bride and now so suddenly a widow, was brave, but of course in complete despair. Gilbert would write

> For my brother was destined to prove, in a dark house of doom, that he alone of all the men of our time possessed the two kinds of courage that have nourished the nation; the courage of the forum and of the field. In the second case he suffered with thousands of men equally brave; in the first he suffered alone. For it is another example of the human irony that it seems easier to die in battle than to tell the truth in politics .... and I continued to the editing of my brother's paper, if you can call it editing, and all the other financiers and politicians showed no signs of dying in any faith, or indeed of dying at all ...

He would exploit travel as a way of overcoming his grief, though in reality the pain of the loss would never leave him. Ireland had been visited before his brother's death, with the hope that a lecture tour would provoke interest in the *New Witness*. Gilbert had made up his mind on the Irish question before he set foot in the country, sure that the North and the Protestant faith signified urban modernism and all that was bad, while the rural Catholicism of the South was where the true path to political contentment and happiness lay. His conclusions were later published as *Irish Impressions,* and reviewed by Bernard Shaw in the *Irish Statesman*

> These Irish impressions are not, as the title page states, impressions by Mr Chesterton. They are impressions by Ireland on Mr Chesterton. I am tempted to recommend the book in which he has recorded them as a proof that an Englishman is a much pleasanter, jollier, kindlier human variety than an Irishman; and though I am checked by the reflection that all Englishmen are unfortunately not like Mr Chesterton, and that he describes himself as a blend of Scotch, French, and Suffolk Dumpling, still, the net result is the sort of man that England can produce

when she is doing her best. Like all such Englishmen he is a thoroughgoing Irish patriot, and will not hear of romantic Ireland being dead and gone. It exists still for him; and he holds us in an esteem which would make us blush if so conceited a nation knew how to blush; for we are very far from deserving it. Our vices are so obvious that they have troubled him though they have not estranged him. Of Dublin he tells us faithfully that though the inhabitants can dream they cannot sleep, having all the irritability of insomnia and all the meanness and jealousy of perpetual wideawakeness, and that they slander one another with an abnormal ungenerousness. In Belfast he is staggered into laughter and horror at the mad pride and wicked selfishness of the purse proud commercial Irish Calvinist; and if he had travelled south instead of north, he would have discovered that the kindlier life and thought of Catholic Ireland does not save it from the infatuate and deadly-sinful conviction that it lives in a world of its natural inferiors . . .

Back at the offices of the *New Witness* Ada Chesterton could face the long hours no longer, and W.R. Titterton came in as an industrious and enthusiastic assistant editor. Things at Essex Street, the home of the magazine, became more stable as the staff realised that without Cecil Chesterton around everybody involved would have to work harder. Gilbert spent less time there, and decided to take his travels farther afield than Ireland. The *Daily Telegraph* asked him if he would go to Palestine with Frances, and write a series of articles on what he saw, now that the British once again were in control of the region. The proposal was God-sent, and readily accepted. Friends played a part in all of this, knowing that Gilbert had to find adventure, and work through the death of his brother. E.C. Bentley, on the staff of the *Daily Telegraph,* was instrumental in awarding the task to his boyhood friend, and Maurice Baring made sure that his military contacts would welcome Gilbert in the Middle East. The excitement at the Chesterton household was as if a child was awaiting Christmas; Gilbert, if not childish, was always childlike.

Gilbert's weight fluctuated, and at its peak was over 320 pounds.
It was a strain his surprisingly meagre frame could not tolerate.
This photograph was taken shortly before a physical collapse,
and shows Gilbert at his most cumbersome.

Immediately after the death of his brother Cecil and the end of WWI, Gilbert traveled to France, Italy, Egypt, and Jerusalem. The snow fell to welcome him. His tour of Palestine and subsequent anticipation of the future of Zionism was perceptive and sensitive. Here he stands in front of the walls of the Old City.

As illness became more frequent, the Chestertons became increasingly confined to Top Meadow. The strain of Gilbert's decreasing health clearly shows both on his and Frances' face.

His last public appearance, May 1936. Opening St Joseph's.

Frances (left) in her prime and (right) after Gilbert's death. "We were always lovers."

Monsignor O'Connor with Gilbert's portrait, after the death of his friend.

The couple travelled through France and Italy, then took a ship across the Mediterranean to Alexandria. From that magnificent city they took the railway to Cairo, and then concluded their journey in Jerusalem. They were treated as honoured guests in Jerusalem, both by the British authorities and by the Zionist organisers who Gilbert was so anxious to meet. It snowed in Jerusalem while Gilbert was there, and he was completely captivated by the romance and beauty of the city. He came to the conclusion that Christmas cards, with their depiction of Christ being born in a snowy Bethlehem, may be more authentic than he had thought. Gilbert visited the holy shrines, delighting in the Church of the Nativity in Bethlehem, and the Church of Ecce Homo in Jerusalem. When he travelled to Bethlehem he was quite overcome

Never have I felt so vividly the great fact of our history; that Christian religion is like a huge bridge across a boundless sea, which alone connects us with the men who made the world, and yet have utterly vanished from the world . . . . I can never recapture in words the waves of sympathy with strange things that went through me in that twilight of the tall pillars, like giants robed in purple, standing still and looking down into that dark hole in the ground. [He refers to the entrance to the stable where Christ is supposed to have been born.] Here halted that imperial civilisation when it had marched in triumph throughout the whole world; here in the evening of its days it came trailing in all its panoply in the pathway of the three kings.

He returned to Britain to write *The New Jerusalem* and discover that the *New Witness* was in dire trouble once again. For the first time circulation figures were dropping with an alarming regularity. The magazine had triumphed in the bitter years before the war, had done relatively well during the war, but had failed to adapt to a new world of new peace-time conditions and attitudes. By August a public appeal was made to *New Witness* readers for donations; the result was the raising of £1,000, generous but far too small a sum. Gilbert was tired of the petty problems of his inherited project, and had become mildly addicted to the travel bug. A lecture tour of the United States was arranged for 1921, and no amount of difficulties on the *New Witness* was going to postpone that. Frances's ill health may have done, and she was going through a bad spell of illness. X-rays revealed further arthritis in her spine, with much consequent pain and suffering. She decided to make the trip.

Gilbert was already something of a celebrity in New York – which until recent times accounted for most of America's reading public – with his books widely read and the large Catholic community interested in his spiritual works. As his ship docked reporters were already clamouring to interview him, asking him questions which he had no way of answering: such as what did he think of the crime wave in the city? He did not think of it at all. The Chestertons drove directly to their hotel, the Biltmore, and began a rest before the stormy days of the tour. His first lecture was at the Times Square Theatre, and was a great success. Gilbert fulfilled the expectations of his American audiences; he was as eccentric, unique and witty as they had hoped. The paradox was new to them, and they were delighted. A lecture entitled "Shall We Abolish the Inevitable?" attracted an amazed, curious group. He liked Americans, enjoyed their youthful willingness to be pleased and entertained; cynicism had not yet tainted the East Coast character. The aggression of American journalists was not so pleasing to him; Frances would sometimes leave the hotel room before her husband to ensure that it was safe for him to leave without being accosted by noisy reporters.

On one subject, of course, he was more than willing to speak his mind. His apparent desire to drink alcohol was partly based on physical need, partly on what people expected of him: the English journalist who would not be able to tolerate any ridiculous drinking laws. He wrote: "I went to America with some notion of not discussing Prohibition. But I soon found that well-to-do Americans were only too delighted to discuss it over the nuts and wine. They were even willing, if necessary, to dispense with the nuts."

After New York came Boston, that very Catholic and

lovely city. He had formed an opinion of the American people by now, and believed that "there is nothing the matter with Americans except their ideals. The real American is all right; it is the ideal American who is all wrong." Such comments, as part of his larger reputation, went before him. He spoke about Ireland, and was cheered. In Nashville and Oklahoma, Omaha and Albany he experienced the wide difference in American culture, the different identities that each state, each city, cloaks itself in. He thought that the cheering Americans took him "absolutely too seriously, though they make the best audience to lecture to in the world." In Canada the reception he gained was little short of magnificent. It was a triumphant tour, and when he returned to Britain he was full of praise for his foreign hosts. He wrote his opinions down for publication in book form in *What I Saw In America.*

Travel not only widened his knowledge of other countries, but also his own convictions. He had written to Father O'Connor at the time, informing him that Frances was unwell, and also that, "I feel it is only right to consult with my Anglo-Catholic friends; but I have at present a feeling it will be something like a farewell." He was writing regularly to Belloc and Baring, both Catholics, and searching for affirmation, for support. They gave the latter, but knew that Gilbert had to make up his own mind.

His letters reveal a commitment to convert to the Roman Catholic Church, surrounded by fears that such an act would hurt his friends, and Frances, and that the new home he desired so much might be a little foreign, "alien." He was reassured by friends that the Catholic Church was as foreign, and as English, as he wished to make it; it was universal, and only the British prejudice towards the faith gave it a European feel and flavour. His wife's views on the subject were of more importance. He discussed the matter with her, sensitive to her feelings but conscious that he needed conversion as a thirsty man needs water. Father Ronald Knox, that great and good priest, advised him, and began to instruct him. Would Frances tolerate his conversion? Finally, it must not matter.

He was still nominally an Anglo–Catholic, within the body of the Church of England. As such he was asked to talk to a

Congress at the Albert Hall, and felt very uncomfortable so doing. He wrote to Maurice Baring, explaining how he felt at the gathering

> To those to whom I cannot give my spiritual biography, I can say that the insecurity I felt in Anglicanism was typified in the Lambeth Conference. I am at least sure that much turns on that Conference, if not for me, for large numbers of those people at the Albert Hall. A young Anglo–Catholic curate has just told me that the crowd there cheered all references to the Pope, and laughed at every mention of the Archbishop of Canterbury. It's a queer state of things. I am concerned most however, about somebody I value more than the Archbishop of Canterbury; Frances, to whom I owe much of my own faith, and to whom therefore (as far as I can see my way) I also owe every decent chance for the controversial defence of her faith. If her side can convince me, they have a right to do so; if not, I shall go hot and strong to convince her. I put it clumsily, but there is a point in my mind . . .

Frances was becoming more reticent on the subject, knowing her husband's ways, and his determination. She knew that he would journey into the Catholic Church, and she could do nothing about it; his discussions with her were as much to satisfy his own feelings as hers. Before any conversion could take place came a loss. Gilbert's father became seriously ill. Ada Chesterton described the sudden attack as an "obstinate cold," but there was evidently more to it than that. He would not get out of bed, became nervous and sullen. His death came before anybody in the family could prepare themselves for it, if that is indeed possible. Gilbert's grief was tempered by the fact that he had to cope with the business affairs left outstanding by his father. Nevertheless, he was heartbroken. Edward Chesterton was buried at Brompton, the Chesterton grave; he had been extremely proud of both of his sons.

The death almost coincided with Gilbert and Frances's move to Top Meadow, their long awaited home. The house was not completed, but enough had been achieved for the couple to live there quite happily. Frances was ill again, and had to be carried straight to her bed in the new house. Ada Chesterton went to see them shortly after the move, and was shocked by what she saw at Top Meadow

> ... the stage, on which amateur talent used to shine, some feet above the auditorium – or should I say floor level? – had been made into a dining-room. It was reached from the small front hall by a narrow passage and you entered, so to speak, by the doorless wings direct on to the dining-table, almost flush with the proscenium curtains. The place was heated by an anthracite stove backstage, which could not be kept at a pressure suffi-cient to warm the whole, as those with their backs almost against it would have been slowly roasted ...
> Beyond the stage, and at the lower level, the audi-torium stretched through a hinterland to Gilbert's cub-byhole. In the front of the hinterland there was an open brick fireplace with space for a small low chair on either side, where Frances would sit for hours, watching the logs crumble into fiery particles ...

Gilbert seemed distracted during the move, surprising since he had been anxious to settle down for months. There were other things on his mind; at least one other thing on his mind. He wrote to Father O'Connor

> ... I write with a more personal motive; do you happen to have a holiday about the end of next week or there-abouts and would it be possible for you to come south and see our new house – or old studio? This sounds a very abrupt invitation; but I write in great haste, and am troubled about many things. I want to talk to you about them; especially the most serious ones, religious and concerned with my own rather difficult position. Most of the difficulty has been my own fault, but not all; some of my difficulties would commonly be called duties; though I ought perhaps to have learned sooner to regard them as lesser duties. I mean that a Pagan or Protestant or Agnos-tic might even have excused me; but I have grown less

and less of a Pagan or Protestant, and can no longer excuse myself. There are lots of things for which I never did excuse myself; but I am thinking now of particular points that might really be casuistical. Anyhow, you are the person that Frances and I think of with most affection, of all who could help in such a matter. Could you let me know if any time such as I name, or after, could give us the joy of seeing you?

Father O'Connor arrived on 26th July, and immediately listened to Gilbert's fears and hopes. He walked with Frances through the town, and told her that it was Gilbert's concern for his wife that was holding him back from conversion. She was delighted to hear that Gilbert had been so forthcoming, answering that "Oh! I shall be infinitely relieved. You cannot imagine how it fidgets Gilbert to have anything on his mind. The last three months have been exceptionally trying. I should be only too glad to come with him, if God in His mercy would show the way clear enough for me to justify such a step." Father O'Connor gave Gilbert a penny catechism, which he read avidly throughout the day. All was now set, and the location for the ceremony would be the local church, then merely an annexe to the Railway Hotel.

Gilbert carried with him that Sunday afternoon the swordstick given to him in the United States by the Knights of Columbus. He made his first confession to Father O'Connor, took a last look at his catechism and prepared for the service. Dom Ignatius Rice officiated. Frances began to weep. After the baptism was administered Gilbert was left inside the chapel on his own for a while; he came out, and immediately began to comfort Frances. He wrote to his mother, Belloc and Baring, informing them of what had happened. Only Baring gave his full approval, and full enthusiasm. After the news appeared in the *Tablet*, letters of encouragement began to arrive. Father Vincent NcNabb, that sturdy priest who wore army boots and survived many a heckler in Hyde Park, wrote to O'Connor, enthusing with "You, my beloved Father, must feel as if the birth pangs of a score of years were now nothing, for the joy that a man-child is born to Jesus Christ." Gilbert himself wrote

> When people ask me, or indeed anybody else, "Why did you join the Church of Rome?" the first essential answer, if it is partly an elliptical answer, is "To get rid of my sins." For there is no other religious system that does really profess to get rid of people's sins. It is confirmed by the logic, which to many seems startling, by which the Church deduces that sin confessed and adequately re-pented is actually abolished; and that the sinner does really begin again as if he had never sinned . . .

He was given life anew, as he expected. Friends detected a new energy in his step and in his approach to work and pleasure. A great burden, that of indecision, was removed from his shoulders, and in its place was now certainty, abso-lute faith and belief. All his writings would now have a con-crete purpose, the road ahead was clear, if not always easy. He was confident that Frances would follow before long; she always did.

While Gilbert was deciding his future, the *New Witness* was also deciding its own; it would close, financially smashed. Frances breathed a sigh of relief, and then a sigh of disbelief. Cecil's child would not die, but would live again in another form. Gilbert stated

> In this day and hour I haul down my flag, I surrender my sword, I give up a fight I have maintained against odds for very long. No; I do not mean the fight to maintain the New Witness, though that was a fight against impossible odds and has gone on for years. I mean a more horrid but hidden conflict, of which the world knew nothing; the savage but secret war I have waged against a proposal to call a paper by the name of G.K.C.'s Weekly. When the title was first suggested my feeling was one of wild terror, which gradually softened into disgust.

The first requirement was money, and as the *New Witness* had made so many enemies the raising of finances was a difficult proposition. Some of the absurdities which Cecil Chesterton and Belloc had believed about the Jewish control of City of London money began to haunt Gilbert, as both Jewish and gentile companies and individuals halted their philanthropy at the front door of "G.K.C.'s Weekly." He was forced to ask his family lawyer to raise money on the family estate, in which he had a considerable number of shares. After this enterprise more money was still needed, and he knew that could only be achieved by writing more books. Having to write to order, for cash, obviously damaged the quality of some of his work; friends told him this, but he would not, could not, change his decision.

The Man Who Knew Too Much was a collection of magazine stories, all concerning an aristocrat named Horne Fisher. The tales are centred on crime and politics, with Fisher solving all the problems with a cynical detachment. Some had it that the central character was modelled on Maurice Baring – class and height were certainly similar – and if so Baring would have been most upset. It is an eminently forgettable little book.

In 1923 two books appeared; the first, *Fancies Versus Fads,* was a further collection of essays and articles. The second made a much larger impact: it was his biography of St Francis of Assisi. The first book actually written after his reception into the Catholic Church, it drew upon his biographical sketch of the Saint in his previous book, *Twelve Types.* The intention was to provide a portrait of St Francis for the "ordinary" man, and to flesh out his previous hypothesis that Francis had anticipated most of what modern liberalism cherished as being unique to its own age. Gilbert believed that the nineteenth and twentieth centuries had discovered little that was spiritually or politically new, or worth knowing, and that Francis was one of the great medieval fathers of contemporary invention. In typically Chestertonian manner, he was able to speak volumes about his subject without mentioning its name

The modern innovation which has substituted journalism for history, or for that tradition that is the gossip of history, has had at least one definite effect. It has insured that everybody should only hear the end of every story. Journalists are in the habit of printing above the very last chapters of their serial stories (when the hero and heroine are just about to embrace in the last chapter, as only an unfathomable perversity prevented them from doing in the first) the rather misleading words, "You can begin this story here." But even this is not a complete parallel; for the journals do give some sort of a summary of the story, while they never give anything remotely resembling a summary of the history.

Newspapers not only deal with news, but they deal with everything as if it were entirely new. Tutankamen, for instance, was entirely new. It is exactly in the same fashion that we read that Admiral Bangs has been shot, which is the first intimation we have that he has ever been born. There is something singularly significant in the use which journalism makes of its stores of biography. It never thinks of publishing the life until it is publishing the death. As it deals with individuals it deals with institutions and ideas. After the Great War our public began to be told of all sorts of nations being emancipated. It had never been told a word about their being enslaved . . .

Thus it was that he prepared to explain why we could not understand St Francis, the Inquisition or earlier forms of Catholic Christianity without coming to terms with the history of all of these things. He explored the world of St Francis, the environment which he knew and experienced. The book was brief, but full and sweeping in its explanations and interpretations. *Tales of the Long Bow,* the volume which followed, was a book of magazine stories, each one centred on the contradiction of a proverb; pigs do fly, water can burn. It is a gentle, charming selection; but was entirely forgotten with the publication of what is perhaps Gilbert's masterpiece, *The Everlasting Man.*

As with some of his other works, this one was written as a response. H.G. Wells, who had been involved in a running debate with Gilbert for years, had brought out his *Outline of*

History as a complete volume in 1925; it had appeared in separate sections earlier. Wells was very much the poor man's historian, writing readable history for young men who were epitomised in books such as his *Love and Mr Lewisham* or *Kipps*. Wells was a rationalist, a believer in self-improvement and materialism. He perceived history as a process of evolution, inevitable and desirable. Man had begun as a primitive, had improved his lot over the centuries, and had in the twentieth century reached a near pinnacle, a position of scientific and political progress, and was able to at last achieve universal happiness and world peace. It was an optimistic analysis of history, and a proud one; the arrogance of modern man was once again on display, the belief that only at that point in history could problems be solved, answers found. God was not relevant, science had produced the answers, and hence done away with any need for a substitute panacea. Gilbert's reply was not long in coming.

The Everlasting Man has as fundamental qualities its strong flavour of humour, of taking a serious matter seriously, but also with a light heart. It was readable. Wells discussed Man's beginnings in the caves, so Gilbert looked closely at what actually went on in the caves. In a section of the book entitled "The God In The Cave" he wrote

> This sketch of the human story began in a cave; the cave which popular science associates with the cave-man and in which practical discovery has really found archaic drawings of animals. The second half of human history, which was like a new creation of the world, also begins in a cave. There is even a shadow of such a fancy in the fact that animals were again present; for it was a cave used as a stable by the mountaineers of the uplands about Bethlehem; who still drive their cattle into such holes and caverns at night. It was here that a homeless couple had crept underground with the cattle when the doors of the crowded caravanserai had been shut in their faces; and it was here beneath the very feet of the passers-by, in a cellar under the very floor of the world, that Jesus Christ was born. But in that second creation there was indeed something symbolical in the roots of the primaeval rock

or the horns of the prehistoric herd. God also was a Cave-Man, and had also traced strange shapes of creatures, curiously coloured, upon the wall of the world; but the pictures that he made had come to life.

Gilbert's history of man's story has the life of Jesus as the focal point of the world, the "crisis of history." The development of the Roman Catholic Church is the guiding line throughout history, a guide by which we can judge progress and advancement. Science has no place here, other than as a by-product of the spiritual centre, and man is no more near perfection in 1920 than he was in 1290. There has always been a path to heaven, and a road to somewhere else. He concluded the book as follows

> For it was the soul of Christendom that came forth from the incredible Christ; and the soul of it was common sense. Though we dared not look on His face we could look on His fruits; and by His fruits we should know Him. The fruits are solid and the fruitfulness is much more than a metaphor; and nowhere in this sad world are boys happier in apple-trees, or men in more equal chorus singing as they tread the vine, than under the fixed flash of this instant and intolerant enlightenment; the lightning made eternal as the light.

The publication of *The Everlasting Man* took Gilbert away from journalism for only a short while; *G.K.'s Weekly* – the "G.K.C." was abbreviated – was calling him back, loudly and clearly. Its appeal was obvious; the staff were dedicated, prepared to work for low wages and were committed to the magazine's fortunes. W.R. Titterton recalled a visit to the offices of the paper by Gilbert

> I am sitting in the editorial chair, when the door opens, and discloses Chesterton, floppy hat in one hand, sprouting cigarillo and sword-stick in the other. Of course, his pince-nez hangs sideways on his nose. A beaming smile, half of surprise, half of joy is on his face, as if, on a long and hazardous voyage of discovery, most unexpectedly he'd found us!

The next few moments are taken up with his depositing his impedimenta carefully anywhere and his apologies for disturbing us. And then he is seated in the editorial chair, happy and at ease.

Usually he feels in an inside pocket and takes out some manuscripts done in that marvellous Gothic handwriting. He hands the articles to me, and probably his work in town is finished. But now and then he'd say to the secretary, "Oh, Miss Dunham, would you mind taking down this for me?" And he'd stride up and down the small office, hands behind his back, while Bunny Dunham typed his conversation.

Every now and then would come a chuckle, ending in a roar and a squeak. When his talk had ended, and he'd quickly read it through, he'd chat for a while and then with infinite reluctance vanish. Afterwards I have (but not often) seen him in a dim corner of a Fleet Street tavern, or in El Vino's wine shop, blissfully contemplating the universe.

But the paper was "made-up" over the phone. G.K.C. would say: "I thought of doing the leader on Gas-and-Gaiters" – or whatever it was. "And I could do three or four notes on so-and-so. Will you do the rest? And have you thought about a second leader?" And so on. But much was the stuff he did each week, such as Top-and-Tail and his current series, such as The Outline of Sanity, or Straws in the Wind. I said I supposed that Straws in the Hair would do, and he burbled and said it was too near the truth.

Gilbert was to be paid £500 a year for his work on the magazine – Shaw thought him mad, writing that he should accept "at least £1,500 a year, plus payment for copy," and adding that he was better off writing plays, perhaps on Joan of Arc or George Fox. Gilbert usually contributed the leading article, between 1250 and 1600 words, as well as a middle-page major article of some 2000 words. Friends were introduced to fill out the pages, with Wells, Shaw and Compton Mackenzie writing articles and commentary pieces. Circulation did not manage to reach over 5000 however, and that was not sufficient to pay all the staff's wages and invest for the future. The general advice was now to close down *G.K.'s Weekly* while there was still time to salvage reputation if nothing else. Gilbert would have none of it.

In 1926 Dorothy Collins arrived at the Chesterton household, and set about maintaining Gilbert as an author. Without this remarkable and versatile lady he would not have written so much during the last ten years of his life, and would probably have collapsed under the strain of his work load. She was a trained secretary and accountant, and could also drive a car – in Gilbert's mind a quite remarkable attribute. The result was that he became far more mobile, and less dependent on third parties for transport to London, or to public meetings. She became an integral part of the family, a trusted friend and companion for both Gilbert and Frances. For all her superb efforts she could not remove Gilbert's feelings of depression about the future of his magazine, or his brother's magazine. He was often irritable at this time, less tolerant than in the past. W.P. Flynn, now eighty years old, recalls meeting him in Westminster's Victoria Street. He was with a friend who knew Gilbert and was introduced to the man who he regarded as something of a hero. Gilbert was asked where he was staying. "Artillery Mansions" was the reply. "Well," said Mr Flynn, "you'll have to be careful then, or they'll canonise you." No laughter, not even a smile; only a sad look of disapproval and a rapid change of conversation. Frances found him difficult at times, and learnt that it was pointless to raise the subject of the future of *G.K.'s Weekly*.

The saviour of the Chesterton magazine was a political philosophy. Distributism was in Gilbert's eyes a natural and inevitable extension of his own religion. It had been discussed and debated by Cecil and Gilbert for years, but had never crystallised into a conscious theory until now. *G.K.'s Weekly* was to become the virtual mouthpiece of Distributism and the Distributist League, and thus ensure a loyal readership. Gilbert was elected President of the League and remained until his death the leading figure of the movement, its symbol and public light. What was it? K.L. Kenrick, Secretary of the Birmingham branch of the league and a leading Distributist,

239

wrote a pamphlet with Gilbert on the subject. He explained it as follows

There are three economic theories struggling for supremacy in the modern world. They are Capitalism – the doctrine that property is best concentrated in large masses in the hands of a few people; Socialism – the doctrine that property is best owned and controlled by the state; and Distributism – the doctrine that property is best divided up among the largest possible number of people. Broadly speaking, we may say that Distributism means every man his own master (as far as possible); Socialism means nobody his own master, but the State master of all; Capitalism means a select few their own masters and the rest of us their servants. Again, broadly speaking, Capitalism may be said to be the economic creed of England, Germany and U.S.A.; and Distributism the economic creed of Ireland, Denmark, Belgium, France, Spain, Italy and Poland. Socialism, as Communism, had until recently a strong hold on Russia, but the latest news from that country seems to indicate that it has been compelled to capitulate to Distributism. We may say, therefore, that Socialism is more or less of a phantom; the real world-struggle is between Capitalism and Distributism; and the economic realist is bound to choose between these two. He can only take a passing glance at Socialism or Communism.

The principal object of G.K.'s Weekly and the League associated with it, is to rally and unite such scattered forces of Distributism as are still to be found in England and the United States. In its foreign policy it sides, generally speaking, with the Distributist countries against their Capitalist aggressors, believing this struggle to be the main international problem of today. If funds were forthcoming it would keep a correspondent in each of those countries, whose main business would be to report on international economic affairs from that point of view.

In its home policy it recognises that England is the hotbed of Capitalism. Here Capitalism was born; here it learnt its tricks; and although it has found apt pupils in Germany and America, it is here that it has wrought its greatest havoc, and here that its natural history may be best studied . . .

The predictions made in the piece are of course ludicrous, as is the arrogant boast that three economic ideals were existent in the world. The nations identified as "Distributist" were, with the exception of Denmark, poorly developed and unable to deal with the poverty of their citizens. The remaining paragraphs of the tract deal with "the writing and speeches of the financiers . . . . rhetoric of the politicians," "enormous blocks of capital" and "a deep-seated evil." The nasty flavour of economic fascism, with its rejection of both capitalism and socialism, is strong indeed, and Distributism died as a creed as soon as the fascist parties built themselves a solid platform. Distributism was naïve rather than unpleasant, relying on wishful thinking and ignorance of world affairs and trends. There were some first-class minds inside the Distributist League, as well as some first-class imaginations. It was heavily Roman Catholic, influenced by the encyclical letter of Pope Leo XIII of 1891, which called for an alternative to the two emerging forms of economics, and stressed that it was "within man's right to possess things, not merely for temporary and momentary use, as other living things do, but to hold them in stable and permanent possession." The number of individual Catholics divided the League, alienating non-Catholics. The tendency for reactionary views to creep in also turned potential members away. Father Brocard Sewell, a young enthusiast in the offices of *G.K.'s Weekly* and inside the Distributist League, is today someone who laments that "Oswald Mosley did not manage to become Prime Minister of this country;" hence it was that young radicals searching for an outlet for their energies and unrest rarely turned to organised Distributism.

Outlining the purposes of the League, formally known as the "League for the Preservation of Liberty by the Restoration of Property," Gilbert made two leading points

241

That the only way to preserve liberty is to preserve property; that the individual and the family may be in some degree independent of oppressive systems, official or unofficial.

And

That the only way to preserve property is to distribute it much more equally among the citizens; that all, or approximately all, may understand and defend it. This can only be done by breaking up the great plutocratic concentration of our time.

He went on to say that the inevitable result of industrial progress was the swamping of the individual. Nobody, according to Gilbert, could or would reverse the trend of capitalism becoming increasingly powerful, and placing ever larger amounts of money in ever smaller groups of people. He concluded

This problem of centralised wealth has produced a great many interesting things. It has produced proposals that what is thus centralised should be used for good instead of evil; that what is centralised should be simplified; that it should be centralised even more, in a new national centre. But it has not produced the perfectly simple proposal that what is centralised should be decentralised. It has not produced a single political party or political programme based on the idea that if property is in too few hands, it ought to be put into many more hands. This truism has been left for us to defend; and we have been obliged to defend it like a paradox.

The object of the League is to form branches or groups all over the country for the defence of this principle and the discussion of the practical application of this principle. A list of proposals already made for its practical application will be found in the Text Book of the League, a pamphlet shortly to be published at 20/21 Essex Street, Strand; and written in collaboration by Mr Hilaire Belloc and the undersigned. But the authors of the pamphlet and the executive of the League desire that the groups and individual members should discuss these proposals in the light of their own local experience and personal judgement; as the work required, which is the re-establishment of small proprietors, small farmers, small shopkeepers and the rest, is a work which must be considered in relation to locality; which is but the geographical aspect of liberty. Unless some such solution is found, there is nothing before us but a choice between communist and commercial slavery.

For those who were set alight by the spark which was Distributism this was a time of hope, ambition and hard work. Confusion was everywhere in the years after the First World War, the years of unemployment, great affluence and social change. The great cause was to come, in the struggle against a genuine darkness, the evil of fascism. Until that time bright young men searched and explored. At the Devereux pub beer would flow, songs would ring out and political debate would go on till the latest hour. It was all so fulfilling; it was all so ultimately empty. Branches of the League were set up throughout the country, and the circulation of *G.K.'s Weekly* rose to over 8000. Its real achievements were minimal. The reality of the situation was that socialism was the advancing cause, and within a generation half of Europe and much of the developing world would identify itself with Marxist Leninism. Capitalism adapted itself, became social democracy, the mixed economy, or authoritarian, state-controlled enterprise. Distributism left no significant mark, its influence is long dead outside of a small group of devotees. In fact Gilbert's death signified the end of the philosophy, if that is what it was, as a serious proposition. He had kept it alive; squabbles and lack of direction tore the movement apart.

The only important debate is concerned with how much the League and the magazine distracted Gilbert from the more important vocation of his books and serious articles. Age would have diminished the number of books he could have written irrespective of the time he spent on Distributism; as an outlet for his political aspirations it served a useful pur-

243

pose. If nothing else, it got him out of the often stifling atmosphere of Beaconsfield, and exposed him to the Fleet Street he loved all of his life. His *William Cobbett* had appeared in 1925, and was as much a biography as an explanation of Gilbert's political views. Cobbett was an early Distributist, campaigning for the real British people. For Tory and Whig read Capitalist and Socialist. It was a contrived book, and some of the interpretations of Cobbett's life are so weighted as to support Gilbert's position that much of it cannot be taken seriously.

1926 was a busy year for publication. *The Incredulity of Father Brown* appeared, to positive reviews and a grateful readership. This was followed by a book of articles, many of them having previously appeared in the *New Witness*, entitled *The Outline of Sanity*. The year's offering was completed by a book of poetry, *The Queen of Seven Swords*, dedicated to, and in part inspired by, Gilbert's friend J.S. Phillimore, who had recently died.

More important for the Chestertons, in 1926 Frances joined the Roman Catholic Church. "I am feeling my way into the Catholic fold," she told Father O'Connor, "but it is a difficult road for me and I ask for your prayers." Her instruction was a confusing experience for her, and a little frightening. "I don't want my instruction to be here," she wrote. "I don't want to be the talk of Beaconsfield and for people to say I've followed Gilbert." She was eventually received on All Saints Day in High Wycombe. For the first time in months she felt close to Gilbert again, a partner with him on a long, marvellous journey.

Of course, her conversion did not save her from illness, and she once again fell into a deep physical decline. Gilbert was afraid of her illnesses, afraid of how he could deal with them, and how he could cope with himself. Not until December could Frances take her first communion and be confirmed in the Church, a "wrench" she found "rather terrible." When she recovered from her ill health Gilbert was prepared to go to any lengths to make her feel secure and loved, both within the Church and within his own heart. It was a time of re-building, of working again at their marriage.

Gilbert had long been fascinated with Poland and its problems. Here was a large, vibrant Catholic country in between the giants of Germany and Russia; it was a victim state, a valiant state. He received the opportunity of visiting Warsaw in 1927, a guest of the P.E.N. Club. Gilbert, Frances and Dorothy arrived at the end of April, greeted by an enthusiastic crowd which included a delegation party from the Prime Minister. If Gilbert was anxious to see Poland, Poland was even more anxious to see him. He was treated as if he were a royal visitor, a representative of the culture which Poland was determined to identify itself with. The *Literary News* of Warsaw wrote of his visit at the beginning of May

... But this admiration would never have reached such an intensity had it not been for a truly exceptional affinity which exists between our distinguished guest and the Polish nation. No other Western writer understands Poland's aspirations and movements as Chesterton does. He understands her today and understood her in the past, during the years of bondage. Only an intuition that sprang from so great a heart and mind as his could span the abyss that exists at the time between fortunate free England and the tragically struggling Polish nation, which can be likened to "the Man in Green" in that it loved its country even at the moment of its greatest downfall. When we fought for and won our independence, Chesterton always stood with us, a staunch friend, wielding his pen for our cause and branding our bondage as an historical crime. By placing the fervour of religious faith, love of truth, concreteness of life as well as the courage to defend these truths above all things, he at once named those which have constituted and constitute the foundation of the Polish spirit.

This has brought it about that, alongside of Conrad, Chesterton today is our most popular English writer. Just as he found a deep spiritual relationship in us, so have we found it in the heart of the author of "The Ballad of the White Horse." This explains why each of his books has been received by us with especial enthusiasm. For our love for the great English writer is based not

245

upon esteem and admiration alone, but upon a deep spiritual and mental kinship.

And this enables us to extend an exceptionally hearty welcome to a great poet and friend . . .

The tour involved a series of lectures, meetings and meals. The meals were, in the best Slavonic tradition, long and full; a delight to Gilbert but something of a chore to the frail Frances. The speeches were equally long, full of praise and flattery. The Poles were surprisingly knowledgeable of Gilbert's work, and as is so often the case with a people who are not given books and magazines on a free and easy basis, they savoured and relished every word they could find. During his visit copies of his book were sold on a virtual black market for extremely high prices – his publishers had no idea of his popularity outside the English-speaking world. Gilbert seemed to make an impression on most of the Polish men of letters he met on the visit. Dr Adam Zielinski was a student of law at King John Casimir University at the time, and since he had some knowledge of English was asked to introduce Gilbert at a meeting of the local Literary Circle. The heat was terrible, with Gilbert visibly affected by the stifling weather. He was asked if such heat made him sweat, and replied that "Only horses sweat. Men perspire and ladies bloom." It was a harmless, not particularly memorable, response but such was Gilbert's charisma, and so great was the impression he made on his Polish hosts, that that simple answer has left its mark for sixty years.

The effect was reciprocal. Poland now became an obsession. In his *Autobiography* Gilbert writes with passion about the country and the people, recalling being "honoured" and stressing the nobility of the Poles. He remembered one incident with special delight

I was driving with a Polish lady, who was very witty and well-acquainted with the whole character of Europe, and also of England (as is the barbarous habit of Slavs); and I only noticed that her tone changed, if anything to a sort of coolness, as we stopped outside an archway leading to a side-street, and she said: "We can't drive in here." I wondered; for the gateway was wide and the street apparently open. As we walked under the arch, she said in the same colourless tone: "You take off your hat here." And then I saw the open street. It was filled with a vast crowd, all facing me; and all on their knees on the ground. It was as if someone were walking behind me; or some strange bird were hovering over my head. I faced round, and saw in the centre of the arch great windows standing open, unsealing a chamber full of gold and colours; there was a picture behind; but parts of the whole picture were moving like a puppet-show, stirring double memories like a dream of the bridge in the puppet-show of my childhood; and then I realised that from those shifting groups there shone and sounded the ancient magnificence of the Mass.

On 3rd May the National Festival of Poland, commemorating the Polish Constitution of 1791, was held. The entertainments were lavish, with the Chestertons being guests of one of Poland's élite and famous cavalry regiments. The party also travelled to Krakow, "even more the national city because it is not the capital," and there saw a performance of "Acropolis." Adam Harasowki, who now lives in Newark, England, met Gilbert during the visit.

The main Polish cities which G.K.C. visited were Warsaw, Poznan, Krakow, Lwow and Wilno, in that order. From Krakow he made an excursion to the salt mines of Wieliczka; he also visited the beautiful mountain resort of Zakopane in the Tatra mountains . . . . I remember being very nervous before meeting such a famous man as Chesterton and making my maiden speech of welcome. I need not have been, as from the word "go" he was very cordial, charming and extremely witty, with a strong sense of humour. I remember that he asked me (after my speech) what Polish word would be most useful for him to remember. I told him he must learn to say: "psia krew," which means "dog's blood" and is really a mild swear word, but it is used often to express anger, as well as surprise or admiration. All the students roared with laughter and Chesterton laughed with us. Mrs Chesterton did not laugh and was far less at ease during the rest of her stay in Lwow. Miss Collins was the ideal, super-efficient secretary . . . . I accompanied them everywhere during their two-and-a-half days' stay in Lwow. The highlight of it was a reception (on 19th May, 1927) at a club of local writers and artists, at which Chesterton was the guest of honour . . .

Gilbert's inscription in the Polish P.E.N. Club album was the ringing "If Poland had not been born again, all the Christian nations would have died." It was hyperbole, but also an honest indication of his love for the country. When he arrived in Britain he wrote an article for the *Illustrated London News* entitled "On Poland" in which he expressed his regard for the Polish people, his admiration of their bravery – he reminded his readers of the war of 1920 when the Poles defeated the stronger and larger Russian army – and the Christian nature of the Polish will to exist and survive. He wrote and lectured, debated and pleaded the case for Poland. He did not live to see the German rape of the country, and the Soviet smashing of it; that is probably for the best. Although even then, Gilbert may have been the only man to confidently predict the rise of Solidarity some time in the future.

X

Best of Enemies, Best of Friends

Gilbert clung to friendships, aspired to them, all his life. It was as though they were spiritual and intellectual lifelines to him, providing an opportunity for stimulation and succour. This had shown itself as early as the appearance of Cecil Chesterton, and later in Gilbert's alacrity in accepting so much – and so much nonsense – in what Belloc said. It was Gilbert's incredulity, not his credulity, which was the crux of his genius. How astounding it was then that he should accept so readily the polemics of those he perceived as friends! Part of this was due to his modesty; a harsher description would be insecurity. He could never quite believe in his own brilliance, but would frequently believe in the brilliance of others. It was what made him so likeable, and so easily exploited.

The most curious bond which developed in Gilbert's life was with George Bernard Shaw. It was curious because it was unlikely, as unlikely as two opposing champions clawing through their animosity to embrace and respect each other. It was unlikely, and it was good. They met for the first time in Paris in 1901. Lucien Oldershaw had taken Gilbert to visit Auguste Rodin, that doyen of late-nineteenth-century sculptors whose famous work, "The Kiss," had at this point been captivating the artistic communities of Europe for fifteen years. He was now sixty-one, but still an imposing figure and an approachable man. It was not, however, the venerable Frenchman who attracted Gilbert's interest, but his model on that occasion. Shaw was posed in perfect subject form, and remained so while he lectured Gilbert on the theme of the Salvation Army. Shaw was forty-five years old, Gilbert twenty-seven. Their relationship had just been born.

Shaw would come to forget the initial meeting, recalling only a letter he wrote to Gilbert after reading one of his reviews in the *Daily News*. He wanted to know "who he was and where he came from," but received no reply from the overworked and overmodest young journalist. When the friendship did blossom it occupied both men's time and thoughts to a considerable degree. "My principal experience, from first to last," wrote Gilbert, "has been in argument with him. And it is worth remarking that I have learned to have a warmer admiration and affection out of all that argument than most people get out of agreement. Bernard Shaw, unlike some whom I have had to consider here, is seen at his best when he is wrong. Or rather, everything is wrong about him except himself." As for Shaw, he never doubted his own righteousness, and never doubted Gilbert's good-hearted, brilliant, witty, invincible ignorance.

After only two years of the friendship Gilbert agreed to write a biography of his kindest enemy for his publisher, and enemy he most certainly was: Shaw the Fabian socialist, Shaw the atheist, Shaw the vegetarian and eschewer of alcohol, Shaw the thin. They wrote and met, seldom agreeing and never hating. In February 1908 Shaw wrote a piece in the *New Age* entitled "The Chesterbelloc." It analysed H.G. Wells as well as Gilbert and Belloc, alleging that Gilbert was plain French on his mother's side, and Belloc was determined not to be an Englishman. Together, and they could not be considered as separate entities, they were a conspiracy, a pantomime spectacle, the Chester-Belloc. "To set yourself against the Chesterbelloc" he wrote, "is not merely to be unpatriotic, like setting yourself against the *Daily Mail* or *Express:* it is to set yourself against all the forces ... of humanity." The Chesterbelloc pained him, because he saw in it those very qualities – goodness, democracy, authentic Christianity – which he coveted, and never genuinely understood.

Part of this attack was a plan, a scheme to dissuade Gilbert from writing Shaw's biography, and provoking him into composing a play which Shaw had discussed with him some time earlier. There was, of course, more to it than that, including a growing antipathy towards Belloc. In March 1908 Shaw wrote to Gilbert

> My dear G. K. C.,
> What about that play? It's no use trying to answer me in the New Age: The real answer to my article is the play. I have tried fair means: The New Age article was the inauguration of an assault below the belt. I shall deliberately destroy your credit as an essayist, as a journalist, as a critic, as a liberal, as everything that offers your laziness a refuge, until starvation and shame drive you to serious dramatic parturition. I shall repeat my public challenge to you: vaunt my superiority: insult your corpulence, lecture Bellow, if necessary, call on you and steal your wife's affections by intellectual and athletic displays, until you contribute something to the British drama. You are played out as an essayist: your ardour is soddened, your intellectual substance crumbled . . . . Another five years of this and you will be the apologist of every infamy that wears a Liberal or Catholic mask.

Gilbert wrote the biography. It was published in August 1909 by John Lane. In the Introduction Gilbert wrote: "Most people either say that they agree with Bernard Shaw or that they do not understand him. I am the only person who understands him, and I do not agree with him." The book was more an analysis of Shavian ideas and ideals than a life of a man. That was typical of Gilbert's biographical aspirations. He saw Shaw as the "greatest of modern Puritans and perhaps the last," and thought that it was "because he is quick-witted that he is long-winded." It was full of the brief, excoriating and wonderfully perceptive remarks which Gilbert's readers now expected. He didn't so much blacken white sepulchres, as tone down one or two red ones. Shaw, he wrote, would "lure his enemy on with fantasies and then overwhelm him with facts;" and that "the truth is that the very rapidity of such a man's mind makes him seem slow in getting to the point;" and that Shaw disapproved of murder "not so much because it wastes the life of the corpse, as because it wastes the time of the murderer."

Shaw reviewed the book in *The Nation*. Gilbert knew that he would; and so did he. "This book is what everybody expected it to be" he wrote, "the best work of literary art I have yet provoked .... Everything about me which Mr. Chesterton had to divine, he divined miraculously. But everything that he could have ascertained easily by reading my own plain directions on the bottle, as it were, remains for him a muddled and painful problem solved by a comically wrong guess." He was hurt. Not by the intensity of the attack — there had been worse in the past — but because an arrow from Gilbert was an arrow which could pierce that contrived shell of Bernard Shaw. Gilbert was aware of the fact, and wrote with some haste to Shaw, hoping to confirm that their "recent tournaments" had not damaged their friendship. It probably had. There would now be a certain guarded flavour in Shaw's attitude towards Gilbert; the door was still open, but the handle was never very far from reach.

Shaw attempted to drown his reluctance in a tidal wave of enthusiasm. He composed a scenario for the still-unwritten play of Gilbert's, dealing with the return of St. Augustine to England. Again, Gilbert refused to put pen to paper. Shaw's enthusiasm for the enterprise was double-edged. He wanted a companion dramatist, and genuinely considered Gilbert to be a literary talent of the highest calibre, although, of course he thought he was better, and this could only be proven by the comparison of two like forms: play to play. If Shaw knew this, Gilbert did as well. Shaw offered to drive to Beaconsfield to help with the opening scenes. Gilbert replied that when the scenes would open, they would open on their own.

The essence of their argument revolved around their personalities: where Gilbert parried and teased, Shaw lunged and cut deep; where Gilbert talked and laughed for conversation's sake, Shaw only ever did things for a pre-arranged purpose. It was the difference between the academic and the practical, between the rolling downs and the industrial cities. Shaw could only see pain and poverty and peasants in the history of Europe, and looked forward to an age of social engineering and constant human improvement. Gilbert, of course, saw no uninterrupted line of advancement of species through the ages, and relied on things past for spiritual guidance. Gregory Macdonald described how the two men seemed to coruscate when they met, how a packed room would appear to become empty but for them when they entered it. Their conflict and their friendship was seen as a tryst, both by Shaw and Gilbert, and by their supporters. London followed them. England followed them. The uninitiated recoiled at some of the dialogue and correspondence between the men, certain that one or other had gone too far. Their fears were not grounded.

Wrote Gilbert in his Shaw biography

I hear many people complain that Bernard Shaw mystifies them. I cannot imagine what they mean; it seems to me that he deliberately insults them. His language, especially on moral questions, is generally as straight and solid as that of a bargee and far less ornate and symbolic than that of a hansom-cabman. The prosperous English Philistine complains that Mr Shaw is making a fool of him. Whereas Mr Shaw is not in the least making a fool of him, Mr Shaw is, with laborious lucidity, calling him a fool. G. B. S. calls a landlord a thief; and the landlord, instead of denying or resenting it, says "Ah, that fellow hides his meaning so cleverly that one can never make out what he means, it is all so fine spun and fantastical." G. B. S. calls a statesman a liar to his face, and the statesman cries in a kind of ecstasy, "Ah, what quaint, intricate and half tangled trains of thought! Ah, what elusive and many coloured mysteries of half meaning!" I think it always quite plain what Mr Shaw means, even when he is joking, and it generally means that the people he is talking to ought to howl aloud for their sins. But the average representative of them undoubtedly treats the Shavian meaning as tricky and complex when it is really direct and offensive. He always accuses Shaw of pulling his leg, at the exact moment when Shaw is pulling his nose.

For "nose" it might perhaps be more accurate to read "noose." When Shaw wanted to be deadly, he was. His debating skills were fine-tuned, rehearsed and practised at Fabian

253

Society meetings and in front of mirrors. He thought on his feet at least as well as he thought at his writing desk. He took pride in what he saw as the traditional, almost atavistic, gift of the gab. Oratory was not a mere annex of the written skills, it was a separate discipline in itself. He revelled in the atmosphere of the debate, the appreciation of the victory, and the vanquishing of the defeated. Gilbert was the amateur incarnate. Frequently late, invariably badly organised and with poorly documented notes, he enjoyed debate as the diarist relishes his nightly sojourns into writing. On one occasion he turned to face an audience with his trouser buttons undone, on another a period chair collapsed under his weight. Vincent Brome described him as

> ... puffing and blowing like a distressed whale, hopelessly late and not altogether repentant. Not infrequently he started by saying he had not prepared the lecture and sometimes ran off into tiresome generalities .... He made far too many jokes about his size, but certainly it deserved some mention since he towered over other men and achieved a Falstaffian girth no one had ever dared to measure. His voice was high and not very penetrating. Given a microphone he sometimes thrust his notes between himself and the microphone, successfully muffling it ...

The two men debated for the first time in 1911, at The Heretics Club in Cambridge. It was to set the pattern for the Shaw-Chesterton meetings: brilliant, confused and confusing, bitingly amusing, and with no palpable results. A great deal of mythology developed around and about these verbal exchanges. Gilbert did not, as had been thought by some chroniclers of the debates with drunken imaginations if not drunken minds, accuse Shaw of "being sober," and neither was ink thrown behind the curtains of the stage. For both men the sense of anticipation and verbal battle was all the excitement necessary. Religion always figured, usually largely, sometimes only in passing. Shaw knew that Gilbert did not like his own faith being attacked, and Gilbert knew that Shaw did not like being accused of having any religious faith at all. Hence it was of no surprise that Shaw began his cannonade with the statement that religion was of little interest to any serious Heretic. The Heretic, he said, was a man with "a home-made religion," and was safe and reliable. The danger in society were the masses, who believed any religious instruction they were given, and had to be carefully watched.

Gilbert's reply reflected what he had written in 1905, in his book *Heretics*. It was his belief that heresy was facile, whimsical, even cowardly. Orthodoxy demanded courage, the courage to appear to be unfashionable. In times past it was perceived as egregious to be a heretic, whereas in the contemporary world men proudly wore the description, relishing its "dangerous and progressive" connotations. He had devoted an entire chapter in *Heretics* to Bernard Shaw, arguing that

Mr Shaw's old and recognised philosophy was that powerfully presented in "The Quintessence of Ibsenism." It was, in brief, that conservative ideals were bad, not because they were conservative, but because they were ideals. Every ideal prevented men from judging justly the particular case; every moral generalisation oppressed the individual; the golden rule was there was no golden rule. And the objection to this is simply that it pretends to free men, but really restrains them from doing the only thing that men want to do.

At Cambridge he decided to interpret Shaw literally so as to demonstrate the ridiculous aspects of his argument. It was an insipid method of argument, one to which Gilbert turned only when profoundly upset by an opponent, or somewhat frightened of him. So Shaw thought that heretics were those people who "found a machine such as a motor car" and transformed it into something completely different, Gilbert explained. He declared his confusion. He had no objection, he said, to people changing machines, but "strongly objected to their finding a bicycle, turning it into a sewing machine and then trying to ride the sewing machine." Shaw responded that Gilbert was deliberately missing the point, and that the only

255

plausible system of religion – if indeed one was required at all, which he doubted – would be one in which God, or god, could be completely understood by his followers. He went on to proclaim that an agnostic was simply an atheist without the courage of his convictions, and that the only practical consequence of a divinity was the evolution of a moral system or network, which could, and he emphasised "could," be of benefit to the people. He continued that the discussion was quite academic, even irrelevant, because God was a direct product of the ignorance of medieval superstition and ignorance, and no such hypothesis was needed in the modern age, when science provided solutions to the long unanswered problems of where, why and when. Gilbert's simple riposte was to state that "He would emulate Shaw's blasphemy, because he thought it was an easy game . . . . if ever God died it was in the middle of the eighteenth century. It now remained for Mr Shaw to explain why God had risen from the dead." Shaw, of course, did nothing of the sort. Gilbert, of course, had not expected nothing of the sort. The meeting terminated in a good deal of hand-shaking, back-slapping and mutual congratulations. Gilbert gripped Shaw's arm and told him he argued well for a Puritan; Shaw grasped Gilbert's hand and told him that it was enough that he, Gilbert, argued at all, considering he was an orthodox Christian.

The popularity of the encounter surprised the protagonists, and provided a focal point for the increasingly polarised literary community. Another challenge was proposed. Shaw wrote to Gilbert

With reference to this silly debate of ours, what you have to bear in mind is this. I am prepared to accept any conditions. If they seem unfair to me from the front of he house, all the better for me; therefore do not give me that advantage unless you wish to, or are – as you probably are – as indifferent to rules as I am. . . . Did you see my letter in Tuesday's *Times*? Magnificent! My love to Winkle [the Chesterton's dog]. To hell with the Pope!

They dined together on a regular basis. Their conversations were long, loud and rambling. One lunch-time conversation was recorded:

SHAW: I'm a likeable old rascal you know – but you really must stop poisoning my mind with all these heresies about God. Otherwise I shall really have to go for you.

GILBERT: It's your intellectual magnanimity which destroys me. If only you were a nasty fellow who lost his temper.

SHAW: Have you ever lost yours?

GILBERT: I've searched hard and long. It just doesn't seem to be there.

SHAW: Then for God's sake cultivate one. You'll never win an argument with me until you're raving – plain, mad, bull-at-a-gate raving – with temper.

They argued about the war, with no tangible result. Shaw thought it useless for anybody to argue with him about 1914: "You might as well differ from the Almighty about the orbit of the sun." Their clash over the war, combined with Gilbert's illness in the early months of it, placed a strain on the relationship. Both men were too busy working and writing on other matters to spend very much time on each other. Contact resumed in the 1920s, and in 1927 came the famous and long-awaited debate at Kingsway Hall. Gilbert was editor of *G. K.'s Weekly,* Shaw was at the pinnacle of his reputation as writer and provocateur. Shaw was concerned that the meeting be properly organised, aware that The Distributist League was notoriously inefficient at such arrangements. "Nothing must be left to well intentioned Godforsaken idiots who have no experience or organising power," he wrote, "and to believe that public meetings are a national phenomena that look after themselves." Gilbert's Distributists and Shaw's Fabian socialists began their propaganda onslaught, encouraging members and supporters to attend the meeting and offer vocal and moral support. This was to be a clash of champions.

It is difficult in today's society of immediate gratification and the electronic media to properly comprehend the atmosphere of anticipation which existed in the weeks before the "Great Debate." Radio had only existed for a relatively short period of time; moving pictures were similarly immature. Politicians could still attract thousands to their meetings – a little over a generation earlier, British Prime Minister William Gladstone had spoken to hundreds of thousands during an election tour – and the author fulfilled the role of intellectual, star, entertainer and politician. Not all of London prepared itself for the event, but all of London that cared about ideas and ideals most certainly did. Shaw would proclaim at the beginning of the debate that "Some of you might reasonably wonder, if we agree, what we are going to talk about, but I suspect that you do not really care much what we debate . . . provided we entertain you by talking in our characteristic manners." There was an element of truth in the statement. What the two men said was interesting, the way they said it was intriguing.

William Titterton, knight-in-waiting of Distributism and its journals, had actively pursued the debate for months. He believed that Gilbert's triumph would be the triumph of Distributism over socialism, whereas Shaw always thought that Distributism was merely an aspect of socialism. The debate's title was Titterton's idea, with a little help from Gilbert. Because of Titterton's earlier involvement and inherent partiality, it was agreed that another should do most of the organisation. The task was given to Gregory Macdonald. He was a young man. Shaw was a massively forward man. Shaw took over virtually everything. It was Macdonald who had the inspired idea of asking the BBC to broadcast the debate, making it the first important aired debate in history. Shaw insisted on the BBC paying a large fee – he wanted at least one hundred pounds – and took control of advertising and ticket sales. The demand for tickets was unexpectedly high, and as they were not numbered Shaw rather pettily placed stewards at the doors to check each entrant. His action bore fruit; such was the passion and the numbers of those seeking to witness the debate that the doors had to be locked and guarded, and some windows were smashed as the unfortunate outsiders shouted "Stop the debate!" By the time the debate began, with the BBC listening in and the crowd busily arguing amongst itself and hoping that the doors of the building would take the weight of dozens of zealous intellectuals, the scene resembled a gladiatorial carnival more than a gentle weighing of concepts.

Shaw had very reasonably agreed that Hilaire Belloc chair the meeting, partly to demonstrate his trust in Gilbert, partly to display his confidence in victory. Gilbert was at ease, complacent rather than confident. He insisted on enjoying such events, always seeing the humour in two grown men arguing with each other in public. During one contest he laughed so hard and for so long that he gave himself chronic hiccups for the entire evening. Both men, however, were influenced by the tension present, and it took the sardonic Belloc to diffuse the situation. "I am here to take the chair in the debate between two men whom you desire to hear more than you could possibly desire to hear me," he announced in his portentous but authoritative tones, still sitting in his chair. "They will debate whether they agree or do not agree .... There is a prospect of a very pretty fight .... You are about to listen, I am about to sneer." Shaw quickly took the initiative, asking Gilbert about the distribution of wealth. "If you take two shillings as your share and another man wants two shillings and sixpence, kill him .... If a man accepts two shillings when you have two shillings and sixpence, kill him. Do you agree?" Gilbert paused, smiled, turned toward the audience and said, "The answer is in the negative." The crowd laughed. The debate had truly begun.

Shaw decided to lead with the socialist case. He dismissed any discussion of nationalisation, of state control over production and exchange; instead he concentrated on the distribution of wealth. "The other day a man died and the Government took four and a half million pounds as death duty on his property. That man made all his money by the labour of men who received twenty-six shillings a week after years of qualifying for their work. Was that a reasonable distribution of wealth? We are all coming to the opinion that it was not reasonable." Gilbert agreed, but wondered why Shaw avoided the consequential question: who should then own the wealth? If the state owned it, the state benefited. The state did not mean the people; it could mean many things, but not the people. He preferred that the "Commons" own wealth and the means of production. "It is not my fault if Mr Shaw has remained young, while I have grown in comparison wrinkled and haggard, old and experienced and acquainted with the elementary facts of life," he humourously stated, employing his notes as a stage prop. He emphasised that a centralised machine owning the means of production and distribution was a potential danger, and in a typically Chestertonian example of forward thinking anticipated the obscenities of social engineering, be they in Hitler's Germany, Stalin's Russia or Communist Cambodia. Shaw's mind was set on narrow collectivism, Gilbert's on liberating devolution.

The two men pounced on the issue of power. Shaw defined it, Gilbert dissected it. Shaw used his umbrella as an example of the limitations of power. "I cannot do as I like with it," he explained with a gesture full of mischief. "For instance certain passages in Mr Chesterton's speech tempted me to get and smite him over the head with my umbrella." He would not, and could not, he said, because there were restrictions upon individual actions, in this case possibly "Mr Belloc's fist." A landlord, on the other hand, could do whatever he liked whenever he liked with his land. Gilbert accused Shaw of propagating fallacies. The real reason why Shaw did not hit him over the head was not because his ownership of the umbrella had certain limitations, but because he did not "own my head." The audience broke into long applause and laughter.

Halfway through the evening Gilbert began to tire. He had lost some of the verve and sheer effervescence which he possessed so abundantly in earlier years. Belloc was aware of this, and his frequent interpolations were in part attempts to rescue his friend and ally. When Belloc was not abusing Shaw or altering the theme of the discussion, he offered penetrating remarks, brilliant in their clarity and incisiveness. He was, however, the neutral chairman of the meeting, and had to be reminded of the fact. Gilbert went on, refusing to lose a round to his nimble opponent. The audience were by now partisan to a man, and cheered their doyens with gusto.

The subject became coal, coal mines, and the nationalisation of the coal industry. Then, as now, the question held both political and emotional value. The coal miners were seen as the vanguard of the working classes, the toil of the miner as the hardest and most proletarian of all trades. Again – then as now – there was a considerable amount of mythology and romanticism about the entire issue. Shaw alleged that Gilbert and his Distributists had called for the nationalisation of coal. This, he purported, was where their argument about socialism and Distributism being separate and distinct dissolved. Could they advocate that the miner's means of production be made his own property? Of course not. It would not be possible, and it would not be required by the miners themselves. He continued: "Under the present capitalistic system the owner has to surrender control to the manager. Under socialism he would have to surrender control to the manager appointed by the Coal Master General. That would not prevent the product of the mine being equally distributed among the people."

Gilbert prepared to make his reply, but in the middle of taking a breath Shaw interrupted him, and continued with his own invective. "Now that Mr Chesterton agrees that the coal mines will have to be nationalised he will be led by the same pressure of facts to the nationalisation of everything else." Gilbert smiled, the audience followed his example. Shaw argued that coal could not be an exception to the general argument, and was essential to both the socialist and the Distributist case. Gilbert waited for Shaw to finish his piece, glanced at him, turned to his supporters in the crowd, and with a gesture indicating inevitable acceptance explained that of course the coal industry was an exception, and that the Distributists were pragmatic in their approach and understood that intransigence was an enemy to progress, not a friend. They would bring coal into state ownership in the same way as they would centralise the design, production and distribution of postage stamps.

Shaw again asked the rhetorical question of why the coal mines were an exception, and again rushed through to his peroration before Gilbert had an opportunity to make his point. The mines were not equally productive, yet people were charged the price of coal according to the cost of mining in the most difficult areas. In the northeast of England coal was relatively cheap to produce, yet in pits in other areas, long, deep tunnels had to be painstakingly and dangerously constructed, making the coal extremely expensive. "Mr Chesterton in arriving at the necessity for the nationalisation of the coal mines has started on his journey towards the nationalisation of all industries," Shaw claimed. "If he goes on to the land and from the land to the factory and from there to every other industrial department, he will find that every successive case is an exception."

He then tackled Gilbert's theory that the British people possessed an instinctive desire to own their own property and live in their own homes. Gilbert's theory was in fact just that. His experience of the "people" was limited, even though he was ostentatiously proud of empathising with their will. He was, however, correct in assuming that home ownership was a natural and inevitable aspiration, as policy and events have demonstrated in Britain. Gilbert's instincts were often reliable. His biographies relied more on inner feelings than intricate research, and were much the better for it. Shaw based his ideas on the experience of looking down upon to learn, rather than trying to stand alongside with and be taught. "People are content to live in houses they do not own," he said. "When they possess them they often find them a great nuisance." And even if they did hang on to such a notion, they could be educated into not wanting property. It was an ominous statement, and would be put into practice with horrible and futile results in generations to come.

Gilbert was annoyed at the idea, outraged by its communal and non-human implications. "We are trying to deal with human beings," he argued, "creatures quite outside the purview of Mr Shaw and his political philosophy. We know town people are different from country people. We know man's irrepressible desire to own property and because some landlords have been cruel, it is no use talking of abolishing, denying, and destroying property." He concluded his contribution to the debate with: "Mr Shaw said that men and women are the only means of production . . . . I quite accept the parallel. His proposition is that the government, the officials, of the State, should own the men and women, in other words that the men and women should become slaves." And so the evening ended. The standing ovation which the two men received was genuine and spontaneous, the newspaper reports following the meeting told of a cathartic, important collision of politics, philosophy and religion. Who was the winner? If anyone won the contest it was Hilaire Belloc, with his impromptu remarks and out-of-place but stimulating and penetrating comments. Gilbert and Shaw shook hands, laughed at something they whispered to each other, and left the stage.

Their friendship continued right up until the end, until Gilbert's death. They met regularly during the 1930s, and maintained a healthy correspondence. After 1936 Shaw remained in contact with Frances, offering her financial and moral support, and visiting Top Meadow to dine and even pay homage. Shaw would mention and refer to Gilbert for many years to come, lamenting his friend's passing as late as the year of his own death, 1950. In *Heretics* Gilbert wrote that Shaw's friends "depict him as a strenuous man of action; his opponents depict him as a coarse man of business; when, as a fact, he is neither one nor the other, but an admirable romantic orator and romantic actor. . . ." It was the romantic in Shaw which Gilbert always drew forth, and it was for that reason that Shaw was so grateful to his contemporary. Romance was as deep in his socialistic, atheistic soul as it was in Gilbert's; it simply took a kindred spirit to release it.

XI

But We Will End with a Bang

The Britain to which he returned was in dire need of a new spirit, a new dynamism and a new leader. To Gilbert's friends Distributism would provide the first two qualities, and would certainly produce the third given time. His own experiences in Poland had only strengthened his belief in the philosophy. He failed to see that apart from the early fathers of the movement, few people were remaining faithful to the League and its purpose. A great many people passed through the ranks, and left after a relatively short period of commitment. In terms of numbers there was no dramatic change in support from beginning to end, and a danger signal was noticed in that a large proportion of eccentrics were becoming attracted. As an "alternative" to the mainstream idea in society, Distributism, like any movement of its kind, would inevitably appeal to the isolated and the searcher. The difference with the League was that this type of person was welcomed, and encouraged. Another problem was that by its very essence the movement opposed too much central authority, resulting in a divergence of views from north to south, east to west. There are many ideologies hiding under the cloak of Distributism.

Gilbert was still writing busily, enjoying the cut and thrust of the debates which went on, and revelling in the camaraderie of the organisation. He was worshipped, and modest as he was that still pleased him to a large degree. It took his mind away from the absurd arguments which were so common inside the League, mostly concerned with tedious matters of intricate policy or bureaucracy. Interviewed by the *Observer* after the appearance of the 500th number of *G.K.'s Weekly,* he was still as enthusiastic as ever

We look like a crank paper . . . when, as a matter of fact, ours is the only paper which isn't cranky. The great papers, like The Observer and The Times, are the faintest little bit cranky – that is to say, they go off on some modern notion and get a little bit out of proportion; as for the ordinary vulgar Press, it is not only cranky but crazy. It has got completely out of touch with reality.

Heaven knows why, but I am an editor. I am a very bad editor, I was never meant to be an editor; but I am the editor of the only paper in England which is devoted to what is a perfectly normal idea – private property.

Most modern property isn't private, and ordinary capitalism makes it even less private if possible than ordinary communism. The system under which we live today is one of huge commercial combinations in which property isn't private, and the system under which we may live tomorrow – God forbid, still it may happen – will be one of Bolshevik organisation in which also property would not be private. What we mean by private property is that as many people as possible should own the means of production; the ground in which to dig, the spade with which to dig, the roof under which to sleep at night, the tools and machinery of production should belong to as many separate individuals as possible.

There is a case for communism; there is even a case for capitalism; but they are both cases against private property. They both mean that it is not a good thing that separate men should own separate farms, and separate shops, but that all should be linked together in one great machine, whether it be a communist State or capitalist business.

Within a certain limited area a man should possess something by which he asserts the difference between man and matter, that man is the master of matter; not mankind, but man. Within that area individual man should decide, and not the manager or the commissar.

And there is no other paper representing that ordinary point of view. You cannot take away from the ordinary man the sense that he is more dignified when he is free, when he has no master but God. And what we complain of is that in England – it is different in other countries – no one is given even a glimpse of that idea.

When asked about the achievements of Distributism Gilbert referred the interviewer to the writings of Hilaire Belloc, and informed him that the transformation to Distributism would be conducted on a constitutional basis, not by bloody revolution. There is no sense of reality in his answers; he expounds his philosophy with consummate skill and charm, but can envisage no obstacle, does not have any doubts as to its success. Such an attitude smacks of one thing: extremism. On this one issue Gilbert would not hear a counterargument. He continued in the article

> . . . we are the only revolutionary paper, in that where the capitalist and the communist agree we disagree. Where both the capitalist and the communist submit we revolt.
>
> We have had ten years of struggle to keep the paper going, with a fine staff and no capital. We have a good circulation for our sort of paper, but we can't get out of the habit of appealing to the intelligence of the human race. That is perhaps where I am old-fashioned; I am that most antiquated of things, a Radical, an ordinary nineteenth-century Liberal, and I have grown old in the delusion that my fellow creatures are rational as well as myself. I am afraid I can't start regarding them as a race of morons or nit-wits; I shall go to my grave believing that if I meet an ordinary sane man he will agree that two and two make four . . .

The year 1927 was a particularly busy and ambitious one for Gilbert, much to the chagrin of Frances and his closer friends. He received letters from people who had read or seen him, but whom he'd never actually met, asking that he take care of his health and perhaps take a sabbatical. Fellow writers suggested that it was preferable for Gilbert to concentrate on longevity and a steady flow of publication, rather than tire himself in an effort to produce as many works as possible in a single year. It was as though he envisaged an early grave, and felt the inexorable need to write all he could, whenever he could. Guests would be asked to excuse him as he left them to add just a few paragraphs to his current book or essay. Frances perceived in Gilbert a fear, an awareness that he had yet to do his best work. Her protestations were in vain, her tears provoked consolation and sympathy, but no change in life-style. She asked him not to work so hard on his play *The Judgement of Dr Johnson,* but to have stopped working at this stage would have been to deny everything that he did, and hoped to, represent. The drama ran for six performances at the Arts Theatre Club. It depicted Dr Samuel Johnson, through the favourable eyes of the author, and fulfilled a long-standing ambition. Gilbert exhibited a childlike glee throughout the run, and was to be seen pacing the floor during the opening night, resembling a neophyte producer or playwright anxious that his child should do, and be seen to do, well. He confided to friends that he would have relished performing the role himself on the stage.

In addition to the play, Gilbert also published three major volumes that year. *The Secret of Father Brown* appeared in September, much to the delight of the priest's devotees, who complained that their hero should come to life more frequently. The book was dedicated to Father John O'Connor, "Whose truth is stranger than fiction, with a gratitude greater than the world." His writing of it had been disturbed by the noise of some building work taking place nearby. His secretary asked the foreman of the workers whether he was aware that the noise was so great that Mr Chesterton could not write. "Yes" replied the foreman, "we are quite aware of that." When Gilbert was told of the exchange he laughed, predicting a sparkling career for this master of repartee. For all the difficulties, the book received sanguine reviews, particularly because of its fuller treatment of Flambeau and the divergence of subject in its ten stories.

Gilbert's biography of Robert Louis Stevenson was to be the first in a series of *Intimate Biographies,* but the promised volumes on Napoleon and Savonarola failed to appear. Gilbert lacked distance from the subject of the book, writing with an overwhelming sense of gratitude for the service Stevenson had done him during those long, lonely days. The

267

book may have lacked impartiality, but it exhibited that congenital perception of character and motive which made almost all of Gilbert's biographical works shine. Sir Edmund Gosse wrote of it

> I have just finished reading the book in which you smite the detractors of R.L.S. hip and thigh. I cannot express without a sort of hyperbole the sentiments which you have awakened of joy, of satisfaction, of relief, of malicious and vindictive pleasure . . .
>
> It is and always since his death has been impossible for me to write anything which went below the surface of R.L.S. I loved him, and still love him, too tenderly to analyse him. But you, who have the privilege of not being dazzled by having known him, have taken the task into your strong competent hands. You could not have done it better.
>
> The latest survivor, the only survivor, of his little early circle of intimate friends thanks you from the bottom of his heart.

The review gave Gilbert more pleasure than almost any other comment on his works, and was a necessary point of support when his next volume was sent to the press.

The Return of Don Quixote was a futuristic fantasy, its qualities diminished by Gilbert's increasing determination to lapse into Catholic apologetics. Reviewers and critics noticed the trend, and insisted on pointing it out. The author was depressed by the book's indifferent reception, and sought solace in the company of friends, and in the comfort of his faith. He began to spend more time at Westminster Cathedral, and other worshippers from the time remember him being escorted along the busy road towards the church by two small boys, "like a huge galleon being guided by two tiny tugs." On one occasion he was stopped on Artillery Row, a nearby street, by two adoring members of the public. They passed the time of day. "You should be careful walking along this road you know," said one of the pair as they were about to part, "otherwise somebody might canonise you." This time

Gilbert did not laugh. He was beginning to suffer from brief but painful periods of depression, and Frances was acutely conscious of this. They took a holiday in the beautifully and quintessentially English Lyme Regis, staying at the Three Cups Hotel, their favourite haven. They were happy, content to be the stylised middle-aged couple walking by the sea. When they returned home, a selection of local children were invited to Top Meadow so as to brighten Gilbert's darker moments. The absence of children from the immediate Chesterton family continued to provoke anguish and sorrow. Gilbert coped with the pain with more stoicism than his wife, as active as ever in the dramas and games of the town's young people. Frances tended to say little, and look on.

In 1928 Gilbert was fifty-four years old. In spite of his size and diminishing health, he retained his youthful appearance, with a fine head of hair, always with its unruly curls and youthful fullness. His countenance was invariably fresh and optimistic, his stance erect and invitingly carefree. In some areas, however, the years had taken their toll. His breathing was at times difficult and even painful, and long speeches became more of a chore than a pleasure; depending on gradients, walking could tire Gilbert for hours, sometimes days, and his capacity to talk and work long into the night was severely curtailed. A Polish academic visiting London made a special effort to meet Gilbert, and finally managed to track him down. The two men were introduced, and evidently shared a number of loves and concerns. But Gilbert tired of the conversation quickly, and finally interrupted a point he was making long before its conclusion with a wave of his hand, indicating that his breath was short and speech was a problem. The gesticulation resembled rudeness, but wasn't. It depicted a deeply sorry man, angry that he could not hold a conversation, frightened that what had once been so natural and facile, could now be so traumatic. Those of Gilbert's friends who thought that he was ignoring his ill health were poor judges of character in general, and of Gilbert's in particular. He was aware of what was happening to him, and equally aware that there was little he could do about it.

The only book published in 1928 was a collection of essays

from the *Illustrated London News* entitled *Generally Speaking*. It appeared in October, and confirmed Gilbert as the paramount essayist of his era. The essays showed that he was more, much more, than a writer of pithy, erudite articles. The staff and voluntary workers at *G. K.'s Weekly,* however, were in the front rank of those protesting that their doyen was a political philosopher and social critic, and that his essays were a mere annexe, something jejune and placid compared to his contemporary journalism. But it was they, with their petty financial squabbles and lapidary statements on policy and position, who restrained his ability and distracted him from nobler enterprises.

In 1929 no book of original writing appeared from Gilbert, only a volume of previously published short stories under the title *The Poet and the Lunatics.* The original pieces had been written to finance Gilbert's eponymous magazine, and the royalties and advances from the book made the same journey.

Later in the year the Chesterton family – for Dorothy Collins was by now considered a virtual daughter, and accompanied Gilbert and Frances on all their holidays and long journeys – organised a pilgrimage to Rome. The enterprise had long been planned, and combined the joys, and needs, of a holiday and a spiritual journey. They lived at the Hotel Hassler, looking down onto the Spanish Steps. They stayed for three months, and Gilbert managed to obtain a private audience with Pope Pius XI. He scrupulously avoided ever writing about the interview, but friends were aware of the state of activity and enthusiasm which he demonstrated for days after the meeting. He also met Benito Mussolini, who had still to begin his anti-Church campaign and was still perceived as a saviour by many Catholics, both in Italy and beyond.

Gilbert recorded his impressions of the stay, and his memories of the encounter with the Fascist leader, in *The Resurrection of Rome.* It was in every sense a product of its maker. Gilbert's frequent insistence on treading the middle road, even when that position was untenable, held the work up to criticism and accusations that its author was naïve, callow, even indifferent to other people's suffering. It was an ambivalent book. Gilbert had found Mussolini to be charming and charismatic, as he was. He also stressed that he would always "prefer English liberty to Latin discipline." His admiration for the new Italian leader was the admiration of a constructive lover of ancient Europe, for a destructive lover of ancient Europe.

If Gilbert was insufficiently analytical or critical of Mussolini's policy at home and abroad – and *G. K.'s Weekly* did support the invasion of Ethiopia – his sentiments were less egregious than the tangible adoration that many British and European socialists poured onto the former socialist editor and leader in Rome, and far less insidious than the tributes which came from Shaw and H.G. Wells and some of their Fabian comrades. The right was equally myopic. Belloc envisaged a united, Catholic Europe under a strong leader, and the rump of the traditional political parties in Britain gave similar backing. Gilbert the socialist only looked to the future, the conservative only to the past, but the Christian to the eternal. For him all answers were to be found in philosophies beyond the material. He was no politician.

While he was overseas *The Thing* was published in London by Sheed and Ward. It was sub-titled *Why I Am a Catholic* and consisted of thirty-five essays, all previously published in magazine or newspaper form. The book was appreciated by Gilbert's co-religionists – Belloc thought it his friend's best and most important book – but neglected by the secular world. It was in every sense a defence and a justification, a support for those who had been "pelted with insults" for their beliefs. In the tradition of *Orthodoxy* and *Heretics, The Thing* outlined Gilbert's attitude towards the church

It is enough to say that those who know the Catholic practice find it not only right when everything else is wrong; making the Confessional the very throne of candour where the world outside talks nonsense about it as a sort of conspiracy; upholding humility when everybody is praising pride; charged with sentimental charity when the world is loud and loose with vulgar sentimentalism – as it is today. At the place where the roads meet there is

271

no doubt of the convergence. A man may think of all sorts of things, most of them honest and many of them true, about the right way to turn in the maze at Hampton Court. But he does not think he is in the centre; he knows.

The book's publication was as important for Gilbert as it was for his readers. It was a cathartic exercise, an enforcing piece of intellectual stimulation. He needed to be reminded of his convictions and their accuracy, even if he "was convinced." He also needed the provocation of travel, and in the September of 1930 the Chestertons and Dorothy Collins embarked for Canada. They sailed on the White Star Line's SS *Doric,* and relished the elegant suite they were given and the space which the half-full ship provided them. Some of the finance for the holiday, or at least the feeling of financial security which hastened the trip, was provided by the publication of *Four Faultless Felons* in August. The Felons are in fact heroes, and they tell their tales to a sympathetic American journalist.

Of the stories in the book, most reflect Chestertonian social and political concerns, and do so with a refined style, but also with a wit and an appreciation which taste more of anger and bitterness than is usual with Gilbert's work. There is none of the exotic and blood-red flavour of Father Brown, more a reminder of things past, or earlier attempts at mystery and imagination. "The Honest Quack" deals with the arrogance of the scientific and the progressive, striking the chord of ecology before that chord was at all fashionable. "The Loyal Traitor" demonstrates the possibilities of benign journalism, and discusses the dangers of revolution. These two stories are the best offerings in the book, and its reviewers in the daily and weekly press gave it fairly short shrift.

On the voyage over to North America Gilbert recovered some of his zest for the smaller, more idiosyncratic things in life. He breakfasted early and began to take walks around the craft, announcing the joys of exercise in a self-mocking manner. He indulged in long conversations, dined well, and took part in the organised games on board. He also composed one of his own, conceiving a treasure hunt in which various clues, usually written or drawn on scraps of brown paper, were hidden in sometimes obvious, sometimes quite impossible places. The solution to the chase was found, but not the clues. The participants insisted on taking them; some for the purpose of remembering a notable day, others for a later sale and a tidy profit.

Gilbert made a speech on behalf of the Sailors' Charity Fund during the sailing, delighting the crew and passengers. He joined in the singing of songs, and took part in horse-racing games. Turbulent seas did not bother him unduly, as they did others on board. Frances noted that the 7.00 A.M. Mass was interrupted a quarter of the way through when the priest suddenly ran from the room to vomit over the side of the ship. She thought it a "great disappointment to the nuns who are on board." Gilbert continued his devotions in private, respectful of the sacrament of priesthood, but mindful of the humour of the situation.

When they arrived in Quebec there was little time to explore very much of the province, or to attempt to come to terms with the then highly Catholic area and its unique inhabitants. Gilbert was fascinated by this oasis of French-speaking, agriculturally based people in the massive bloc of English-speaking North America. He did, however, visit the monuments to Wolfe and Montcalm, and was moved by their respective sacrifices. He referred to General Wolfe as "that noble young man," and thought of his as the best of the British imperial tradition. In Montreal and Toronto enthusiastic audiences of over four thousand people greeted him as the best of the British literary tradition. He was speaking and working well, but Frances was tiring easily and beginning to bring her physically sympathetic husband down with her.

They moved on to Indiana and the University of Notre Dame. Gilbert had been invited to lecture to the students of the University for a six-week period on the subjects of Victorian history and literature. He was by this time in his life turning down the majority of the lecture offers which were proposed, finding the travel and organisation too much of a strain on his health and his home life. The appeal of the

273

American series was that all of the lectures took place in the same university, and hence his peripatetic past could be forgotten. He underestimated his own value, and other people's perception of it, in the United States. Lecture agent Lee Keedick managed to persuade him to undertake a tour, stressing that it would be short and the work load negligible. A more artful man than Gilbert would have realised that both claims could hardly have been true or else it would not have been worth Keedick's trouble to organise such a venture. When the Chestertons arrived at Notre Dame they also found that they were not even to be housed together, with Gilbert living in college rooms, and Frances having to go to the Infirmary, managed by nuns, because no women were allowed into the college itself. Frances was outraged, and Gilbert was incredulous. They refused to tolerate such circumstances, and insisted on alternative arrangements. These took the form of a stay with a family named Bixler who lived at South Bend, and with whom the Chestertons became good friends.

Gilbert's average working day on the tour was finely organised. He would write and rehearse during the day, sometimes writing one essay or book while dictating a second to Dorothy Collins and preparing notes for a third on rough paper. After tea, at around 4.00, he would go to a dinner, usually with local notables or with visiting Catholic or literary celebrities. He drank steadily throughout these meals, without harming his delivery at the evening lectures. At the weekend he would travel to neighbouring institutions to deliver more lectures, much to the annoyance of Frances. His travels took him to Illinois, Michigan and Wisconsin, and later to Ohio. At Notre Dame he delivered thirty-six lectures, to audiences of over five hundred people. On one night he would speak of nineteenth-century morality, on another, the imperialism of the Victorians, on still another, Dickens and his legacy. It was an exhausting itinerary, but one he relished. His ardour was reciprocated, and in November 1930 he was made an honorary doctor of law by the university. The same thing happened in New York, and in Pittsburgh and Philadelphia he was toasted as a "great man" of the century. Such was the success of the campaign that Gilbert was asked to extend his talks to the South and West. He agreed. After a rest period over Christmas and New Year's, he began 1931 with more engagements which took him to Vancouver, San Francisco and Portland. For those votaries who followed him from town to town, the remarkable aspect was that he appeared to alter the theme of his lecture each night. He would write later

My last American tour consisted of inflicting no less than ninety lectures on people who never did me any harm; and the remainder of the adventure, which was very enjoyable, breaks up like a dream into isolated incidents. An aged negro porter, with a face like a walnut, whom I discouraged from brushing my hat, and who rebuked me saying "Ho, young man. Yo's losing yo dignity before yo times. Yo's got to look nice for de girls." A grave messenger who came to me in a Los Angeles hotel, from a leading film magnate, wishing to arrange for my being photographed with the Twenty-four Bathing-Beauties, Leviathan among the Nereids, an offer which was declined amid general suprise. An agonising effort to be fair to the subtleties of the evolutionary controversy, in addressing the students of Notre Dame, Indiana, in a series on "Victorian Literature," of which no record remained except that one student wrote in the middle of his blank note-book, "Darwin did a lot of harm." I am not at all certain that he was wrong; but it was something of a simplification of my reasons for being agnostic about the agnostic deductions in the debates about Lamarck and Mendel. A debate about the history of religion with a very famous sceptic; who, when I tried to talk about Greek cults or Asiatic asceticism, appeared to be unable to think of anything except about Jonah and the Whale. But it is the curse of this comic career of lecturing that it seems to bring on the lighter stage nothing except comedies; and I have already said that I do not think America takes them any more seriously than I do . . .

Anxiety only broke into the proceedings on one occasion. In January, in Chattanooga, Frances was taken ill. Her health began to deteriorate, and after a few days of amateur nursing she was taken into hospital, under the supervision of two specialists. It appeared that she might not live, and Gilbert rushed back to her side. He had had to cancel lectures at the last moment, had lost his ticket, and had not slept in nights. It was pointed out to him that for each lecture cancellation he would have to pay compensation to Mr Keedick of £100. The cancellations were mounting up, and so were Gilbert's bills. The point of the tour had been to earn enough money to maintain *G. K.'s Weekly* and build enough savings for domestic stability. At this rate Gilbert would return to Britain both exhausted and poor. A recovering Frances urged him to continue the tour, with Dorothy as his guide and helper. Reluctantly, he did so. The lectures took him to California and back to New York. He was completely drained. By the time he arrived back in England he was once again an ill man, in dire need of rest and peace. British friends expecting a rejuvenated Gilbert Chesterton were shocked to greet such a worn figure. Frances blamed herself, Gilbert blamed nothing at all. More than that, he initiated another series of talks, speaking to the highly demanding Oxford Union in October. Dorothy Collins finally took matters into her own hands, cancelling short-term engagements. Ronald Knox was one of those disappointed. "It is so maddening," he wrote. "I shall begin to believe you have a down on me . . ."

With his *Illustrated London News* column still in great demand, Gilbert decided to publish a further collection of the pieces. It was titled *All Is Grist,* appeared in late October 1931, and reflected his increasing age and declining ebullience. Articles for *G. K.'s Weekly,* broadcasts for the BBC and occasional free-lance work kept him busy, but the crowning achievement of the period was the biography of Chaucer in early 1932. The subject suited Gilbert more appositely than almost any other. Here was the England of the Roman Church, the England of chivalry, the England of Gilbert's imagination. The idea of the book came originally from Richard de la Mare, the son of a famous father, who was employed by the publishers Faber and Faber. Gilbert received an advance payment of 1000 pounds, the highest of his career, and the writing of the book proved to be equally rewarding. It would be his final tribute to his England. Although the bulk of the Chaucer book was the result of some form of atavistic empathy, a natural disposition, there was still a great deal of research, writing and dictating to be done. By the time of its completion Gilbert's health was in a terrible state, and he was finding relaxation difficult. The Chestertons travelled across the Irish Sea to Dublin, to be present at the Eucharistic Congress in Dublin. The vocal support from the Irish people for the couple, and the comforting atmosphere of a mass meeting of kindred spirits went a little way to restoring Gilbert's mental ease. Physically however he was suffering and deteriorating.

Sidelights on New London and Newer York and *Christendom in Dublin,* based on the recent trip, appeared by the middle of 1932, and Gilbert was fighting his pain to appear on the BBC and speak to the Distributists, the Detective Club and a plethora of Catholic and literary societies. He once more broke down. Dorothy Collins, on holiday in France, wrote to Frances: "It seems almost inevitable that he should have these attacks at stated intervals. I suppose it is Nature's warning to him that he is not made of cast-iron and that he must be careful." It was increasingly apparent to increasingly large numbers of people that Gilbert's health had to break once and for all before too long.

Yet there was still a feeling that something was still to be done, to be achieved, to be finished. The tangible atmosphere of expectation and finality frightened Frances. In 1933 *All I Survey,* another collection of essays, appeared; this was surely not the final statement from such a man. With Hitler about to grip the once-stately, noble Germany by the throat, and Europe about to decay into dictatorial politics and fascistic remorse; and, to the East, with a murderous regime hiding in the obfuscation of social engineering, Chesterton let fly two more shots at the madmen who ran the asylum. The first was a biography of St Thomas Aquinas, that most stable and sensible of saints. If the rules and laws and philosophies of Aquinas had been followed, contemporaries said, the world would not be preparing for slaughter.

In a recent introduction to an American edition of the book Raymond Dennehy stated:

> There is praise and there is praise. It is one thing for a book to be widely praised by laymen, quite another thing for it to be praised by experts in the field and quite another thing yet for it to be praised by the members of both groups. Chesterton's book on Aquinas has not only earned the praise of laymen and expert alike but has also earned the praise of the expert's expert, the late Etienne Gilson, the greatest of all the historians of medieval thought. His studies on Thomas Aquinas are the benchmark for all subsequent Thomistic scholarship. After reading Chesterton's St Thomas Aquinas Gilson remarked: "For many years I have studied St Thomas and written on him and now a journalist writes a better book about him that I have." [Gilson continued] "I consider it as being without comparison the best book ever written on St Thomas. Nothing short of genius can account for such an achievement. Everybody will no doubt admit that it is a 'clever' book, but few readers who have spent twenty or thirty years in studying St Thomas Aquinas, and who, perhaps, have themselves, published two or three volumes on the subject, can fail to perceive the so-called 'wit' of Chesterton has put their scholarship to shame. He has guessed all that they had tried to demonstrate, and he has said all that which they were more or less clumsily attempting to express in academic formulas."

It is a deceptively simple book, relying, not on esoteric analysis and archaic nomenclature, but on strong, clean and sharp penetration of Aquinas and his works. Gilbert "understood" Aquinas, and when he was in such a position he found it relatively straightforward to convey such an understanding. He defends and explains St Thomas Aquinas's realism and common sense, the way in which he stressed the ultimate "goodness" of Christianity and its philosophy, and the link between Aquinas and contemporary Catholic thinking. Far from this being liberation theology, it was the liberating of theology. His approach to the actual writing of the book was delightful. He would break off from other writing and say to Dorothy Collins with a grin on his face, "Shall we do a bit of Tommy?" and then dictate to her and talk to himself. He asked his secretary to obtain some books on Aquinas to aid his research; she replied, quite naturally, that he would have to tell her which books he wanted. His reply? "I don't know." A letter to Father O'Connor resulted in a list of suggested reading, and a trip to London produced the books themselves. Gilbert barely looked at them, and the only mark he made was to draw a picture of Aquinas on one of the pages. There were elements of self-identification in the book. Here was St Thomas, "The Dumb Ox," a large, obese man who as a youngster was laughed at and thought to be stupid. It was a labour of love, a tribute to Aquinas and a tribute to Gilbert. As was usual, he set his subject firmly in the age from which he came.

> Thomas Aquinas, in a strange and rather symbolic manner, sprang out of the very centre of the civilised world of his time; the central knot or coil of the powers then controlling Christendom. He was closely connected with all of them; even with some of them that might well be described as destroying Christendom. The whole religious quarrel, the whole international quarrel, was for him a family quarrel. He was born in the purple; almost literally on the hem of the imperial purple; for his own cousin was the Holy Roman Emperor. He could have quartered half the kingdoms of Europe on his shield – if he had not thrown away the shield . . .

With what energy he had remaining Gilbert delivered some more broadcasts, eased his bulk onto the lecturing platform for the last few times, and then fired his last optimistic, sure, steadfast cannonade. *The Scandal of Father Brown* was published in 1935. It contains few of the thrusts and lunges of the earlier detective stories, and is surely the weakest of the collection. But its essence remains unchanged. Father Brown – unimposing, stoical, witty and wise – continues to tread his path and right other's wrongs. Both Gilbert and Frances's mothers were dead now, and the lustre of younger days had somehow been misplaced down the years; or was it lost? They were happy together, and content. Gilbert continued to work on his autobiography, which was to be published after his death. He concluded it thus

> The story, therefore, can only end as any detective story should end with its own particular questions answered and its own primary problems solved. Thousands of totally different stories, with totally different problems, have ended in the same place with their problems solved. But for me my end is my beginning, as Maurice Baring quoted of Mary Stuart, and this overwhelming conviction that there is one key which can unlock all doors brings back to me my first glimpse of the glorious gift of the senses; and the sensational experience of sensation. And there starts up again before me, standing sharp and clear in shape as of old, the figure of a man who crosses a bridge and who carries a key; as I saw him when I first looked into fairyland through the window of my father's peepshow. But I know that he who is called Pontifex, the Builder of the Bridge, is called also Claviger, the Bearer of the Key; and that such keys were given him to bind and loose when he was a poor fisher in a far province, beside a small and almost secret sea.

Gilbert complained to Frances that he was tired; more than in the past, and more frequently. She understood. The long sleep began. It was so deserved, so full of peace and grace.

> Know you what earth shall lose to-night, what rich
>   un-counted loans,
> What heavy gold of tales untold you bury
>   with my bones?
> My loves in deep dim meadows, my ships
>   that rode at ease,
> Ruffling the purple plumage of strange and secret seas.
> To see this fair earth as it is to me alone was given,
> The blow that breaks my brow to-night shall break

the dome of heaven.
The skies I saw, the trees I saw after no eyes shall see.
To-night I die the death of God: the stars shall die
    with me:
One sound shall sunder all the spears and break
    the trumpet's breath:
You never laughed in all your life as I shall laugh
    in death.

OF YOUR CHARITY
Pray for the repose of the Soul

of

Gilbert Keith Chesterton

who died

JUNE 14th 1936

✠

FACTUS EST

The Lord became my protector and He brought me forth into a large place. He saved me because he was well pleased with me. I will love thee O Lord my strength. The Lord is my firmament and my refuge and my deliverer. *Introit for Sunday within the Octave of Corpus Christi—*
The day of his death

Knight of the Holy Ghost, he goes his way,
Wisdom his motley, Truth his loving jest;
The mills of Satan keep his lance in play,
Pity and Innocence his heart at rest.
Walter de la Mare.

"Red roses full
of rain."

for you - as you
would wish. F.

R.I.P.

Bibliography

Primary Sources

Students of Gilbert Chesterton are privileged enough to have
John Sullivan's two volumes of bibliography within easy
reach. Entitled *G.K. Chesterton, a Bibliography,* and *Chesterton Continued – A Bibliographical Supplement,* these
works are indispensable, if in need of constant updating. The
bulk of Gilbert's note-books, drawings, diary material and
first draft books are still at Top Meadow, under the supervision of Revd Henry Reed. Although some organisation of the
papers has taken place in recent years there is still a lot of
work to be done. Sadly, a great many documents have been
destroyed or lost over the years, partly by accident, partly by
design. This diaspora of Chestertonian work has made research difficult. I attempted to supplement the Top Meadow
collection by writing letters to the Catholic press, the literary
press, major newspapers and various journals within the
areas where Gilbert lived and worked. The result was hundreds of letters from members of the public who had firsthand
or inherited anecdotes and memories. Some of these were
original, others were well-known. The light they threw on
Gilbert's personal life was extremely illuminating. I also used
this method of discovering information in Ontario, Canada,
and New York State, U.S.A.

The chapter on anti-Semitism owes a great debt to the
Wiener Library in London, where a file on Gilbert exists. This
institution catalogues anti-Jewish statements and actions, and
is an essential source both for facts and for understanding.
The *Chesterton Review,* published from Canada, is one of
those rare journals, a literary magazine concentrating on one

285

author, which is not eccentric or foolishly esoteric. It publicises most new findings, often publishing them. Of Gilbert's own works, only a small number are currently in print; of the others, some are virtually impossible to obtain. The Ignatius Press in New York is engaged in issuing the complete works of Gilbert Chesterton, an enterprise which will take years. The first volumes have already been published, and are expertly edited and organised. This will guarantee access to the entire canon.

I have listed Gilbert's published books, in chronological order; so few are currently in print that I have not listed publishing houses.

1900
Greybeards at Play
The Wild Knight and
   Other Poems

1901
The Defendant

1902
Twelve Types

1903
Robert Browning
Varied Types

1904
G.F. Watts
The Napoleon of Notting
   Hill

1905
The Club of Queer Trades
Heretics

1906
Charles Dickens

1908
The Man Who Was
   Thursday
All Things Considered
Orthodoxy

1909
George Bernard Shaw
Tremendous Trifles

1910
The Ball and the Cross
What's Wrong With The
   World
Alarms and Discursions
William Blake

1911
A Chesterton Calendar
Appreciations and Criticism
   of the Works of Charles
   Dickens
The Innocence of Father
   Brown
The Ballad of the White
   Horse

1912
Manalive
A Miscellany of Men

1913
The Victorian Age in
   Literature
Magic

1914
The Flying Inn
The Wisdom of Father
   Brown
The Barbarism of Berlin

Bibliography

1915
Letters to an Old
  Garibaldian
Poems
Wine, Water and Song
The Crimes of England

1917
Lord Kitchener
A Short History of England

1919
Irish Impressions

1920
The Superstition of Divorce
The Uses of Diversity
The New Jerusalem

1922
Eugenics and Other Evils
What I Saw in America
The Ballad of St Barbara and
  Other Verses
The Man Who Knew Too
  Much

1923
Fancies Versus Fads
St. Francis of Assisi

1925
Tales of the Long Bow
The Everlasting Man
William Cobbett

1926
The Incredulity of Father
   Brown
The Outline of Sanity
The Queen of Seven Swords

1927
The Return of Don Quixote
Collected Poems
The Secret of Father Brown
The Judgement of Dr
   Johnson
Robert Louis Stevenson

1928
Generally Speaking

1929
The Poet and the Lunatics
The Thing
G.K.C. as M.C.

1930
Four Faultless Felons
The Resurrection of Rome
Come to Think of It

1931
All Is Grist

1932
Chaucer
Sidelights on New London
   and Newer York

1933
All I Survey
St. Thomas Aquinas

1934
Avowals and Denials

1935
The Scandal of Father Brown
The Well and the Shallows

1936
As I Was Saying

Posthumous

Autobiography
The Paradoxes of Mr. Pond
The Coloured Lands
The End of the Armistice
The Common Man
A Handful of Authors
The Glass Walking-Stick
Lunacy and Letters
Where All Roads Lead
The Spice of Life
Chesterton on Shakespeare

Secondary Sources

Barker, Dudley, *G.K. Chesterton,* Constable, London, 1973
Baring, Maurice, *Puppet Show of Memory,* Heinemann, London and Little, Brown & Co. Inc., Boston, 1922
Belloc, Hilaire, *The Jews,* Constable, London and Houghton Mifflin, Boston, 1922
_____*On The Place of Gilbert Chesterton in English Letters,* Sheed & Ward, London and New York, 1940
_____*The Servile State,* T.N. Foulis, London and Edinburgh, 1912
Bentley, E.C., *Those Days,* Constable, London, 1940
_____*Trent's Last Case,* Harper & Row, New York, 1912
_____*Biography for Beginners,* T.W. Laurie, London, 1905
Boyd, Ian, *The Novels of G.K. Chesterton,* Elek, London, 1975

Canovan, Margaret, *G.K. Chesterton: Radical Populist,* Harcourt Brace, New York, 1977

Chesterton, Ada, *The Chestertons,* Chapman & Hall, London, 1941

Chesterton, Cecil, *G.K. Chesterton: A Criticism,* J. Lane, New York, 1909

Clemens, Cyril, *Chesterton as Seen by His Contemporaries,* International Mark Twain Society, 1939

Coates, John D., *Chesterton and the Edwardian Cultural Crisis,* Hull University Press, 1984

Dale, Alzina Stone, *The Outline of Sanity,* Eardmans, Grand Rapids, Michigan, 1983

Donaldson, Frances, *The Marconi Scandal,* Hart-Davis, London, 1962

Ffinch, Michael, *G.K. Chesterton,* Weidenfeld & Nicolson, London, 1983

Kenner, Hugh, *Paradox in Chesterton,* Sheed & Ward, New York, 1947

MacKenzie, Norman and Jeanne, *The Time Traveller,* Weidenfeld & Nicolson, London, 1973

Mackey, Aidan, *Mr Chesterton Comes To Tea,* Vintage, Bedford, 1978

Maycock, A.L., *The Man Who Was Orthodox,* Dobson, London, 1963

O'Connor, John, *Father Brown on Chesterton,* F. Muller, London, 1937

Sewell, Brocard, *Cecil Chesterton,* St Albert's Press, Faversham, 1975

Titterton, W.R., *G.K. Chesterton: A Portrait,* A. Ouseley, London, 1936

Ward, Maisie, *Gilbert Keith Chesterton,* Sheed & Ward, New York, 1944

——*Return to Chesterton,* Sheed & Ward, London and New York, 1952

Wells, H.G., *The Outline of History,* G. Newnes, London, 1920

Wilson, A.N., *Hilaire Belloc,* Hamish Hamilton, London, 1984

"The Mind of Chesterton" Christopher Hollis, (Hollis & Carter, 1970).

"Paradox in Chesterton" Hugh Kenner (1948).

"Chesterton, Man and Mask" Garry Wills.

"On the Place of Gilbert Chesterton in English Letters" Hilaire Belloc (1940).

"The Laughing Prophet, the Seven Virtues and G.K. Chesterton" E. Cammaerts (1937).

"Hilaire Belloc: Edwardian Radical" John P. McCarthy, (Liberty Press, 1978).

Index

Gilbert: The Man Who Was G.K. Chesterton by Michael Coren
NOTE: References to Gilbert K. Chesterton are abbreviated as G.K.C.
in the index.

293

Index

Whitman, Walt, 58, 59–60, 61, 62, 84, 120
Wiener Library, 214–15
Wilde, Oscar, 61, 62, 199–200
Wild Knight and Other Poems, The (Chesterton), 118, 119–21; reviews of, 121; sales of, 121
William Blake (Chesterton), 187
William Cobbett (Chesterton), 244
Williams, Ernest Hodder, 53, 107, 108
"Wine and Water," 184–85
Wine, Water and Song (Chesterton), 221
Wisdom of Father Brown, The (Chesterton), 212–13, 218, 219
Wise, Rabbi, 215

Wolfe, Humbert, 216–17
Wolfe, James, 273
Women's liberation movement, 186–87
World War I, 201, 220, 222–23, 224–25, 257; Cecil Chesterton's death in, 200, 201, 225

Xavier, St. Francis, 40

Yeats, Willie, 78, 110
Yorkshire, England, 146, 147, 148

Zangwill, Israel, 214
Zielinski, Dr. Adam, 246
Zionism, 196, 210, 211, 213